THE MAKING

AND UNMAKING OF THE

HAYA LIVED WORLD

BODY, COMMODITY, TEXT

Studies of Objectifying Practice

A series edited by

Arjun Appadurai,

Jean Comaroff, and

Judith Farquhar

THE MAKING

AND UNMAKING OF THE

HAYA LIVED WORLD

Consumption, Commoditization,

and Everyday Practice

BRAD WEISS

Duke University Press

Durham and London

© 1996 Duke University Press
All rights reserved
Printed in the United States of America on acid-free paper ∞
Typeset in Minion by Keystone Typesetting, Inc.
Library of Congress Cataloging-in-Publication Data
appear on the last printed page of this book.

CONTENTS

ACKNOWLEDGMENTS

In the course of preparing this study I have had the good fortune to receive the support and encouragement of a great number of friends and colleagues. As is probably the case for any researcher who drops in on an entire community for an extended visit, my greatest thanks must go to the many Haya neighbors and friends I made during my stay in and around Rubya. In addition to indulging and enduring my endless questions, we shared many remarkable times, both painful and joyous. The experience of entering their lives, if only for a brief period, has stayed with me. I trust that Ma Carolina and Ta Gregory, Isiah, and especially Kyabona will not be offended if I mention them by name and single them out for special thanks. My memories of Laurean and Mzee Juma will be among the most long-lasting and poignant of my life. I must also point out that I would never have had the opportunity to meet these friends or, indeed, to carry out this research, if it had not been for the tremendous generosity of Severian and Anatolia Ndyetabula, who allowed me to stay in their home for the tenure of my research.

My preparation at the University of Chicago was aided by the university through a Special Humanities Fellowship. Research in Tanzania was funded by a Fulbright-Hays doctoral dissertation fellowship. The Tanzanian National Institute for Science and Technology (UTAFITI) enabled me to live and work in Tanzania. A generous Faculty Summer Research Grant from the College of William and Mary allowed me to complete my revisions of this book. Bibi Lyaruu, the director of UTAFITI, provided valuable and rapid support of my project at crucial times. Joseph Mbele of the University of Dar es Salaam was my faculty sponsor, and offered encouragement and advice throughout my research.

The staff and employees of Rubya Hospital were also especially kind to me. Numerous conversations with them not only provided me with a wealth of information, but offered hospitality and warmth. In particular, Drs. Kam Mann and Margaret Hargrave could be relied on for companionship and conviviality when they were truly needed.

In Chicago I have enjoyed the commitment of faculty and friends alike. I am grateful to the members of my dissertation committee—Jean Comaroff, Nancy Munn, Bill Hanks, and Jim Fernandez—for their extremely thoughtful insights and great encouragement at all stages of my work. Nancy Munn's rigorous methods of analysis and her concern for the specific form of particular social worlds is in many ways an inspiration for my own project. Bill Hanks was a wonderful mentor to me while I was in Chicago and continues to be an enormously important colleague and friend. He has always been able to take seriously and illuminate both the fine grain of some rather detailed ethnographic interpretations, as well as to sharpen the broader theoretical aims of my writing; he also has an uncanny capacity to see the connection between the detail and the wider work, even when the links aren't very clear to me! Jean Comaroff's engaging intellect and energy were enormously influential in my decision to study in Africa—a decision I'm glad I made. Her contributions to this work, and to my own sense of its significance are too many and varied to enumerate.

I am also grateful to the members of my writing group: Mark Auslander, Misty Bastian, Adeline Masquelier, and Debra Spitulnik. I learned a great deal from their always helpful suggestions, as well as from reading their own ethnographies. Judy Farquhar has offered good counsel and shown real support for my work at crucial moments. Arthur Knight has proven to be a fast friend, and his comments on the introduction to this work were astute as well as generous. My thanks as well to Sondra Jarvis for her figure and map illustrations.

Lastly, and most importantly, I want to express something well beyond thanks to Julie Corsaro. She has offered wonderful encouragement and enthusiasm, not only for this project but for our making a life together. I could not have hoped for more.

Briefer versions of chapters 6 and 7 have appeared previously—chapter 6 in *American Ethnologist* 19(3):538–52, chapter 7 in *Africa* 63(1):19–35. Permission to publish these chapters here is gratefully acknowledged.

THE MAKING

AND UNMAKING OF THE

HAYA LIVED WORLD

1 AN ORIENTATION TO
THE STUDY

Changing Perspectives

From plateau atop the escarpment in the Muleba District of Tanzania one can look out over a long slope to the valley below. This valley presents a vast hilly expanse, a field of broad savanna plains interspersed with rocky outcrops and compact villages, whose verdant flora stand out sharply against the surrounding terrain (fig. 1a and b). The sloping face of this escarpment leads down beyond the valley and villages to the western shores of Lake Victoria. In the Haya language (*oluhaya*) Lake Victoria is *Lwelu*, "the great out-there," and from this plateau it does indeed seem a distant place that lies beyond the lands tended to by Haya villagers.

However, such a view is possible only from a particular perspective, a perspective that is not merely a topographical vantage point but also, and more importantly, a particular *way* of perceiving this region. This description of that view represents what was often my own way of looking at a landscape. And the very idea of a "landscape," approached in this way, presupposes a distance between an observer and a visual scene, and a perspective that exemplifies a separation between subject and object. There are, however, ways of apprehending this region that do not reduce it to an observable backdrop. These Haya villages and the lands between them are not merely an arrangement of positions, for they are dynamically integrated into a unified order of space and time. Haya do, in fact, recognize distinctions between the regions I referred to. Valleys and plateaus present different life possibilities for those who reside in one or the other. The savanna grasslands that predominate are not treated like the villages they surround. But these contrasts within the region are conjoined in the course of actual Haya activity and experience. Savannah encroaches on untended village land, or villagers may attempt to reclaim farmland from the desiccated bush. Migrations from plateau to valley or from village to village

Figure 1 (a and b). Two views looking out from villages *omugongo* ("on the back") across the valley with Lake Victoria on the horizon. Amid the savannah are densely settled villages.

occur with every generation as social relations alter the contours of these physical spaces. The material environment thereby becomes incorporated into the practical organization of Haya society and culture.

The same is true for Lake Victoria. While the lake is distinctly "out-there," it is also clearly a part of the regional world configured in Haya experiences.[1] As a place of trade and travel, Lake Victoria is also a means of establishing concrete connections between the Kagera Region[2] and the rest of Tanzania and East Africa as a whole. The image of rural isolation on the shores of the imposing lake, implicit in the objectification of the "scenic" landscape, is undermined by Haya interactions with their world.[3] Through these interactions, Lake Victoria becomes in fact metonymic of the interpenetration of "local" and "global" communities, a "great out-there" that is simultaneously inseparable from the lives of rural Haya villagers.

This book explores Haya ways of inhabiting their locales, and examines the forces that shape and transform these processes over time. I argue that in the course of mundane, everyday activities the Haya construct a lived world, an order of concrete spatial and temporal relations that is not only *imbued* with cultural meanings but also serves to *direct* creative cultural activities. This lived world is therefore a product of everyday practices at the same time that it produces these practices (Bourdieu 1977; Certeau 1984; Lefebvre 1971).

By drawing particular attention to the productive dimensions of this spatial and temporal world, I am also attempting to highlight the importance of human agency in the Haya (or any) sociocultural order. While numerous studies address the construction of subjectivities, as dictated by the rigors of specific spatiotemporal "regimes" (a field of inexhaustible grist for the now legion Foucauldian mills), the fact that the lineaments of these regimes are themselves generated through creative human activity often remains unexamined.[4] Central to my analyses, in contrast, are the ways in which Haya actions and experiences (i.e., their capacities as subjects and agents) are anchored in their physical locales and built spaces (Merleau-Ponty 1962; Munn 1971; J. Weiner 1991). Through these anchoring processes, the lived world comes to incorporate and integrate both objective and subjective dimensions. Actual locations like a domestic hearth, a grave site, or a river are configured in the course of Haya activities as recognizable places, and in turn the spatial and temporal parameters of "place" shape the agents of those activities. The lived world is simultaneously an objectification of social agency and intentions as well as a field of material relations that situates and informs these specific forms of subjectivity.

This emphasis on the mutual construction of human agency and concrete orders of space and time in lived experience also leads me to explore the interrelation of persons to their world and its objects as a central feature of this ethnography. Throughout this work I offer analyses of the ways in which Haya men and women are implicated in or confront an array of material forms and items (e.g., food and money, houses and crossroads, automobiles and buckets) as part of a more general interest in processes of *engagement* as they are culturally constituted. I find the concept of engagement productive because it nicely captures the sense of reciprocal interchange between persons and the world that is entailed in any activity. A Haya person who engages in uprooting a tree, buying a fish, or naming a child (to cite three examples discussed at length below) approaches and appropriates such objects and others from a particular perspective, but at the same time this person is *appropriated by* these features of the world. The form of activity or practice itself directs and configures—indeed, engages—the person who carries it out. Because of this reciprocal character of engagement, when people act to define, transform, and *make* the world they inhabit, they also work to make themselves (Comaroff 1985b; Munn 1986).

The process of engagement as I have described it here also provides a focus for my analysis of transformations in the Haya sociocultural order. These transformations can be assessed at a number of levels. To begin with, any particular action may always have an unforeseen outcome, and this can have real consequence for the persons engaged in that action. A man's attempts to feed his wife and children may prove unsuccessful, which will diminish his standing as a household head. Courtship gifts may be rebuked, or accepted from more than one suitor—leading to suspicions about a man's ability to control money or a woman's ability to control herself. Each of these instances (explored in the following chapters) suggests that as an action unfolds, it presents the possibility for redefining and repositioning (reengaging or disengaging) the agents they involve. Such transformations, in turn, have consequences for future actions and future outcomes.[5]

At another level, the cultural constitution of engagement can most forcefully *reveal* the effects of widespread sociocultural transformation. As distinctive kinds of action become possible and even commonplace (as with the emergence of new forms of housing or new agricultural techniques), the terms in which persons interact with each other and their world are necessarily altered. Most analyses of social change examine the use of money or the introduction of a variety of consumer goods into a regional world, and these phenomena are explored here as well. What I hope to contribute to such studies is a recognition of the specific capacities and potentials for making and remaking the Haya sociocultural world that are introduced by the practices that surround these commodity forms. The sense of dislocation that characterizes Haya views of selling certain kinds of land or the experience of excessive heat and desiccation many Haya associate with certain media both exemplify transformations in the manner in which Haya men and women encounter their physical environment. Exploring Haya forms of engagement through such practices allows me to trace the changing character of social action *and* experience; and to ground the relation between action and experience in an object world whose qualities are dynamic and often ambiguous.

These theoretical issues—the interrelation of action and experience as processes that both generate and are anchored in a meaningful order of spatial and temporal relations—motivate the ethnographic analyses presented in this book. In the remainder of this introduction I spell out more precisely some of the terms that recur in these analyses and discuss some of the arguments that have influenced my thinking on these questions. To orient the reader to the organization of my argument and to suggest some common themes that can be traced through the ethnographic discussions of its chapters, I also provide a brief synopsis of the book as a whole. Finally, I offer some background on the Haya in order to locate them in the context of East Africa.

The Lived World

I began this chapter with a description of a Haya landscape in order to convey a contrast between this way of perceiving a visual scene and the process of inhabiting a world. This notion of *inhabiting* space and time is essential to my ethnographic analysis. My understanding of what it means to inhabit a world and how this is relevant to cultural constructions of space and time derives directly from Merleau-Ponty's phenomenological descriptions of consciousness and being, as well as from a number of anthropological studies that develop and apply these concepts in specific cultural contexts (Hanks 1990; Hugh-Jones 1979; Lass 1988; Munn 1986; J. Weiner 1991). Recent ethnographies of sub-Saharan Africa that explore the connections between inhabiting and embodying a social world—an important dimension of Merleau-Ponty's arguments—have also been especially influential to my thinking about this as an issue for ethnographic analysis (Boddy 1989; Comaroff 1985b; Devisch 1983, 1985; Jackson 1989).

Merleau-Ponty's discussions of space (and, less centrally, time) proceed from a critique of both "empiricist" and "intellectualist" epistemologies (Merleau-Ponty 1962). He characterizes such theories as positing a separation between an objective "spatiality of positions" (100) as against an independent consciousness that exists "*in* space, or *in* time" (139). This separation suggests that space is "the setting in which things are arranged" and implies that consciousness becomes merely the "content" of this "container" (243). In contrast, Merleau-Ponty asserts that space and time are inseparable from the active consciousness that inhabits them. Indeed, consciousness *is* being in the world:

> [S]pace and time are not, for me, a collection of adjacent points, nor are they a limitless number of relations synthesized by my consciousness, and into which it draws my body. I am not in space and time, nor do I conceive space and time; I belong to them, my body combines with them and includes them. (140)

In Merleau-Ponty's work, this process of being-in-the-world is rigorously grounded in bodily experience. For Merleau-Ponty, the body not only mediates all experience, it is "our general medium for having a world" (Merleau-Ponty

1962, 146). The body is not *detachable* from a surrounding spatial *context* because "To be a body, is to be tied to a certain world . . . our body is not primarily *in* space: it is of it" (148). The fact that the body is in the world in this way means that spatiality is not configured by a set of "external co-ordinates" (100) or independent positions that determine the locations of objects "in" it. Rather, spatiality exists as a set of *orientations*. The anchored perspective of the body *inhabiting* space establishes the orientations that define a spatialized world. And this spatialized world is also, as Lefebvre makes clear, a *social* world:

> For the spatial body, becoming social does not mean being inserted into some pre-existing "world": this body produces and reproduces—and it perceives what it reproduces or produces. Its spatial properties and determinants are contained within it. (1991, 199)

Bodily being, then, configures a world, at once lived and thus necessarily social, in the body's ability "to make out boundaries and directions in the given world, to establish lines of force, to keep perspectives in view, in a word, to organize the given world" (Merleau-Ponty 1962, 112).

The analyses in this book attempt to illustrate some of the ways that Merleau-Ponty's conceptions of inhabiting, anchoring, and establishing orientations of space and time are important not only to an anthropology of the body but to an understanding of sociocultural activity and practice more generally. Phenomenological approaches in anthropology, and in the social sciences more generally, have often been criticized for focusing on individual experience and failing to situate that experience in the context of wider social forces and relations (see Lévi-Strauss 1987). The advantage of the kind of phenomenology offered by Merleau-Ponty is that it insists on the *simultaneity* of "being" and the "world," a position that makes it impossible to reify individual experience, or to isolate it from the encompassing order of activity in which it is engaged. This perspective does not attempt to define a particular "type" of experience and identify it with a particular cultural pattern. Indeed, Merleau-Ponty's understanding of the temporal character of consciousness that "always finds itself already at work in the world" (1962, 432) seems compatible with many contemporary perspectives on the processual and dynamic character of culture.

Certainly Bourdieu's notion of the *habitus*, fundamental to his theory of practice and enormously influential in numerous ethnographic analyses, can be traced directly to Merleau-Ponty's account of the "body image" as a set of dispositions and "potential source" of habitual actions (Merleau-Ponty 1962, 98).[6] In my descriptions of a Haya world I argue that there are important orientations that are built into a lived order of space and time and which therefore extend *beyond* the body. I identify certain kinds of practices that situate a given location as a recognizable place, and thereby establish a meaningful orientation to the space and time it inhabits. For example, through certain routine ritual procedures, or by offering important media like food, coffee, beer, or money, a Haya person can instantiate a concrete set of orientations in the world. That is, any particular practice establishes a certain organization of directions, sequences, expectations, or potential relations to other persons and places; in turn, this organization gives a determinate form to ongoing Haya activity. These orientations provide the bearings for Haya social life.

These orientations are tangibly laid out, and constituted in social practice. They have their ultimate origins in the situation of the body and, in Merleau-Ponty's words, in "the body in movement [which] inhabits space, [and] because movement is not limited to submitting passively to space and time, it actively assumes [space and time and] takes them up in their basic significance" (1962, 102). At the same time, I attempt to demonstrate that orientations grounded in the body's situation can also be concretized in certain physical places. The Haya house, for example, has a concrete set of orientations embedded in it, orientations that are not imposed on it by a fixed, objective map, but that derive from the ways in which the house inhabits a world. The internal organization of the house and its relation to other houses, and the encompassing environment (which are intrinsically connected dimensions of a house) situate a Haya house as a recognizable place. Similarly, a grave site is a physical place that projects important orientations *of* time (and space). That is, the identifications of Haya generations with particular graves or with the agricultural cycle of banana crops (all of which are detailed below) do not merely exist *through* time, they actually produce and organize temporality itself. These physical places establish orientations (e.g., of sequence, direction, periodicity, beginning, and ending) that constitute the concrete form of Haya space and time. The Haya lived world, then, is an oriented space and time that emerges through the process of inhabiting a world. This process is anchored in the situation of the active body and may be concretized in meaningful places and objects. As we shall see, sociocultural activity is continuously *making* and *unmaking* dimensions of this lived world, as the orientations embedded in persons and places become intensified or diffused, empowered or dismantled.

Commoditization

The second principal theoretical focus of the work is the significance of commodity forms and commoditized transactions for Haya men and women. This interest in the meanings of property, marketed goods, and commoditized exchanges in Haya culture is not merely a secondary or "additional" concern of mine; rather, questions about the place of commodities in Haya action and experience emerge directly out of my more general interest in the cultural problems of constituting and inhabiting a lived world. Commoditization, as it is discussed here, includes not only the emergence of commodities and market exchanges in Haya communities, but also the possibility of *making* any object into a commodity by transacting it in the appropriate (or inappropriate) manner. I do *not* conceive of commodities and the commoditization process as elements that are alien to inhabiting a lived world or as forces that by their very nature eradicate or subvert that world. For commoditization emerges within the process of inhabiting the world and commodities themselves derive their significance from being engaged in practices that make up this process. As Marcus has correctly observed, "the world of larger systems and events has . . . often been seen as externally impinging on and bounding little worlds, but not as integral to them" (1986, 166). My coupling the two theoretical emphases of this study is an attempt to demonstrate that the "larger systems" associated with markets, money, and modernity are very much an integral dimension of this specific regional (but *not* little) world.

Because the particular, local significance of any commoditization process is constructed in the course of actions—which, as I suggested above, may always have unforeseen consequences—the meanings of commoditization and of particular commodities often do pose challenges to those who are engaged in this process. In particular, the experience of *agency*—a person's or community's sense of their own capacity for making the world—can be undermined or enhanced through the commoditization of things and persons. Through my analyses, I argue that commoditization and commodities can be central to sociocultural *transformation* without being seen as an anathema to meaningful sociocultural practices and relations.

Theories of historical transformation that focus on the economic forces of markets and money often rely on teleological notions of change. They presume that the systematic incorporation of "local" societies into wider economic relations must necessarily result either in a "rationalization" of cultural values or in a pervasive sense of "alienation," as local values become increasingly irrelevant to metropolitan projects (Taussig 1980; Wallerstein 1974). Moreover, commodity production and commodities themselves come to embody the "disenchantment" of symbolically nuanced orders of activity and experience (Bourdieu 1979; Weiner and Schneider 1989, 13). From these teleological perspectives, a uniform, systematic incorporation of any particular lived world can only lead to the effacement of meaningful practice. However, a detailed consideration of commoditization as an integral feature of a lived world challenges such theorizing. The commentaries of the people whose actions construct this world tell us that precisely what is essential to any process of social transformation are the experiences and meanings through which it is realized. From this perspective, commodities can be seen to present new possibilities and potentialities for making the world, while they are simultaneously being remade by the activities in which they are deployed.

As I suggested earlier, my approach to the meanings associated with commoditization emerges out of my identification of the lived world with oriented social activity. The spatial and temporal orientations of these activities are routinely concretized in specific features of the physical world, and especially in objects. In my view, both Marx, in his discussion "The Fetishism of Commodities" (1906), and Mauss, in his essay "The Gift" (1954), also conceptualized the problem of objects in terms of the capacity of certain objects to condense within themselves qualities that are characteristic of their wider social worlds. Both of these theorists (whose arguments remain central to the contemporary spate of anthropological discussion of objects and commodities in particular) further link the qualities embedded in commodities and gifts to the forms of social *practice* in which they are engaged.

For Marx, commodities exemplify a particular form of consciousness that is characteristic of capitalist production. Commodities conceal the "definite social relation between men" that creates the commodity, and assume "the fantastic form of a relation between things" (1906, 83). In a commodity "the social character of men's labours appears to them as an objective character stamped upon the product of that labour" (83). Commodities, therefore, appear to have an independent existence, standing apart from their producers and seemingly able to "[enter into relations] both with one another and the human race" (83). This attribution of independent agency is what Marx calls fetishism.

In his view, the fetishization of commodities arises out of the "peculiar social character of the labour that produces them" (83). The culturally constituted qualities of that labor—that is, "the specific social character of private labour" (85)—are expressed and equated through the commensurable values attributed to labor's products. Since laborers work independently of one another under capitalism, the social character of their labor acquires its value

only by means of the relations which the act of exchange establishes directly between the products, and indirectly, through them, between the producers. To the [laborer], therefore, the relations connecting the labour of one individual with that of the rest appear not as direct social relations . . . but as . . . material relations between persons and social relations between things. (Marx 1906, 84)

Therefore, in Marx's formulation, commodities are objectifications of the very practices—and the specific, meaningfully oriented *form* of the practices (e.g., the condition of private labor, the marketed exchange of commodities)— through which they are produced.

Mauss is most interested in objects as "*total* social phenomena," phenomena that embody "all the threads of which the social fabric is composed" (1954, 1). In particular, Mauss explores the implication of things in the identity of persons. He suggests that "the confusion of personalities and things" (18) is characteristic of gifts or "total prestations," according to which "to give something is to give a part of oneself" (10).

However, in Mauss's analyses this identification of persons with things is less clearly grounded in sociocultural *practices*. For Mauss, the "spirit of the gift," its animate character that compels the receiver to make returns to the giver, derives from the collective representations of those societies that exchange prestations. In keeping with this Durkheimian perspective on the religious origin of economic value, Mauss in fact argues that such archaic societies "are in a state of perpetual economic effervescence" (70). In spite of this essentialist conceptualization of value, Mauss's theories remain significant for my analysis. In addition to his crucial recognition of the ways in which objects can be extensions of persons, Mauss's focus on the moral dimensions of economic activity is of major importance. This aspect of his theory may not seem terribly novel, but what I find significant is his understanding of the *experiential* nature of morality, the fact that the obligation of givers and receivers, in Mauss's description, is so tangibly felt as an active force. Moreover, all of the specific kinds of prestations described—gifts and potlatch, *sacra* and pledges—are objects that serve to *orient* social relations. They do not merely instantiate principles of social solidarity or represent collective ownership, they give direction to those bonds and obligations. Thus, while in Mauss's view prestations may derive their significance from collective religious representations, they also clearly objectify the active dimensions of sociality.[7]

I have described certain commonalities in the perspectives of both Marx and Mauss, but contemporary debates about the significance of objects have more often pointed to contrasts. Most often cited in comparisons of the two perspectives is the fact that Marx and Mauss were describing two very different kinds of objects, namely, commodities and gifts. From this difference a wide range of conclusions has been inferred. Gregory, for example, draws a fundamental distinction between gifts and commodities, arguing that "gift-debt" and "commodity-debt" are grounded in two opposing systems of production and exchange (1980, 639ff). Perhaps the most important contrast between gifts and commodities—according to Gregory, who cites both Marx and Mauss when making this assertion—is the suggestion that

> [commodity-debt] is created by the exchange of alienable objects between transactors who are in a state of reciprocal independence, whereas gift-debt is created by an exchange of inalienable objects between people in a state of reciprocal dependence. (Gregory 1980, 640)

One of the problems with this characterization is that it makes it difficult to account for the routine *coexistence* of both kinds of objects and debts within the same economy, often between the very same social agents, which is typical of most sociocultural systems. Indeed, even Gregory, in his ethnographic evidence, recognizes this coexistence. If a man offers bridewealth for the daughter of a family from whom he often purchases beer or fish or other products of that family (a situation that I encountered with some of my Haya neighbors), is the wife he receives an "alienable object" or is the produce he buys with cash ultimately "inalienable" from the family that sells it? Are these transactors in a state of reciprocal dependence or *in*dependence? It might be suggested that the state of social relations between the transactors can be determined only *relative to* the kinds of objects they exchange. That is, to use the example above, with respect to affinal exchanges these families are in a state of reciprocal dependence, while relative to produce purchases those same families are reciprocally independent. But this argument is simply tautological; it defines the properties of the objects (gift or commodity, inalienable or alienable) in terms of the kinds of relations they mediate (dependent or independent) and defines the nature of those relations in terms of the kinds of objects exchanged.

Another approach to the contrast between gifts and commodities suggests that each kind of object is the product of a different system of production. Gregory's own argument cites this difference when he claims that "[gifts] must be explained with reference to the social conditions of the reproduction of *people,* [commodities] must be explained with reference to the social conditions of the reproduction of *things*" (1980, 641). In one of the most important examples of this kind of approach, Taussig argues that fetishized commodity images of Colombian and Bolivian rural peoples—as well as the magical realism of Latin American literature—are "the creative response to an enormously deep-seated conflict between *use-value and exchange-value* orientations" (1980, 21; emphasis added). According to Taussig, precapitalist societies, or those

organized by the "peasant mode of production" (25) are "based on the production of use-values" (21), with the "aim of satisfying natural needs" (29). He
further follows Mauss in asserting that the objects produced in these societies
are "intermeshed" with or animated with the life-force of those who produce
them (36). For Taussig, however, this sort of "precapitalist fetishism" arises
from the "organic unity between persons and their products" (37) and must be
clearly distinguished from the "fetishism of commodities" as Marx described it,
which emerges in societies based on the production of "exchange-values."

Taussig's strict opposition between use-value and exchange-value and his
identification of these values with two distinct modes of production and, indeed, distinct types of society are especially problematic. To begin with, this
identification of use-values with precapitalist societies has the unfortunate (if
undoubtedly unintended) consequence of naturalizing "peasant" practices and
small-scale societies (Appadurai 1986, 11). Taussig's emphasis on the "satisfaction of natural needs" and the "organic unity" of products and producers
implies that productive human activity in precapitalist societies is somehow
more authentic than capitalist labor, as though precapitalist social relations and
practices were unmediated by sociocultural orientations (see also Willis 1991,
41–60 on the apparent "inauthenticity" of certain [postmodern] forms of labor
and value). Indeed, Taussig claims that "[i]n the precapitalist mode of production . . . the connections between producers and between production and
consumption are *directly intelligible*" (1980, 36; emphasis added) and not, by
implication, culturally constructed phenomena. This naturalization seems less
an explanation of commodity fetishism than a fetishization of precapitalist
production.

A further difficulty with the distinction between use-value and exchange-
value, apart from their association with precapitalism and capitalism in Taussig's exposition, is that it fails to account for their co-implication in any system
of *production*. Quite aside from the fact that objects are put to use and exchanged in every society, the more important point is that exchanges can
produce specific meanings (like status, reputation, style, etc.), while utilities are
constituted through social interchanges that are oriented by those very meanings (cf. Baudrillard 1981; Certeau 1984). In contrast to the productive dimensions of sociocultural *practice* and *agency* that I outlined above, Taussig's naturalization of use-values seems to abstract and privilege one dimension of a total
system of production.

The final point that I want to make about Taussig's argument relates directly
to my analysis of the objectification process in the Haya lived world. Taussig
asserts that corresponding to the two different value orientations in precapital-

ist and capitalist societies are two very different forms of fetishism. Precapitalist fetishism, according to Taussig, exemplifies a kind of Maussian personification in which objects are inextricably bound to their producers. This "organic unity," he argues, stands in "stark contrast to the fetishism of commodities" which derives from a "split" between producers and the products they exchange, and results in "the subordination of men to the things they produce, which appear to be independent and self-empowered" (Taussig 1980, 37). This argument clearly implies that alienation is a product of capitalist transformation and that personified objects in noncapitalist contexts are not experienced as alienated things whose independent powers can subjugate their human producers. My guess is that the Nuer informant who told Evans-Pritchard "day by day Cow avenges the death of her mother by occasioning the death of men" (Evans-Pritchard 1940, 49) would be surprised to hear that "the subordination of men to the things they produce" is a result of capitalism. My point, which is crucial to many of the analyses that follow, is that the potential for *both* personification and alienation is intrinsic to the process of objectification (Miller 1987). I argue that Haya things such as food or beer, land or bridewealth, can be understood as personifications (e.g., as extensions or embodiments) of those who give and receive them. But they can also serve to undo and subvert the identities of those who seek to control them, and Haya do experience their own subordination to the demands of such things. By the same token, commodities produced for the market are understood by many Haya through the ways in which these commodities implicate themselves in the most intimate aspects of bodily being and physical health. Far from instantiating a split between persons and things, commodities like cement and zinc, cars and plastic, or money itself are often tangibly entwined in the persons who possess them. Taussig's theory of inevitable alienation in the transformation to hegemonic capitalism should not, therefore, be smuggled in with the commodity.

A recent response to the long-standing theoretical dichotomy between gifts and commodities has been to obliterate the distinction altogether. In a thought-provoking essay, Appadurai argues that exchange is *the* source of value in objects, and that the social and historical significance of commodities must be found in these objects as "things-in-motion" (1986, 5). One of the important benefits of this view—aside from its laudable refutation of fundamental oppositions between alienability and inalienability, or use-value and exchange-value—is the way in which it incorporates the potential for transformation in the "life" of a social "thing." That is, commodities, according to Appadurai, have distinctive "trajectories" (5), and tracing the course of these trajectories allows us to gauge the motivations, calculations, and intentions—that is, the human *agency*—that activates and becomes embedded in these objects. Appadurai's perspective thus conjoins both the productive (and especially the political) and the symbolic potential of objects to concretize human activity in the world.

A further advantage of Appadurai's focus on the trajectory of objects is that it recognizes that the same object can be entered into a range of exchanges and activities. One of the examples he cites are "enclaved commodities" (22), objects that are removed from circulation or withheld from certain kinds of transactions. This kind of practice is especially crucial when, as Appadurai observes, different kinds of commodities coexist in a given sociocultural context or when "the capitalist mode of commoditization . . . [interacts] with myriad other indigenous social forms of commoditization" (16). Such a process of "enclaving" is central to the ways in which Haya engage with a wide range of objects, as indicated in my discussions of "subsistence" foods as compared with marketed produce, or the relation of land to money.

The difficulty that remains with Appadurai's argument is that while collapsing the intrinsic *opposition* between gifts and commodities as types of objects, he has also obscured the real *differences* in the potential of objects to embody value. Indeed, the very purpose of enclaving or diverting[8] a particular commodity, as Haya examples will illustrate, is to prevent that object from being associated or equated with other kinds of commodities, especially with the kinds of transactions that characterize their trajectories. These practices, therefore, seem premised on the understanding that different objects embody, generate, and retain value in different ways. In other words, certain objects have social lives that are qualitatively different from others as well as correspondingly distinct potentials for constructing the lives of the persons who control (or are controlled by) them. The Comaroffs make such an argument with respect to Southern Tswana understandings of cattle and commodities, noting that

> both cattle and money are *particular* sorts of goods, with a peculiar aptitude for abstracting and congealing wealth, for making and breaking meaningful associations, and for permitting some human beings to live off the backs of others. (Comaroff and Comaroff 1990, 211; emphasis in original)

As I noted above, all objects have the potential for alienation or personification, for diffusing or condensing value. But not all objects do so *in the same way*. I intend to demonstrate the ways in which the distinctive potential of different objects is realized in Haya culture.

My analysis of Haya everyday activities addresses different objects' distinctive capacities for producing certain effects in the world, but it is centrally concerned with the interpenetration of these different capacities. Appadurai, as already noted, is quite correct to draw attention to the interaction of multiple forms of transaction that is characteristic of most sociocultural orders. What is especially interesting about this interaction is its uneven and highly contingent character in these contexts. Thus, the interpretation of and negotiation over the specific exchange form or category of a particular object (e.g., If I give you a hoe, is that part of my bridewealth payment, or am I offering you credit and expecting to be paid when your coffee is harvested?) become principle contexts for everyday politics. Political concerns can also be encountered in Haya efforts to resist the fusion of different exchange relations, to avoid selling land, or to restrict the purchase of certain kinds of food in the market, while seeking to assure their circulation through more appropriate forms of transaction. Again, these forms of resistance indicate that not all modes of transaction can be evaluated in the same way.

While I appreciate the importance of avoiding a dichotomy between gifts and commodities, in my account of Haya culture I do use the term commodity (and commoditization) to refer to particular kinds of objects. In his discussion "The Money Form," Marx notes that gold began to "monopolise" the position as "the money commodity" not because of its *intrinsic* value but because it was

> a simple commodity . . . capable of serving as an equivalent, either as a simple equivalent in isolated exchanges, or as a particular equivalent by the side of others. Gradually it began to serve, within varying limits, as a universal equivalent. (1906, 81)

According to Marx, then, money is any commodity capable of assuming "the universal equivalent form" (81). And it is this capacity for creating universal equivalence, or commensurability—which, as Marx demonstrates, is embodied in money simply by virtue of its being a commodity like any other—that I find useful for characterizing the commoditization process.

This is not to suggest that a commodity is anything that can be exchanged for money. The reverse is true, since money can arise only when commoditization has established the potential for equating the value of different objects. Commoditization, then, is a process that defines the universal equivalence, or commensurability, of objects. But as the ethnographic record of "resistance" shows, it is a universal equivalence that is never universally applied. Commoditization never fixes all objects in the commodity form—that is, the trajectory of any object can be diverted over time, an heirloom can be sold, a 5,000 shilling goat can be sacrificed. Nonetheless, commoditization does open the potential for a broad range of transactions through the commensurability of objects that can seriously challenge attempts to restrict, define, displace, and *control* the trajectory of an object. This latent potentiality, which emerges through commoditization, infusing every object with the possibility of being remade and equated with all other objects, underlies much of the ambiguity and uncertainty present in the Haya lived world.

Historical Perspectives: An Overview

What today is known as the Kagera Region of Northwest Tanzania (see maps 1 and 2) has over one million inhabitants, according to 1989 census figures.[9] From at least the seventeenth century through the early colonial period, the people of this region were organized into small, but rather highly centralized kingdoms (*engoma* in *oluhaya*) (Kaijage 1971, 545; Katoke 1975, 17; Schmidt 1978, 85ff). In the precolonial period there were never fewer than three and as many as eight separate Haya[10] kingdoms (Curtis 1989, 47). The hierarchical sociopolitical organization of these kingdoms exhibited a pattern characteristic of interlacustrine cultures (Beattie 1970; Oberg 1940; Maquet 1954). A small number of "noble" patrilineal clans (*oluganda*), known as *abalangila* or *abahima* (depending on the kingdom), ruled over a large majority of commoner clans (*abailu*). Each of the kingdoms was presided over by a single king (*omukama* singular, *bakama* plural—literally "milker," a common term for any authority in the interlacustrine region), who appointed members of the nobility to administrative posts with authority over territorial divisions within the kingdom.

According to the so-called "Hamitic hypothesis," this division between ruling and commoner clans was attributed to the invasion of nomadic pastoralists from the Nile Valley, who conquered the indigenous Bantu-speaking agricultural clans and established hegemony over them (Cory 1949; Richards 1959).[11] However, recent scholarship has demonstrated that whatever invading forces may have arrived in Buhaya (i.e., "the place of the Haya") seized power in an *already* hierarchical political order (Kaijage 1971, 550; Katoke 1975, 17; Schmidt 1978, 90–107; Ishumi 1980; Curtis 1989, 46–48).

In the nineteenth century, the rapid rise of the Buganda kingdom to the north had a profound effect on the organization of these smaller Haya states, as they sought to ally themselves with this powerful patron. The Baganda were especially adept at exploiting the internal divisions of Haya and other states around the lake. In Buhaya ("the place of the Haya"; *Bahaya:* "the Haya people"; *Muhaya:* "a Haya person"), the Baganda supported the claims of some contenders for *omukama* over others and also abetted *abalangila* rulers of smaller territorial divisions in their efforts to establish their own independent kingdoms. The balance of power between the three largest kingdoms (Kiziba in the North, Ihangiro in the South, and Kyamutwara between) shifted over the course of the century, and also resulted in the division of Kyamutwara into three smaller kingdoms (Maruku, Bugabo, and "Lesser" Kyamutwara).

Later in the century, other external powers became important to these kingdoms. The western kingdom of Karagwe early on had become an important location along the Zanzibari trade route from Tabora to Buganda (Katoke 1975, 70ff). Indeed, when Speke traveled through Karagwe in 1861, he both noted the prosperity of the region and was able to converse with its King Rumanyika in Swahili, the language of the East African coast (Speke 1863). The kingdoms along the lake became engaged with the Zanzibari trade nexus much later, through an interregional trade around Lake Victoria. This trade was controlled largely by "royal monopolies" on the most important goods—coffee and bark cloth to Buganda and (to a much lesser degree) slaves and ivory to Zanzibar (Hartwig 1976; Curtis 1989, 54).

The ascendance of the Baganda and the influence of Zanzibari trade in Buhaya were further complicated by the arrival of European forces. For the Haya kingdoms, the Germans in fact had a strategic significance similar to that of the Baganda. German military intervention and allegiance was sought out in the struggles between the smaller kingdoms of Kyamutwara (Austen 1968, 39). The most important effects of colonialism on Haya economy and society throughout the colonial period, under both German and British administrations, were realized in the area of coffee cultivation. These effects continue to be of overwhelming significance to this day. As the regional trade during the nineteenth century indicates, coffee was cultivated in Buhaya in the precolonial period. Extensive coffee growing on a commercial scale began in 1904 with the introduction of arabica varieties to supplement indigenous robusta coffee. This cultivation was complemented by the expansion of the hut tax, designed to induce cultivators into marketing their coffee in order to acquire cash (Austen 1968, 95). Coffee exports increased steadily from this point until World War II.[12] Throughout the colonial period, coffee production was the focus not only of colonial administrators' agricultural and commercial policies but of Haya efforts to organize themselves politically and commercially (Austen 1968; Hyden 1969; Curtis 1989).

The significance of this administrative history has to be seen in terms of Haya efforts to control certain categories of land. Haya villages (*ebyaro,* plural) are composed of a number of family farms (*ekibanja,* singular). These farms are also places of residence, and all households occupy farmland. The primary produce of these family farms are perennial tree crops: bananas, which provide

Map 1. Tanzania (from Coulson)

the edible staple, and coffee, which provides the principal source of cash. All the farms within a village lie immediately adjacent to one another, so the village as a whole is a contiguous group of households on perennially cultivated land. These residential villages are dispersed across and clearly contrast with open grassland (*orweya*).

Control of cultivable village land and of individual *ekibanja* farms was, and continues to be, the focus of political relations in Buhaya. According to Haya men's and women's own accounts of these relations, each family farm is held individually and inherited patrilineally; but, as Haya debates and litigation also demonstrate, specific understandings of "individuality" and "descent" are clearly created in the course of social practices (practices like landholding itself). A man who is a household head will attempt to insure that his clan descendants continue to occupy his farm after his death. In the precolonial

Map 2. The Kagera Region in Tanzania

period, if a household head were to die without any surviving male agnates to inherit his farm (*okuchweka*, "to leave off"), control of that land would revert to the king. Such lands were routinely redistributed to allies and *abalangila* administrators. These appointees became the owners of the land and established relations of patronage with tenants in need of land to cultivate. This system of royal land accumulation and distribution was known as *nyarubanja*, literally "large farm." This royal tenure system was the subject of a great deal of political reform throughout the colonial as well as postcolonial periods. While this system never accounted for more than 10 to 20 percent of all farmland held in Buhaya (Reining 1962, 63), it was administered in different ways and with different consequences during the history of the region. As coffee cultivation became increasingly commercialized, Haya kings often sought means of alienating villagers from their lands, claiming that they were to become tenants (*omutwarwa*) of the newly appointed landlords (*omutwazi*). The creation of new *nyarubanja* was officially forbidden in 1928, and a series of acts passed after independence sought to restore all such lands to their tenants.[13]

The *nyarubanja* system clearly illustrates that the control of land was integral not only to the exertion of political authority in each Haya kingdom but also to the articulation of that administrative authority with the descent system of Haya clans. Clans in the Interlacustrine area are often described as exogamous totemic classifications that are dispersed throughout a given region (Beattie 1970). Although some (but by no means all) Haya claim that the members of a clan can trace their descent to a common ancestor, there is little evidence to suggest that Haya clans were ever localized in particular places or ever functioned as corporate groups. Indeed, I know of many cases in which two Haya neighbors could claim that, despite being members of the same clan, they shared no common ancestry or place of origin. In some instances, clan members would not recognize a common totem or even maintain exogamous relations. While marriage might not be "officially" permitted between such clan members, Haya recognize ritualized ways of legitimating such marriages.[14] This pattern of dispersed clan affiliations is characteristic of interlacustrine cultures more generally. Indeed, clan classifications often cross ethnic regions. Many Haya could trace clan affiliations from Bunyoro through Ankole in what is now Uganda.[15]

The dispersed and fluid character of Haya clanship is equally critical to the control of the *ekibanja* lands. If descent was ensured through the maintenance of household farms (an issue discussed at length in chapter 7) then inmigrating clansmen from other regions in Buhaya and beyond could be accommodated through inheritance as a way of assuring lineal continuity. Also relevant is the fact that Haya farms are generally quite small,[16] and the grassland surrounding Haya villages is not easily converted into the arable land necessary for household occupation.[17] This combination of variables meant that households with many potential heirs would not be able to provide tracts of land adequate to support descendant generations. Such cases contributed to the migration necessary for those *without* heirs to pass on their estates to those who could not inherit land within their natal villages. Moreover, the displacement of persons without access to inherited lands resulted in the formation of other forms of tenancy that generally gave tenants rather tenuous attachments to the lands they cultivated (Reining 1962, 63ff).

In addition to tenancy and inheritance, land could be acquired through purchase. With the rapidly expanding market for coffee, which was grown on family farms, such lands soon acquired a high commercial value. Because of their fears that the sale of such lands would produce a landless proletariat without a labor market, when peasant producers were necessary for the commercial success of coffee, the British administration prohibited the sale or mortgaging of land in 1928. This legislation was difficult to enforce, although the fact that native courts would not recognize land sales made purchasing land a risky proposition (Curtis 1989, 115). Land sales did continue in Buhaya, and in the 1950s an administrative effort was made to both recognize their existence and regulate them more closely. In 1957, Bahaya Land Rules were passed, which not only recognized the right of landholders to sell their land but also preserved the rights of clan members to repay the purchase cost to the buyer and thereby redeem the farm (Curtis 1989, 538–41). To this day, Haya recognize the right of individuals to sell land to those outside the clan only when members of their own clan are unable to match the purchase price offered. This complex of rights surrounding the sale of *ekibanja* is the focus of the vast majority of litigation in Kagera.

The final point I want to make about the disposition of the family *ekibanja* is that women were, and continue to be, systematically denied access to farmland. Widows' and daughters' rights as heirs to their husbands and fathers were recognized only in 1944 (Curtis 1989, 112). Women marry virilocally, and divorced women were not assured of access to the land from their natal home. Women do, however, have access to surrounding *orweya* lands at both their natal and marital homes. While this land is allowed to fallow after each harvest, and women do not retain rights to specific plots of land, their control over the products of such land is crucial to Haya daily life. Women who work these lands together often establish regional "associations" (*ebyama*), which make central contributions to marital relations, mortuary activities, as well as the purchase of everyday consumer goods like food and clothing. I describe the significance of the products of women's activities that center on these *orweya* fields in some detail throughout part 1 of the book. In chapter 7, I also focus on the systematic exclusion of women from clan-based family farms, a position that actually induces women into assuring access to land through both buying and selling.

These dimensions of the administrative and clan-based control of land form the broadest structural parameters of Haya society and economy. Relations of domination between royals and commoners, as well as within commoner clans, were articulated through the spatial and temporal dimensions of the physical terrain. Clan continuity and dispersal were and continue to be constituted by the disposition of the land. Access to arable lands, especially residential farm lands, serves to motivate and orient the movements of people within and between regions of Buhaya. This movement, in turn, establishes the flexibility of clan identifications, as descent relations are split off and recycled in the course of inheritance and dispossession, sale and purchase. Land thus provides a critical form for anchoring Haya identity in the world. The mobility and/or fixity of persons on the landscape are what constitute landholding and clanship. To confirm Merleau-Ponty's insights, we might say that Haya social relations do not exist *in* space, rather they are relations *of* space itself.

This perspective on the relations between clans and the landscape poses a challenge to conventional structuralist and functionalist premises about social organization. Haya agnatic and affinal relations are rife with tensions, and attempts to control land reveal the points of negotiation characteristic of these structural relations. The status of the land itself, the forms of transaction that engage it, and the very identity of the persons who occupy it can all be called into question. Haya efforts to assure descent through incorporating "clan" heirs, migrating to areas where "clan" lands are available, or redeeming the lands of clan members are not *mechanisms* that assure the "reproduction" of this structure; rather, they are strategic practices with systematic potentials for altering the relations between persons and places, thereby redefining the identities of both. The fluidity of these relations, as exemplified in *nyarubanja* tenancy or the increasing commercialization of family farms and their products, has been characteristic of the Haya sociocultural order throughout this century.

Yet these are only the broadest structural features of Haya culture and society. The central purpose of this study is to address the ways in which these relations are constituted and made meaningful in the course of Haya activity and experience. The significance of Haya sociality is explored through the establishment of domestic viability and through the efforts of Haya men and women to define and create the values that orient them to the land they inhabit. The spatiality and temporality of generational, affinal, and residential relations are worked out in meaningful ways through these practices, not merely as the principles of a social order but as tangibly embedded and embodied dimensions of a lived world.

Contemporary Perspectives: The Late 1980s

I lived and worked in Buhaya from September 1988 to March 1990. For the entire length of my research I lived in a village in what was once the kingdom of Ihangiro, the southernmost region of Buhaya, approximately 100 kilometers south of the regional capital, Bukoba. To reach Kagera from Dar es Salaam, one has to take a train to Mwanza, a journey of nearly two days. From Mwanza, there is a daily steamer across Lake Victoria to Bukoba. To get from Bukoba to Rubya, a bus runs on most weekdays; it takes about six hours to travel the sixty miles. In the rural areas of the Muleba District there is no running water (although a very few homes have storage tanks that collect rain water) and no electricity (although a few homes and public buildings do generate their own electricity; see chapter 8). All the Haya men and women I met who lived in the district spent at least some time doing agricultural activities—especially weeding, which is a never-ending task. There was no mechanized agriculture on the small household farms, and agricultural inputs in the form of either animal manure or chemical fertilizers and pesticides were extremely rare. Most houses were of wattle and daub, although baked and unbaked brick homes were not uncommon. Many homes had corrugated zinc roofs, although woven thatch was still widely used.

The life histories of Haya men and women, however, belie this pastoral vision. While many Haya from this southern district had never been as far away as Bukoba, many others had traveled for trade or labor to other parts of East Africa, in spite of the transportation difficulties described above. Haya women have worked in urban areas all across East Africa selling domestic and sexual services since at least the 1930s, and the number of women living or working outside of Buhaya today, at least according to my Haya neighbors' accounting, is greater than the number of men.[18]

The linguistic context in Buhaya literally bespeaks the interpenetration of these regional worlds, as well. Seven years of primary education are required in Tanzania. Secondary education is highly desired by most of the Haya I met, but positions are virtually unavailable. A friend of mine who taught primary school told me that there were only 500 positions in private and public secondary schools in all of the Kagera Region for the 17,000 graduates of primary school (although I have been unable to confirm these statistics). The language of instruction in all primary schools is Kiswahili, the official and national language of Tanzania. Broadcasts by the state-run Radio Tanzania are in Kiswahili and English. I found that, with very few exceptions, all Haya could be considered native speakers of both Kiswahili and Oluhaya.

My own linguistic situation in the community further demonstrates its multivocality. I had studied Kiswahili for the equivalent of three academic years prior to my research in Tanzania, and I could converse freely when I arrived in Kagera. I spoke and was spoken to in Kiswahili throughout my time in Buhaya. Both Kiswahili and Oluhaya are Bantu languages, and I did manage to learn Oluhaya well enough that I could follow—but not fully participate in—most Haya conversations. I never worked with a "translator" in my research, except in the sense that I might ask someone to tell me in Kiswahili what they had just told their interlocutor in Oluhaya.[19]

In all respects, the Kagera Region of the late 1980s, even in the most remote

Figure 2. The largest weekly market in the region. Printed textiles (*kanga* and *kitenge*) are laid out for display or exhibited across the bicycles that their merchants use to transport their inventory.

rural areas, is an immediately recognizable part of the "modern" world. Haya men's clothing style is clearly derived from Western fashions. In most cases, the very clothing itself comes (used) from Europe. Women's dress may appear "exotic" at first blush, but the *kanga* and *kitenge* they wear are produced in textile factories in urban parts of Tanzania and Kenya—and some of the most prized cloth comes from Holland.[20] Ironworking in Buhaya has been traced to the fifteenth century (Schmidt 1978, 235ff), but the axes and *pangas* used in Buhaya today are made in China. So are the bicycles that facilitate trade and transport for those who can afford them. All of these goods are available *omujajalo*, "at the market." Going to market is the social event of the week in rural Buhaya (fig. 2). Markets are held only once a week, but even the smallest market attracts hundreds of people, as most villagers live within a few miles of two to three different market sites.

Coffee remains the single greatest source of income for the vast majority of Haya households (Smith and Stevens 1988, 557). I found that the median house-hold cash income from coffee for 1989 was approximately $30.[21] Moreover, the world market price for coffee hit a fifteen-year low in 1989. The price for a kilo of coffee rose from 46 shillings in 1988 to 48 shillings in 1989. However, from

September 1988 to December 1989 the Tanzanian shilling was devalued by 100 percent, meaning that the price per kilo received by Haya who sold their coffee in 1989 was roughly half of the 1988 price. In spite of these tremendous obstacles, many of my neighbors felt that the economy was in better shape in the late 1980s than it had been earlier in the decade, when consumer goods were virtually unavailable at any price in most of rural and much of urban Tanzania.

Thus, apparent contrasts between an isolated rural, agrarian locale and a world of consumer goods, mobility, and migration are tangibly *conjoined* in contemporary Haya local life. This study should be seen as an attempt to address this conjuncture, *not* by teasing apart what might seem to us its disparate elements but by elucidating their integrity in the actual practices and experiences of Haya men and women.

A Précis

This book is organized as follows. The chapters of part 1, "Making the World," present a detailed ethnographic examination of Haya daily practices focused around domestic production. In particular, the production and provision of viable households in space and time are explored through analyses of food-related activities. Chapter 2 develops a model of what I call *focal* space and time as it is constructed in recognized Haya places, in particular in the Haya household. Chapter 3 explores the centrality of the hearth in the Haya household as a concrete locale that condenses crucial social dimensions of productive action. Chapter 4 extends the discussion of culinary practice to the totalizing procedure of providing, presenting, and consuming a meal. Part 1 concludes with chapter 5, a discussion of the place of food and food-related actions (especially eating and feeding) in the construction of Haya understandings of value and wealth. Throughout these chapters I address the ways in which food—as a material substance, a highly transformative product, and a commodity—figures in the creation of Haya forms of sociality and viability.

In part 2, entitled "The World Unmade," I examine the forms of sociality and productivity embodied in the Haya practices discussed in part 1 and explore what many Haya perceive to be insidious threats and indices of disruption and dislocation to these crucial forms. My analysis focuses directly on commoditization, not as an imposed transformation that simply and irrevocably subverts Haya cultural values but as a process that is infused in all aspects of the lived world, and which leads to the creation, enhancement, transformation, as well as subversion of local understandings of effective personal and collective action.

In chapter 6, I discuss an affliction called "plastic teeth," which many Haya fear is plaguing their infants. Chapter 7 extends my discussion of affliction and commoditization by dealing directly with Haya understandings of both AIDS and money, and the relation between them. The final chapter treats a local rumor or legend concerning "greedy people" who make their living by stealing and selling human blood. Ultimately I argue that all these diverse images of consumption are concrete forms of consciousness that articulate a wide set of forces, local communities and global economies, rural villages and urban scenes, and embodied commodities and commoditized bodies. In conclusion I argue, in contrast to Bourdieu, that far from being a scourge of meaning and "authentic" value, Haya sociocultural activities indicate that commodity forms present novel possibilities, which reciprocally reformulate subjective experience as they reconstitute the physical world. "Making" and "unmaking," then, can be contrasted analytically as different dimensions of these activities, but in phenomenal terms they are always conjoined in this dynamic constitutive and creative process.

1 MAKING THE WORLD

Part 1 of this book focuses on everyday practices surrounding Haya households and domestic production. As a means of approaching this vast topic in a more or less coherent fashion, I devote considerable attention to Haya interests in and activities concerned with the production, provision, and consumption of food. To understand how the activities in which food is engaged make food so central to the organization of Haya sociocultural processes and to appreciate the ways in which food motivates people's actions, we have to consider the specific forms that these actions, and that food itself, can take. As we shall see, not all edible things have the value of food, and not just anything can be done to acquire the values that food provides. What is important about food in this respect are the ways in which the concrete means of providing and using food open onto an entire way of life. While I begin my analyses at the level of the household, I go on to demonstrate that a wide range of culturally configured practices, concepts, and debates are entailed in food-related activities (Bourdieu 1984, 176–200). The concrete form of these activities must be specified in order to assess the constitutive dimensions of food for a lived world of meaning and experience. Food, I am suggesting, is integral to making this world.

But food's capacity for making—for generating both a tangible world of objects as well as the potential for a variety of experiences as a part of that world—is not easily assessed in terms of the standard categories of production, distribution, preparation, and consumption, which focus on food strictly as a resource or functional necessity (cf. Goody 1982, esp. 40–96). For the implications of food lie in its potential both to objectify the creative processes that produce it and also to serve as a vehicle for activities that extend beyond the contexts of production or provision. An entire order of experience, power, and meaning is condensed in immediate food contexts—growing and harvesting, cooking and preserving, presenting and selling, eating and feeding.

Moreover, the qualities generated in these immediate contexts, and the meanings that inform the organization of these contexts can also be traced through numerous levels of experience and action. Food is clearly a kinesthetic medium, and this has made it a rich topic for detailed anthropological investigation (Appadurai 1981, 494). Health, sexuality, bodiliness, and more general aspects of the person (Battaglia 1990; Bourdieu 1984; Dubisch 1981; Laderman 1981); the landscape, architecturally constructed space, and residential obligations (Hugh-Jones 1979; Malinowski 1935; Munn 1986; Richards 1939); an encompassing political economy and the local community's place in it (Appadurai 1981; Douglas 1966; Mintz 1985; Weismantel 1988)—all are inflected with practical understandings of value that, as I hope to demonstrate in the Haya case, are formulated in terms of concrete experiences of food. In short, food is a central symbolic vehicle *in,* as well as an objectification *of,* constitutive collective practices. Food is a locally privileged means of organizing and experiencing the material and immaterial features of a lived world.

2 "EVIL FLEE, GOODNESS COME IN": CREATING AND SECURING DOMESTICITY

Lighting and Entering

"Have they already built a house?" This is a common question in Buhaya, one that is most often asked of young married men. The question suggests a certain status and sense of achievement that accompany building a house (in Haya, *eka,* or *enju*) and thereby becoming a household head (in Haya, *nyineka, nyinenju,* literally "mother of a house"). One may have access to abundant resources, be recognized as hard-working, or enjoy a reputation for being honest and reliable, but to fully exercise the authority (in Haya, *obushobola;* in Swahili, *utawala*) that is the prerogative of the head of a household, you must have a house.

To draw attention to the significance of what I will call "viability" in the organization and orientation of a household, let me begin not with house building but with the acts that open a house as a residence. *Okutaa omunju,* "to enter into a house," is a ceremony that serves to acknowledge and safeguard a home and those who live in it.[1] Neighbors, friends, and relations gather for this occasion, and they share coffee, beer, and conversation as they would at almost any festive event. But the most important activity in the house entering ceremony, in the view of those who discussed this with me, is lighting the home's first fire—*okuemba omulilo* ("to light the fire"). This fire ideally is lit by the father of the new household head. Any senior agnate—a father's brother or father's sister, each of whom is equally one's father—is just as acceptable. It was also insisted that it was not appropriate for one's mother to light this fire—one man even suggested that he would sooner light this fire himself than have his mother do so. In the Haya patrilocal system, the new house has been built on land provided by agnates, and so it seems that the identity and integrity of that house, which are assured by this fire, must also be grounded in agnatic relations.

The fire is built, not at the hearth back in the kitchen, but in the sitting room (*omulyango* in Haya or *sebuli* in Swahili) in the front region of the house. Only after the fire has been lit and allowed to burn for a while, are the embers (*ebisisi*) from this fire carried back to the kitchen hearth, usually by women, and never by the senior agnate who lights the fire. This fire contains medicinal plants and is made from special woods that are themselves medicines. As the fire is lit, a blessing (*ekigasha*) is offered: *Ekibi kishoholaha, ekilungi kitaamu,* "Evil flee, goodness come in." This blessing is intended to insure tranquility in the household, not only over the long term but also in the short term, for the period of the house opening ceremony itself.

This is only a brief, schematic account of an important event. But these elementary procedures exemplify certain *potentialities* of action (see Munn 1983, 1986) and the form that such actions can and should take. These potentialities concern the generation of productive, viable domesticity, its spatial and temporal organization, and the ways in which it engages social relations.

The house is an abiding interest of anthropological analyses, and the present consideration should be situated in that tradition. The "close relationship between the structure of the house and the structure of the group that it shelters" is central to Mauss's study of Eskimo social morphology (1979, 44). In recent years, the house and household have been described as basic units of social structure and process, units that embody collective principles of hierarchy, opposition, segmentation, and the like; and whose symbolic configuration, as a tangible representation of these principles, serves to orient those who inhabit the house to the production, reproduction, and transformation of collective life (see esp. Bourdieu 1979; Hugh-Jones 1979; Fernandez 1982; Daniels 1984; Comaroff 1985b; Hanks 1990). The interpretation offered here is equally concerned with the house as a "representation" or "embodiment" of sociocultural processes in the sense suggested by these analysts. Moreover, I am especially interested in focusing on the house as a means of initiating a discussion of the significance of food in Buhaya. The material form of a house not only orients persons to each other, but it orients them to other material objects. And in Buhaya food is an object of particular interest to a household. This first section of this study concerns the relations between food and households, and uses food as a central medium for explaining and exemplifying the practices and processes of domestic organization, production, and generativity. In short, I argue that food is integral to household viability, and provides a concise means for examining what such viability entails.

This initial account introduces the Haya household in what is occasionally a rather technical discussion of spatial and temporal relations and orientations as well as of very specific linguistic forms and practices. Some of my formal language (e.g., my account of "within-ness," or relative vs. absolute cardinality) is intentionally abstract, although I am always attempting to relate these formal terms to a specific ethnographic set of activities. These abstractions emerge out of an attempt to grapple with the subtleties of indigenous processes, processes that are quite pragmatically realized in a range of sociocultural practices, but less frequently discussed by Haya men and women directly—or, more importantly, seen as worthy of discussion.

In this chapter I am less concerned with tracing the significance of the values and orientations I discuss across a wide array of Haya cultural practices than I am with narrowing my focus to a particular set of activities, in order to see how they form a meaningful pattern in space and time. Thus, while I do not explore the significance of (for example) "within-ness" to everything from sexual relations to food security, I do attempt to specify very carefully some of the meanings of this concept to the particular Haya acts of lighting a fire and entering a household. This narrow focus—coupled with my attempt to demonstrate the richness of these few, superficially "simple" procedures—necessitates a degree of abstraction. In any case, while the material discussed and presented here helps me to construct an analytic model, evidence for the applicability of this model, as well as challenges to it, are explored in much greater detail in subsequent chapters.

Basic Orientations

Lighting the fire in these house entering rites presumes and instantiates a distinction in the basic form of the house, a distinction between the front and the back of the house. Contemporary Haya houses are built on a four-sided plan, with a sloping roof. Most houses have corrugated zinc roofs, although some roofs are thatched with grass and plant fibers. Many houses are built with bricks, although (in my sample) most are wattle and daub, constructions of mud packed on a wood and fiber frame. In these four-sided houses (*ekibanda*, singular), the front room (*omulyango*) is enclosed on all sides, and a doorway leads to the back room or rooms (fig. 2). If there are storage rooms, these are also separated by doorways off to the sides of the front room. The effect of this design is to make each room in the house a separable enclosure. This is an effect that is made even more pronounced by the way in which internal doors are kept closed when guests are met in the front room (figs. 3 and 4).

The point of this discussion is not to describe the importance of doors in contemporary housing, but to indicate the fact that divisions within the house are clearly recognized, marked, and maintained in routine activities. The divi-

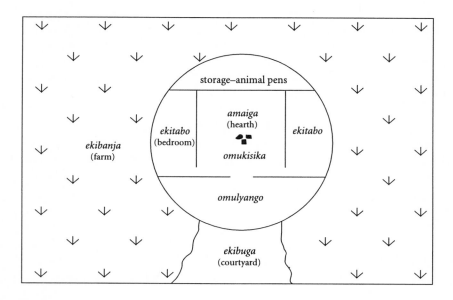

Figure 3. *Omushonge* housing.

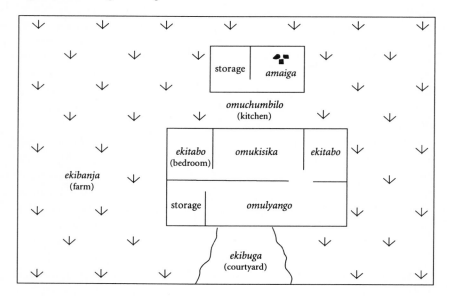

Figure 4. *Ekibanda* housing.

sion between the front and rear rooms of an *ekibanda,* which is instantiated in the house entering, is equally important to the historical design of Haya houses. The "beehive" form of house (*omushonge*), built on a circular plan out of woven fiber and wood and covered entirely with grasses (fig. 3), was in wide use in Kagera up through the early 1950s (see Reining 1967),[2] but is virtually nonexistent in the 1980s. My neighbors were familiar with this design (many had been born and raised in an *omushonge*), but they spoke of this style of house as an antiquated relic, and an example of Haya "cultural tradition" (*kitamaduni*).[3] However, in the *omushonge* the distinction between front and back was equally marked; the greeting area in the front part of the house (also called *omulyango*) was separated from the rear of the house by large woven screens hung from the posts that supported the house frame. The rear region of the house was called *omukisika*—literally "inside the screen." In contemporary houses, this area behind the front room is also called *omukisika,* despite the absence of screens. These transformations indicate that division, enclosure, and exclusion remain central features of architectural design, regardless of geometric configuration.

The back area, called *omukisika* in both round and four-sided houses, is an area associated with women and, especially, with affinal relations. As we have seen, the fire is moved from its agnatic inception in the front of the house and taken back to the kitchen by women, usually matrilaterals of the household head. Moreover, when a new bride is taken into a household, she is sequestered for a period of time (in some cases I know of, up to a full year) and refrains from work in her new household. During this time, the woman is said to be *omukisika* ("behind/inside the screen") and spends her time in the inner rooms in the back region of the house. In fact, I was friendly with a teacher living in a small residence on the school grounds who actually constructed a screen around his quarters when he brought in his new wife.

These rear rooms are the area in which married women continue to spend much of their time (when they are actually inside the house) while they live in their husbands' homes. Indeed, the most respectful position for a woman to greet and converse with guests in her home is reclining on the floor of the back room, peeking out from its doorway, lying between the front room and the door that is pulled close behind her. In these ways, the rear rooms of a house are sites of affinal incorporation and occupation. But these areas are more than simply sites, for the spatial relation between front and back gives a concrete orientation to social relations. The specific content and character of affinity itself are defined and generated through the ways in which it is situated *in* particular spatial contexts as well as through the ways in which affinal relations are integral to the definition *of* household space itself. As the movement of the fire from front to back implies (and as the uses of that fire in the household, described below, make clear), it is the actions of affines in a house that establish these differences between front and back. The movement of the fire from front to back, which completes the house entering, thus confirms and constitutes the spatial orientation and coordination of the social relations that make up a household.

While the fire built in the front room helps to establish important divisions within the house (front and back, lineality and affinity), as well as the sequencing of those relations (*from* front *to* back, etc.), it is equally concerned with the relations between houses. The medicated contents of the fire and the blessing that accompanies the fire suggest this connection of the newly entered house to the world around it. The simple phrase (*Ekibi kishoholaha, ekilungi kitaamu* ("Evil flee, goodness come in") invokes a contrast, not only between evil and goodness but between "right here" and "elsewhere," a distinction that has ramifications for a much wider order of relations and practices in which the house is implicated. The spatial form of contrast presented in this blessing is more apparent for Haya speakers. The verbs *okushohola* ("to go away or flee") and *okutaa* ("to enter") are stated in this rite with distinct verbal extensions— *aha* and *omu,* respectively—both of which have important locative implications. *Aha* used in this way refers to "there" as a nonspecified but delimited place, direction, or duration. So, for example, one can reply to the question *Nogy'ai?* ("Where are you going?") by saying *Nagendaha* ("I'm going there"), which suggests that one is going to some unspecified place other than here (or, perhaps as likely, a place that is being concealed from the questioner). The extension *aha* is used in contrast to *aho,* a related extension that refers to "here" as a nonspecific locus—as, for example, in the greeting *Alioki?* ("What is here?") and its response *Tulio!* ("We are here!"). As an extension, *omu* not only contrasts locus relative to speaker (i.e., *aha* vs. *aho,* "here" vs. "there") but defines a specific directionality as well. *Omu* is used to express "within-ness," and as a verbal extension, it has a centripetal quality, directing the action to the *interior* of a given locus. In this way, goodness is directed to enter *inside* (*kitaamu*) the house, while evil is sent off away from this "inside, here."

This point is not merely a trivial observation that there is a contrast between "here" and "there" relative to which any speaker situates him or herself in any act of reference. What I am suggesting here is that the contrast of "inside, here" and "some other place" encoded in this blessing is a *dynamic* one. There is always a tension between "inside" and "elsewhere" that is implicit in the configuration of any recognizable location. The particular spatial qualities of the "inside, here" invoked in this utterance are determined by their orientation to the "somewhere else," not merely as an opposition (as, for example, "here" vs. "not here") but as an interrelation of spatial directions. The inside space addressed here is significant precisely because it is defined as distinct from but also *a part of* the wider world that lies "somewhere else." That is, "entering inside" (*kitaamu*) is necessarily a movement situated within an unspecified "elsewhere." Generating the inside space referred to therefore entails a dual orientation, a "within-ness" that is intrinsically "away from" an external location. I suggest that this reciprocal interrelation of spatial orientations is what makes this blessing efficacious, for it allows a home to be recognizable and distinguishable as a "place" (*omwanya*).

Of course, simply willing these interrelated contrasts into existence is not (generally) enough to make the world conform to one's desired ends. The dual orientation of inside and elsewhere is not wholly created by this ritual invocation. Indeed, it is the encompassing meaningful situation of these contrasts that informs these references—the fact that "within-ness" and "somewhere else" are practical dimensions that concretely orient people's experiences, ideas, and actions (i.e., that they are a part of a wider cultural context)—that allows this invocation to work. In order to address this wider situation, and to specify some of the concrete meanings embedded in the form of the house as an inside space with a dual orientation of this sort, let me turn to the contents of the house opening fire itself, and to the qualities of fires more generally.

Woods and Weeds

The house entering fire contains medicines (singular, *omubazi;* plural, *emibazi*) that serve to safeguard the house and effectively make "evil flee and goodness come in." The principal wood used to construct the fire (according to informants) is a thin bamboo reed—*olubingo,* or *matete* in Swahili. Bamboo of this kind can be used as a medicine or amulet to safeguard a person. It is also a very important component of house building. Storage areas in the space immediately under the house's roof, called *ahadari,* are constructed out of long, narrow lengths of bamboo. These materials form the floor of a kind of attic in which household implements are commonly stored.[4] The other plants I was told are burned in the fire are *omwetango* and *eibuza,* which were described simply as "weeds" (*omwata*) that are readily available on almost any farm. There are a number of different contexts that I am aware of in which each of these different medicines could be used, contexts that certainly could be usefully explored in order to tease out the significance of these plants. But, what is equally interesting are the names of these medicines and their derivations.

Like the words that bless these plants as they burn, the names of these medi-cines have a locative significance. The bamboo, *olubingo*, is derived from the verb *okubinga*, "to drive off." To drive off something—or, perhaps more likely, someone—in this way is not simply to send them away but to actively remove them and keep them away from a particular place. Thus, diseases are "driven off" through therapy, and I often heard former husbands say that they had "driven off" their wives to dissolve a marriage. The weed *omwetango* gets its name from the verb *okutanga*, "to prevent"; *eibuza* is from the verb *okubuza*, the causative form of *okubula*, "to be lost."

It is not sufficient simply to note that each of these plants embodies an action.[5] The argument could be made that the significance of any object derives from the ways in which it evokes the actions through which people engage it (an argument that I'm inclined to make myself). Here I am arguing, instead, that these particular forms of medicine, rather than being objectifications of the potential positive outcomes of actions (e.g., in the form of goodness, wealth, peace, etc.) focus specifically on the *process* that will lead to these outcomes. What is especially important is that each of these actions—driving off, prevent-ing, and losing or making lost—has a concretely spatial and temporal implica-tion. Simply stated, these medicines have to do with removing and keeping things out.

The use of these medicines in the house opening fire thus deepens the significance of the spatial contrasts invoked in the blessing, for the actions of removing and keeping things out are complementary aspects of the dual spatial orientation in and *through* which the house is situated. Driving things off or making them lost are actions that derive not necessarily from an "inside" position (one can, for example, drive off goats that are eating out in a peanut field) but from a determinate place *out from which* the action is oriented. Reciprocally, acts of prevention may also *derive* from a determinate position, but they are *oriented* toward other (possible) acts and agents that come from beyond that position. The coordination of these distinct orientations—driving off and keeping out—through the specific qualities embodied in the compo-nents of the house opening fire is further evidence of the ways in which the house is situated as a dynamic interrelation of spatial dimensions.

Temporal relations are equally critical to these acts and orientations, since they are centrally concerned with *motion*. The acts of driving out and keeping away not only connect the internal position protected through these invoca-tions to an encompassing external context by preventing penetration (from the outside) and reciprocally removing intrusions (from the inside), these acts also establish temporal connections between the inside as a place of *origin*, and the encompassing context toward which that which is excluded is oriented and (should) ultimately *end up.* These acts *initiated* at the interior are directed toward "driving out" as their *final* consequence. The reciprocal spatial dimensions of these invocations are therefore complemented by the dynamic interrelation of origins and endpoints over time.[6]

Moreover, these particular forms of action—the concern with movement out of and into a definitive place—suggest important experiential and meaningful aspects of a house's spatiality. These rites, and other activities discussed below, suggest that when an area is created and recognized as a particular *place,* the reciprocal orientations of inside and outside can become antagonistic, and this potential for antagonism must be managed.

The nature of this antagonism, and the wider significance of the house opening fire to its spatial and temporal dimensions can be seen in other contexts in which the qualities of these practical dimensions are acted upon. For example, the medicines used in the house opening fire (particularly the *omwetango,* in my experience) are often used by beer brewers. My Haya neighbors claimed that medicines should be used in this way because one needs "to prevent disputing" (*okutanga abalwana;* or *kuzuia magomvi,* more common in Swahili) which is an unpleasant possibility when beer is served. These medicines can be rubbed over the vessels in which the beer is fermented or distilled or can be placed in the household fire, as they are in the house entering rites. Moreover, a similar utterance accompanies the use of medicines in these contexts: those who are causing trouble are sent off with the words *Ababi, abalwana bagende!* "Evil ones, those who argue must go!"

The importance of medicating those contexts in which beer is served in order to prevent dispute can be accounted for, to a certain degree, in terms of Haya understandings of the effects of drunkenness on the spatiotemporal orientations of the body (see Carlson 1989, 241–48). A proper level of drunkenness allows one to feel full (*okuhaaga*), to be expansive in a way that extends the experience of life itself—Haya often say *Twalola!* ("We are living!") while they drink.[7] This sense of fullness and expansion is also the household's motive during ceremonial celebrations that provide drink for numerous guests. But, just as the spatial form of housing is placed at risk by these expansive activities (as the necessity of "driving out" and "keeping away" evil indicates), bodily integrity may also be violated by excessive drunkenness. When a person has far too much to drink, according to my many drinking partners, "you forget yourself" (*kujisahau* in Swahili). This degree of drunkenness is commonly associated with becoming lost and dislocated, itself a critical index of having "forgotten yourself." People often told me of occasions when, having become excessively drunk, they would end up spending the night "sleeping out in the bush."

That preventing dispute is a particular concern for the Haya during beer drinking has, perhaps, less to do with the effects of inebriation than it does with the consequences of sociality. Haya friends often told me that fights break out when beer is served because you can be sure that "a mixture of different people from different places" will show up at a home where beer is available. As one beer brewer put it, "It only takes one drunk stranger to ruin a celebration." Thus, all manner of ceremonies have to be "medicated" because the "mixture" of people, and hence the probability of "strangers" showing up, in itself poses uncertainties. Moreover, such a concern is sensitive to the fact that *places* have qualities as well. And the mixture of places entailed by this mixture of people presents a situation that is especially problematic when the viability of a particular location is at risk. As we have seen, the house opening rites themselves serve to protect the house from conflicts between guests that might arise during the course of this ceremony, and they do so by clearly defining the coordinate spatial dimensions of that place. The significance of this concern with preventing dispute, then, has to do with the spatial configuration of social relations that becomes embedded in any house that is recognized as a distinct place. This spatial configuration, as I have described it, is characterized by a *dual* orientation. Inwardly directed action is intrinsically separated from a wider world, which is kept at a remove; yet that separation also recognizes the necessary connection to that external world in order precisely to *demonstrate* that an *internal* focus can be secured. In fact, a successful beer drink is one of the best ways of making such a demonstration. Offering beer proves the viability of a household *in relation* to those whom it provides with drink. Guests/strangers (plural, *abagenyi*; singular, *omugenyi*), therefore, are a dangerous necessity. While they make the offer of beer possible, the presence of guests in a house also entails a risk, not only of "opening out" the properly inward focus of a house but also of "opening" the guests to each *other*. The integrity of the household as a relational field, one that asserts its viability through its ability to successfully *separate* itself from yet *integrate* itself into a broader social field, can be literally dis-integrated in the conflicts of drunken strangers.[8] Haya concerns with preventing dispute, then, suggest that both bodily and household forms of spatiality are similarly engaged and at risk during beer drinking. In this situation, assuring the proper management of antagonistic spatial orientations could be called the essence of "prevention," an essence that is conveniently embodied and manipulated in the form of *omwetango*.

This feature of Haya sociality—the susceptibility and antagonism of households, persons, and wealth (such as beer) to "others" who are intrinsically a part of and frequently necessary to one's own identity and integrity—is a pervasive dimension and problematic of social practice, one that is particularly relevant to discussions of food provision, production, and consumption; gifting; and, not surprisingly, affliction and sorcery. Here, I want to point out that this concern is inscribed at the most fundamental levels of Haya spatial orientation, through the contrast between inside and outside as it is constituted and controlled in the form of the house.

Binding Circles and Cardinal Foci

The use of medicines in these ways and on ceremonial and collective occasions such as these is most commonly called *okuzinga,* "to bind, coil, or surround." Wedding ceremonies must be bound (*okuzinga obugenyi,* "to bind a wedding") to insure their tranquility, and binding death (*okuzinga olufu*) in order to "keep it away" is essential at the conclusion of mortuary rites. The verb *okuzinga* suggests a kind of encompassment—for example, an island is an *ekizingo,* that is, land encompassed by water. The form of encompassment is equally important. *Okuzinga* is an encircling activity[9]—thus, *enzingo* is a variety of plantain, widely recognized as a powerful medicine, whose individual fruits coil around the stalk in a continuous line (i.e., not in a pattern of discontinuous rows, for those of you less familiar with banana bunches). This quality of encompassment as an encircling or coiling procedure is significant for the Haya. A door may be closed and firmly locked. In the Haya vernacular, however, one would not say that the lock "binds" the door shut. A door is "closed/locked" (*oluhigi lwakinga*). But a large pole that is secured in place and tightly wrapped by coiling fibers (as a housepost might be) would be said to be "bound" (*enyomyo yazingwa*). "Binding," then, as I am translating the term *okuzinga,* entails this specific spatial form.

The encircling action of *okuzinga,* or "binding rites," adds another dimension to house entering ceremonies. To begin with, these rites can themselves be called *okuzinga enju,* "to bind the house." This circular form suggests an identification of this form of ritual with the form of the house itself, as the *omushonge* beehive style of housing is built on a circular plan. Moreover, all "binding rites" work to protect a given location, event, or identity by manipulating a particular spatial configuration; that is, they encompass such phenomena in order to situate them in a meaningful, powerful, and, thus, effective way.[10] The significance and efficacy of encircling to these binding rites suggests that the interrelated orientations of "within-ness" and "somewhere else," whose coordination, as we have seen, is worked out and represented by a range of objects and practices, are also articulated with circular form. That is, inward and outward directionality must both be understood as dimensions that are generated as necessary constituents of the wider circular and encircling spatial forms that characterize particular Haya places. A contrast between inside and outside is intrinsic to the creation of circular enclosure.

The importance of circular form and encircling actions to the establishment and protection of Haya locales requires us to move beyond the dual dimensions of inward and outward orientations. The encompassment that is effected by binding rites presents a more complex order of spatial relations than the simple opposition between "within-ness" and "somewhere else." At the same time, the form of this encircling action tells us more about the Haya construction of directionality and spatiotemporal orientations in ways that illuminate the characteristics of this inward/outward contrast. The Haya sense of "within-ness" is not defined merely through its tensions with the wider world in which it participates and from which it withdraws; it is not merely a *direction,* however significant this aspect of interiority might be. Rather, as the circularity of these binding rites suggests (and as I hope to make clear below), internal space and enclosure more generally have a determinate form as well as a processual structure. The dimensions of this form and process, and the qualities embedded in them, are in turn essential to a house's capacity to create and sustain its own integrity and viability within a wider community.

The internal space that is created and protected by binding rites is an order of spatial and temporal dimensions that, I suggest, can be considered a kind of integrated totality. Constructing this totality involves many of the techniques and substances that have already been discussed, as well as additional means that entail a more complex set of dimensions and possibilities. Medicines, for example, can be used and blessed in binding rites simply by placing them in the fire and invoking the separation of inside and outside. This technique is considered sufficient to orient a place properly, and its brevity may be necessary to deal with immediate conflicts—a drunken dispute needs to be settled rather quickly. But a more effective means of safeguarding a location involves using the same medicines in a precautionary fashion. Typically, Haya men say that "those old women" know about the best ways to protect places. These women (according to their own description of their techniques) will light the ends of medicinal plants in the fire, and then carry the plants to the place that is to be protected. A woman then shakes the burning medicine in four directions; in front of her, behind her, to her right, and to her left. In some (but not all) accounts of house opening rites, I was told that the senior agnate may use the fire medicines in this way. Moreover, in house opening ceremonies, millet (*omugusha*) and coffee berries (*akamwani*) are often used in similar ways. The "father" of the new household head will chew millet and spit it in the four directions mentioned. Next, coffee berries are tossed in the four directions. Furthermore, tossing coffee berries in this way is perhaps the most common kind of blessing or of propitiation in Buhaya.

The significance of millet and coffee cannot be summarized easily.[11] Millet is used to ferment banana juice into beer, and coffee berries are cooked to create a masticatory. These two products are the most pervasive substances of social interaction in Buhaya and figure in almost every single act of exchange or encounter. Suffice it to say that millet (in beer) and coffee berries could be called the quintessential Haya objects for guests, and their exchange marks the establishment of a vast array of social relations, from blood brotherhood pacts to bridewealth payments. The practices that employ millet and coffee, therefore, suggest that, like the burning medicinal plants, they are media that help to realize and objectify the interrelated contrast between "insiders" and "outsiders." As objects for guests, the use of beer and coffee is premised on the difference between insiders and outsiders, while such tokens simultaneously attempt to overcome that difference by mediating between insiders and outsiders.

However, the ways in which millet and coffee, as well as these other medicines, are used entail a more comprehensive set of spatial dimensions than these. By directing these substances in four directions, the inward orientation is not only contrasted to the outward direction (which the very substances, medicinal and otherwise, confirm), but this internal focus becomes systematically differentiated. The dual orientation that characterizes any particular Haya location as a *place* distinct from its surrounding context is expanded by these actions and through them such a location becomes what might be called a "fuller" space. Internal space is constructed, by such actions, as a set of cardinal directions whose systematic coordination is essential to the identity of a house.

The implications of these cardinal dimensions are tremendously important for the qualities of house space and the processes that go on within the house, for the forms of identification and representation that become appropriated by the subjects and objects that inhabit a house, and for the social, spatial, and temporal relations that exist between houses. To begin with, I should point out that the four directions acted upon (or enacted) in this way necessarily entail a fifth position, namely, the center. Each direction—front, back, right, and left— can be determined only *relative to* some center position. This means that the cardinality created through the motions toward these four directions is a system that orients a *specific place*—that is, a central position—to the world. The human body is an obvious exemplification of this kind of relational orientation, as any particular body provides the central position relative to which these cardinal directions become interrelated and a determinate set of orientations (i.e., left/right, front/back) is defined. And, clearly, each human body carries with it a system of orientation that is *uniquely* relative to it—for what lies in front of men and to my right, may be behind you on your left.

The *relative* cardinal space of the body—or of Haya houses centered in this way—are not, therefore, like the *absolute space* of, for example, latitude and longitude or the points of a compass. These latter are spatial forms that define a set of coordinates relative to which any specific place can be situated. In his discussion of household space and cardinality in Yucatec, Hanks identifies a critical social dimension of these contrasting spatial systems. He differentiates between "grid" and "centered" systems of representation, the former characterized by "relations among objects . . . computed relative to fixed axes and dimensions," while the latter consist of "spatial relations [that] are defined relative to activities and speech events" (Hanks 1990, 295). This difference not only corresponds to the distinction I am drawing here between relative and absolute cardinality, it also points to the fact that centered spatial systems such as the Haya house are defined with reference to concrete sociocultural practices.

The cardinal system defined in this way is a relative system of orientation, one that can be created in the course of activities from any given position relative to which other positions can be located. But there are also indications that through binding rites this form of cardinality, and especially the position at its center, achieves a kind of fixity or enduring integrity. While binding a position may not generate an absolute space, it can produce a relatively fixed and recognizable place that has consequences for ongoing action and events. This much is evident in the very idea of coiling or encompassing, for the central position is encompassed as a part of a delimited place. Given the encircling effects of binding rites, the cardinal directions constitute and orient a center that is enclosed and secured.

The relative fixity of this cardinal system can also be seen in yet another kind of practice, also called *okuzinga,* in which cardinal directions are less created through ritual actions than they are "found" and deployed in protective measures. In Buhaya, crossroads (*emyanda etana,* literally "paths that call each other") are used as sites at which particular phenomena—disease, misfortune, death, and the like—can be bound.[12] Objects identified with the victims of misfortune—for example, a sick person's shirt, or the leftovers from a funerary meal—are often left at crossroads in order to bind the misfortune, thereby keeping it away from those who have been afflicted. I was told that binding rites at a crossroad are effective because crossroads are the conjunction of different paths, and are, therefore, certain to have some (human) traffic on them. Thus, the misfortunes bound at a crossroad will be *removed from* those who are afflicted and *sent on* to those who come across them, conjoining, once again, the interrelated practices of driving off and keeping away.

The use of crossroads in this way suggests a degree of fixity even to relative cardinal systems, or cardinal places. The crossroad serves to fix objects in space in a particular way. Misfortune can be removed and transformed because these central positions are bounded spaces. More fundamentally, the crossroads is a bounded space because of the way in which it concretizes cardinal relations. The crossroads is both a central space relative to which directions are defined, but also the center itself is *defined by* the relation between directions. The alternate pathways come together to create, and locate a particular center. Indeed, the relation between the roads is the crossroads itself. The crossroads, then, is both an encompassing center and an encompassed site, a center that is located and determined by the convergence of roads. Furthermore, the kinds of mobility characteristic of this encompassed and encompassing position are also reciprocally constructed. The crossroads is a place of coming together, as well as moving apart. As Haya neighbors told me, a crossroads is a place of "going and coming" (*genda nakuija*), a conjunction that assures that people will be passing through. Just as the bound household conjoins the motion of keeping off and driving away, so too the crossroads articulates convergent and divergent movements. Indeed, the fact that the crossroads connects these centrifugal and centripetal movements allows it to hold on to or fix aspects of one's identity, because of the assurance that these will be passed on to others. This reciprocal quality of the crossroads, as a space that both encompasses and is encompassed by cardinality, makes this site a relatively integrated position in relation to the directions it coordinates. The integrity that inheres in cardinal orientations provides a grounding for sustained identity, an integrity that can be appropriated by binding rites that make use of crossroads or invoke the cardinal space of the house.

This system of orientation has a totalizing effect, one that helps locate a particular *place* as something more than a site in opposition to others. Establishing a cardinal space through binding procedures not only generates a stable position, it creates an internally integrated place, one that has an independent configuration. This configuration gives the "here" of the house a more complete orientation to its encompassing context of near and distant neighbors and strangers and, reciprocally, situates this context with respect to that particular household "place." Cardinality is characteristic of an integrated and total spatiality. Each house, as we shall see, becomes its own *center* of its social world, a focus for locating relations between selves and others, and for securing a perspective on the world.

Houses in Villages

These features of cardinal relations, the ways in which they establish a certain fixity and totality in spatial form, can be more fully demonstrated through an understanding of the forms of identification and representation that are embedded in the ways in which the Haya inhabit household space and the ways in which households occupy village space more generally. It is worth pointing out that the form of cardinality enacted through these binding rites within the house are achieved by and through the human body. This is no mere obvious fact, for the correspondence between Haya household and bodily spatial form reveal a great deal about the meaningful construction of identity and action.

The relative cardinal space inscribed in the house through bodily action is reflexively embodied in Haya bodies, which appropriate its form. The ways in which the house and the body are coordinated is essential to Haya spatial organization. In Haya villages, houses are almost randomly dispersed. There is no fixed, absolute orientation system (such as the movement of the sun from East to West, or landmarks like particular mountains, or Lake Victoria), nor is there any collective spatial form (such as a central plaza, a chief's residence, or a bull's horn configuration) which might serve to coordinate *inter*-household spatial relations.

I am not suggesting that Haya spatial organization is simply arbitrary, but rather that no Haya village forms an absolute "grid" of spatial relations. Villages (*ekyaro,* singular) are made up of household farms, each of which is adjacent to its neighbor. A village of contiguous farmland is surrounded by and clearly differentiated from a kind of savanna (*orweya*), which is the site of annual fields that are fallowed; beyond this savanna lies uncultivated bush and forest (*eiringa*). Household farms, unlike the cultivated savanna regions, are also the sites of Haya houses. Thus, there is a higher level of spatial organization insofar as residential land within the village is clearly differentiated from nonresidential land, both cultivated and uncultivated, that lies outside of the village. However, it is equally important to recognize that *within* any given village, houses are not spatially oriented in any uniform way. If a son wishes to build a home for himself after he has married, he will be shown a place on his father's farm where he can build. But this site is at the discretion of the senior relative. It need not be above, below, to the side, etc. of any other home. When a farm is purchased, the new owner may build a house wherever he or she likes. As a consequence, Haya houses face in all different directions, even when they form part of a single household—as, for example, when a father and son or sons have built houses on the same farmland.

This kind of spatial organization is certainly not random, but it does demonstrate that a Haya village does not form an *absolute space* that systematically orients each house or household within a uniform schema. What does unify Haya village organization is that a *relative cardinal system* serves as a complete system of orientation for each *separate* house. What unifies Haya inter-household organization is that each household's orientation *differentiates* it from other households according to the same cardinal schema. In the same way, Haya persons embody cardinality. Each body constitutes a relative cardinal space, the *values* of which (for example, eating with the right hand, sleeping on the right of the house, being buried to the left or right of the house, and many more)[13] both structure and are structured by household orientations (Bourdieu 1977, 72; see esp. Daniels 1984, 105–62 on the relation between Tamil houses and persons). However, the nature of these cardinal spaces is such that each house and each person forms its *own* coordinate system. As I have said, there is no higher level of interhousehold or interpersonal spatial ordering. This restriction of orientation has the effect of inscribing in these objects and subjects a form of spatial integrity and totality. Persons and houses form totalities that not only embody cardinal directions but also *separate* one body from another and one house from the next. The totalizing system created by relative cardinal spaces means that each locus so defined has a separate orientation from all others—just as, quite simply, what is on my left can be to your right. Each house is its own center, and can be oriented to the wider world independent of the kinds of orientation that configure the other houses or places that surround it. This form of inscription (which is also a form of embodiment) has the effect of establishing social identity as a total configuration, one that is integrated through its differentiation from other similarly oriented identities. When put together in this way, mere building materials or corporal substances become recognizable places that can actively participate in the world of which they are a part. A cardinal space, therefore, is a constitutive schema that informs the identity of the person or object that *inhabits* it by inscribing that identity with a definitive orientation to itself and its wider context.

Inside and Outside

The significance of cardinal dimensions as they are constructed in the house—the degree of integrity, totality, and continuity they instantiate—derives from the way in which a central position is situated with respect to its encompassing context. Being centered allows the Haya house to be oriented as a multidimensional spatial form, a specific place with the potential for engaging in, transforming, and being transformed by this wider context. The center also functions to expand the dimensions of household space by encompassing and grounding the contrast of "here" and "elsewhere" in a more fully developed cardinal space. Moreover, in the culturally specific dynamics of Haya spatial (and temporal) organization, establishing a center is critical to creating an *interior* space. As the coiling and encircling action of *okuzinga* suggests, the position established in this way defines a center *relative to* a periphery that surrounds it. The center position is not only the place relative to which all directions are defined, it is also an inside position, and this interiority is equally important to the integrity of spatial form.

We have already seen that the locative forms of the house opening blessing refer to the house as an interior space. The "inside, here" of the house is dialectically related to the "somewhere/anywhere else" that is driven off and kept away. Yet, again, this interiority is not merely a direction. As the binding rites make clear, interior space is encompassing and encompassed. It is constituted as a cardinal position relative to which directionality itself can be defined. In Haya practices, centrality—and its potential for spatial orientation— is intrinsically interior. To inhabit a center places one in an interior situation. The fact that encircling and encompassing are the essential features of binding rites that establish cardinal spaces suggests this identity between interiors and their centers. The integrity achieved by a coordinating center is necessarily embedded in the *enclosure* that surrounds it.

The significance of interiority to the spatial form and integrity of the house is clearly recognized in Haya practices and experience through the spatial form of the social identities that occupy the house. Not just houses but households are interior "spaces." Haya villagers most often will refer to a household as, for example, *omwaGregory,* "inside (at/of) Gregory's" (the interior locative *omu* here used as a prefix with the possessive *-a-* and the name of the household head); alternatively, one speaks of *abomuka* "those inside the house" (the plural demonstrative concord *ab,* used with the locative *omu,* affixed to the noun *eka,* house). More generally, the distinction between "insiders" (*abomunda*) and "outsiders" (*abahelu*) is a basic aspect of Haya identity (Seitel 1977, 199). Indeed, Haya ways of differentiating "self" from "other" are routinely expressed in this spatialized form. Thus, clan members are opposed to non-clan members, or village residents to non-village residents, as "insiders" to "outsiders." It is interesting to note that the Haya term for the category of "sister's child" is *omwihwa,* literally, "one who has been taken out from inside" (Seitel 1977, 199)—that is, not just a child who has been given birth, but one who has, from the perspective of those in the sister/mother's clan, "come out" from the "interior" of agnatic relations (Beattie 1958b, 21). Furthermore, the word for neighbor, *omutaani,* is derived from the reciprocal form of the verb *okutaa,* "to enter"; hence, neighbors are literally "those who enter with each other." Each of these forms of reference—which is to say, social *practices*—indicates that interiority is characteristic of close social relations, an interiority that is bound up in the physical space of the house itself.

The significance of the fact that the house is a quintessential interior and interiorizing space and the necessary implication of centrality to interiority are well illustrated by further aspects of binding rites and the substances that enter into them. Small rings woven from banana fiber, *ngata,* can be used in binding rites. These rings, which are routinely used as cushions for carrying heavy objects on one's head, can be used in order to bind people to particular places. According to informants, objects associated with the person in question can be burned with medicines. The smoke from these embers is then dispersed in four directions (front, back, left, and right), and these medicated remains are then encircled by a banana fiber ring. Here, the cardinal space created by the medicinal objects is articulated with movement inside, to the center of the ring, and with the process of enclosure. The binding rite aims to keep the person *inside,* to move the person into a space that is simultaneously a grounded center. Moreover, in yet a further exemplification of the correlation between bodily and household forms, the basic *ngata* form and construction technique (that is, the circular woven ring) serves as the interior framework of the *omushonge* house. Circular rings of increasingly wide circumferences are the supports for the woven wood and fibers that make up the dome of this house style. Thus, the house itself is an icon of the process of binding. The small *ngata* at the apex of the home (like the *ngata* used to carry objects on the head) and the wide circumference of the house conjoin the properties of interior space with the integrity achieved by enclosure.

As a speculative aside, it is also worth considering *olubingo,* one of the medicines described earlier. This bamboo reed, which is so critical to Haya house binding rites and which can be used to safeguard even relatively unmarked events (for example, by carrying it in your pocket while on a trip), has a botanical form that corresponds to the Haya pattern of spatial organization I am trying to describe. This bamboo regenerates—sometimes in small plots set aside on family farms, sometimes in larger groves near rivers—through parthenogenesis; that is, it reproduces by putting up shoots. The older plant puts out shoots, which surround it. In turn, each of these new offspring puts out its surrounding shoots. Over time, then, the growth pattern of bamboo resembles a sequence of interlocking circles with the "parent" of each generation of shoots at the center of its offspring, which surround it.[14] This pattern corresponds to the model of spatial orientation that I suggest is constructed in Haya socio-cultural practice, an orientation in which centrality is articulated with encompassment and enclosure. The bamboo growth also highlights the temporal dimension of this process, for each center position is the point of origin for the enclosure of growth that surrounds it. This temporal sequence also corresponds to that of the binding rites described here, in which the inside, central place is the position from which a wider, encompassing orientation is established. While I certainly never heard anyone describe the powers of bamboo by making reference to the way that it grows, this reproductive pattern is at the very least an interesting example of a more general process of perpetual growth, integrity, and viability. Bamboo, whose "medicinal" powers are widely recognized, is a concrete manifestation of the interrelation between centrality, interiority, and enclosure that is characteristic of Haya spatial organization.

Where There's Smoke

While these objects and medicines are interesting examples of Haya spatiality, it is the fire itself, at the heart of these house opening activities and the font of domestic productivity and transformation, that is the principle icon of meaningful spatial organization. The place of the fire in these binding rites, in routine domestic work, and in the phenomenological qualities it generates (such as smoking, heating, igniting, etc.) make fire a critical symbol of enclosure, interiority, and, thus, viability—all of which, I have argued, are fundamental spatial aspects of household form. In binding rites, the fire is a place of incorporation and transformation. Medicines are introduced into the fire in order to protect the fire itself and the entire house that contains it. These medicines are actively remade by the fire. The smoke (*omwiko*) from the medicines allows this incorporation to be effective, and, further, it gives these medicines a more extensive spatial domain. By being burned, the efficacy of these woods and weeds can be expanded from a single spot (that is, the space of the fire itself) to a much wider region. The effects of fire and burning, then, are to make connections within spatial regions. The areas that are filled with smoke become related back to the source of this smoke.

Although Haya hearths are decidedly not altars to clan-based or any other spirits, the relation between hearths and the limits of household spatial form is similar to that described by Fustel de Coulange for the Ancient City (Fustel de

Coulange 1956, 62). The hearth is clearly a focus, a point of origin that serves to orient other regions to it and to each other. This is evident in the use of smoke and burning medicines in binding rites. The fire not only allows for the spatial extension of protection in these rites, but it facilitates the multidimensional coordination of that extended space. The smoke can be cast in cardinal directions, and the fire can be blessed in order to define and invoke internal and external orientations. Through its transformative potential, fire can literally *fill space*, a space that is configured in a systematic and meaningful fashion.

The charged significance of fire in these rites and in more mundane contexts should also be related to the phenomenal form of fire, smoke in particular. Like water (cf. Comaroff 1985b, 200), smoke has tangible, perceptible form, yet it is also evanescent and easily dissipated. Indeed, smoke is very like a liquid substance for the Haya. When smoking pipes and cigarettes, Haya say they "drink tobacco" (*okunywa akatabak*), a usage common in much of East and Central Africa (cf. Shipton 1989; Taylor 1992), which indicates that smoke itself is imbibed like a drink, and not drawn (*kuvuta* in Swahili) like air (*amayaga*) or breath (*omwoyo*). Smoke can pervade space and can be contained or dispersed.

These powerful qualities are especially relevant to the Haya concern with enclosure, and the relation between keeping (some) things in, and keeping (other) things away. Consider the use of medicines in beer-related binding rites. Here, medicines are placed in the fire, with a rapid invocation: "Evil ones, be gone!" In this case we can see that the smoke from the medicines in the fire pervades the immediate space of beer drinking, and the invocation contrasts this smoky (and liquefied) location with "elsewhere." The smoke both encompasses a household and (with a bit of verbal help) distinguishes and conceals it from its wider context, "driving off" those who bring conflict. In the Haya scheme, then, smoke and the fire that produces it can actually create a space. Moreover, as Newbury notes for Bany'Iju of Ijwi Island understandings of "household smoke" (Newbury 1991, 30–31), the Haya recognize certain generative properties of smoke, and see it as an especially beneficial product of domestic activities that can secure and protect agricultural productivity.[15] In all of these respects—the coordination of internal and external directions, the creation of a cardinal space as an integrated totality with respect to an encompassing context, and the assurance of protective enclosure that originates from a sustaining central source—fire embodies the qualities of spatial orientation that are essential to the house as a recognizable, enduring, and viable place.

In this chapter I have attempted to describe a basic model of Haya spatial organization. In my assessment of house entering rites and related rites of a similar kind, I have argued that certain qualities are implicated in the creation of spatial form, qualities (such as enclosure, interiority, and encompassment) that contribute to the integrity and viability of the Haya house and household in particular. In the chapters that follow I demonstrate the ways in which this basic model of spatiality characterizes a much wider range of domestic activities and is inscribed or objectified in a variety of architectural features. Again, my concern is with the significance of food and food-related processes to household productivity and to the spatial form of the house itself. In the next chapter, then, we move, so to speak, out of the fire and into the hearthplace.

3 HEARTHPLACES AND HOUSEHOLDS: HAYA CULINARY PRACTICE

Fires and Time

In my discussion of house entering rites and their related sets of activities, I focused on Haya formulations of spatial orientations—on the relation between inside and outside, for example, and the significance of contrasts such as this to qualities of space like enclosure and interiority. Implicit (and at times explicit) in my account of these spatial orientations is a temporal dimension to both the actions and practices described, as well as to the qualities of space they create. I now return briefly to the temporal aspects of these phenomena, to suggest further temporal implications in the meanings of Haya household hearths and fires in order to extend our understanding of the ways in which their qualities are objectified in a wider Haya world of experience. This is, then, an extension in two senses: I attempt to deepen my account of spatial form and in so doing expand the analysis onto many other aspects of Haya domestic organization.

To begin with, the house entering rites and the fire that is their principal concern *is* a beginning. Lighting this fire is an act of founding a house. This temporal importance of the fire was made clear to me by my neighbors' discussions surrounding the use of a kitchen in a house whose absentee owners had yet to properly "enter" their house. While a caretaker was allowed to live in this house, he never used the kitchen that was built along with the house but instead prepared his meals in an old, abandoned hut at a further remove from the house itself. It was agreed, by those who were concerned with the propriety of owning a house, that the new kitchen must remain unused, because the actual owners of the house would be upset "to find a new kitchen already dirtied with smoke." The implications of these comments and of the actions of the caretaker are that the use of fire and cooking in a kitchen is of greater consequence for establishing attachments to a household than is merely residing in the actual house. And this consequence, I would argue, derives from the temporal qualities intrinsic in fire. The kitchen can remain "new" as long as it does not reveal its use by a smoky residue. Fire, in this understanding, initiates the attachments of persons to a household. Moreover, this is a process (and substance) that concretely establishes and *marks* time in the form of the objective transformations—the smoke-stained evidence—it brings about.

These temporal implications can also be seen in the earlier discussion of smoke and the creation and orientation of spatial form through the use of smoke. I argued that the smoke from medicinal fires used in "binding" rites served to *extend* the benefits of the medicines through space (i.e., from the fire to the area filled with smoke) as well as to *create* the directional orientations of household space by linking together the focal center of the fire, the encompassed space of the house filled with smoke, and the cardinal directions that guide the smoke (see discussion in chapter 2). Here, I want only to point out that the spatial configuration introduced by smoke has a clear temporal aspect as well, for the fire and smoke coordinate the focus (i.e., the place of the fire) with its surrounding situation by establishing it as a point of *origin*. The fire is both central and temporally *primary* in the construction of the Haya physical domestic world.[1] The significance of centers as origins can also be seen in the form of growth described for the medicine *olubingo,* used in this fire. In this case, the central position is the point of origin that becomes surrounded (spatially) by successive generations of plants.

Points of Origin, Process of Growth

Each of these cases suggests that the orientation of spatial form cannot be disentangled from its temporal features. But, beyond this theoretical point, the introduction of temporality to the discussion of space and places allows us to consider the significance of the fire and hearth in particular, and of spatiality and temporality more generally, to Haya sociocultural organization. The fire, as we have seen, begins in the front of the house and moves to the hearth. The Haya word for hearth, *amaiga,* takes its name from the three stones (*eiga,* singular; *amaiga,* plural) on which cooking vessels are set over fires. But the term *amaiga* also has some other important meanings. A man may have children by several women, and the children of one woman and one man (i.e., a group of "full siblings," or uterine kin) are referred to as an *amaiga,* a "hearth." The hearth, then, is metonymic of the house in general as well as metaphoric of the social relations that rely on it.[2] It also suggests a *set,* a grouping of individuals or things (whether household members or hearthstones) that belong together and form a totality.[3] A less common, but equally recognized meaning of

amaiga is a place of origin. The sense of "origin" in this case is usually flexible—
it may be the place from which all members of a widely dispersed clan are said
to come or it may be the place from which more immediate relations (e.g., one's
grandfather or great-grandfather) moved before arriving at a current village of
residence. In any case, the understanding is that a "hearth" is recognized as a
place from which one has come. I would add that this idea of origin is also
implied in the more generally used sense of *amaiga* as a group of uterine
siblings, since the identity of this group of children lies in their common
maternal origin.

The notion of origins inscribed in these places and objects is also critical to
Haya forms of sociocultural process more generally. As the flexibility of the
amaiga understanding indicates, these places of origin are provisional points
that form a part of a continuous process of development. The development of a
household over time—the passage from ascendant to descendant generations
or the movement from center to periphery, as in binding rites—is comprised
entirely of continuous processes that focus on recognized points of origin
which are then related to subsequent, continuous events, consequences, or
actions. As the relation of points of origin to endpoints might further suggest,
these cultural processes frequently construct cycles that have a periodic form.
For example, when a Haya person speaks of his or her *amaiga* in reference to a
place of origin (as opposed to a group of siblings), he or she will specify a place
that is remembered as the place from which one's immediate ascendant relations, perhaps one's grandfather or great-grandfather, came before arriving at
the village in which the speaker currently resides. Thus, an origin of this kind
has a *proscribed* temporal scope. A person's place of origin is not the house or
village in which they were born; nor is it the locale to which the earliest
remembered ancestor can be traced. Rather, an *amaiga* in this sense refers to the
most immediate precedent, the location at which the movement in time and
space that connects a prior place of residence with a current one was initiated.
Indeed, many Haya men and women insisted that they could not recall antece-
dent places of origin, places from which previous generations had come to their
own *amaiga*. Such places would have been of concern only to their "elders,"
who would have recognized them as their own immediate place of origin.
Other people would recall a named village or specific region as an *amaiga* and
then posit some general, remote region as a possible ultimate origin. (In some
accounts, Uganda, but just as often *Misri*—that is, Egypt—was cited.) Remembered places of origin, therefore, form part of a *periodic* continuum, moving
from a beginning to an ending; each movement to a new village by any given
generation both *initiates* a new developmental process (i.e., the line of genera-

tions that will reside at this new site) and also *terminates* the process that recognized a previous *amaiga* as its place of origin.

The cyclical aspect of these periodic processes is also well illustrated by another term for place of origin, one that suggests a connection to agricultural practices. The term *ekisibo,* for example, can be used for "place of origin" in the same sense I have described for *amaiga*.[4] The word *ekisibo* also (and more routinely) denotes the stump and root system of a felled banana plant. At one level, it could be said that the banana *ekisibo* is the origin of the plant and literally "grounds" the developmental process of its entire life. Indeed, the Haya differentiate between the *ekisibo* as the oldest part of the banana plant, and the supple central leaf that grows out of the apex of the stem and is the newest part of the banana plant.

In Haya agricultural practice the *ekisibo* is also part of a critical, periodic *generational* cycle. At any given time, each banana plant forms part of a cluster of three banana plants. When Haya describe their cultivation techniques, they say that banana plants have three stages of development. The youngest plants grow parthenogenetically, as shoots born of the more mature plants. But only one shoot is allowed to mature to a full plant, as Haya farmers eliminate the others of its generation in order to ensure adequate nutrients for the single maturing plant. At a second level is the mature plant, which is the "parent" of the young shoots. The mature plant will have begun to yield fruit. Once these fruit have fully matured, the stem of the banana plant is hacked through in order to harvest the fruit. This leaves the third stage of the plant, the *ekisibo*. Thus, the *ekisibo* stump that remains after bananas have been harvested is in turn the "parent" of the maturing banana plant that is beginning to bear fruit. In this way Haya cultivation practices produce a three-generation cycle of plants, from young plants to mature plants to harvested stumps. In this agricultural practice we clearly see that there is a *periodicity* constructed through the generational cycle; that is, a total process of banana plant cultivation is completed over the course of these sequential stages. It is not merely a question of duration or of seasonality but a repeated rhythm of sequencing that constitutes the temporal form of banana growth. What is even more important is that each periodic growth process has its own point of origin and completion. When a banana plant is felled at harvest, its "parent" *ekisibo* stump and root system, which nurtured the harvested plant, is simultaneously uprooted. This newly felled stem then becomes the *ekisibo* for the succeeding maturing plant and its shoot. Each *ekisibo* (root/foundation/origin) is, therefore, a new point at which the developmental process is begun. Thus, just as successive memories of the landscape and locality recall immediate antecedents as "places of origin," each new and maturing banana plant can be traced to and is supported by an origin that is initiated anew with each successive harvest.

The place of the fire and smoke in the house entering ceremonies and the significance of the hearth as a cultural form incorporates certain related temporal, periodic features. Hearths and fires are icons of incipient processes. They both *signify* origins (as in the various connotations of *amaiga*) and are themselves *means* of initiating ongoing activities (as in house entering). But, more than merely starting up processes, fires and hearths provide concrete evidence of the ways in which these processes unfold. Smoke, I have argued, can mark the passage of time; similarly, remembering places of origin or acknowledging privileged relations between siblings allow the Haya to make connections over time. Just as the house entering fire is able to both create a contrast between inside and outside as well as set this opposition into *motion* (i.e., by interrelating these orientations), fires and hearths serve to establish contrasts between past and present and then to project this difference through time. That is, the notion of "origins" is a way of signifying time, as well as a way of *making* time; in this way, recognizing an origin, or recognizing that there is some origin, is a way of asserting that time goes on and can be experienced by relating ongoing events to some initial "point." This is what I mean by "projecting" temporal differences over time. And it implies that the contrasts between past and present, origins and futures, are oppositions that are also *processes* through which temporal relations (like events or generations) are constructed.

Objects in the Hearth: Stones and Wood

Let me take these rudimentary dimensions, which I conceive of as a core set of culturally constituted relations, and make them more concrete. The hearth has certain values that are inscribed in the set of ritual practices I have assessed; but a hearth is also, even more clearly, a particular *place*. The hearth thus takes its meanings from the way in which that place is configured (i.e., the architectural form and features of the hearth itself) and from the practices that go on there, as well as from the relation of the hearth to the rest of the house for which it is so important.

In most houses, whether they are made of brick with zinc roofs or of wattle and daub, all floors are carefully swept (even if the floor is dirt, it is swept in order to smooth its surface) and then covered with one of several varieties of grass. But at the hearth, three stones are laid out on a cleared surface. The first stone, according to some informants, is laid by the father of the new house owner, much as the house entering fire is lit by this senior agnate. The hearthstones thus encapsulate time as well, insofar as their sequence is ordered by clan hierarchies. The household fire that originates the household and the first hearth stone that initiates the hearthplace are each grounded in agnatic seniority. Beattie found that part of Nyoro mortuary rites for a household head consisted of removing the hearthstones from the hearth of the deceased, an act that some of my neighbors suggested was once the case in Buhaya as well.[5] The significance of the hearth and hearthstones in relation to other objects in the house, especially house posts, are discussed at greater length in the next chapter. For now, I simply point out that the care taken in selecting and removing hearthstones suggests very strong identifications between household heads and the hearth, identifications which, in fact indicate that the very possibility of domesticity and domestic authority is objectified in the hearth.

The fate of these hearthstones upon the death of the householder is also suggestive when considered in terms of the meanings of the *amaiga* as a place of origin. If a hearth is a means of initiating social relations that will endure and be remembered over time, then the removal of the hearthstones at death suggests a kind of closure, not simply to the life of a person but to the *origin* of the relations that constitute the household. This act gives an indication of what I mean when I say that focal places serve as points of both origin and conclusion. Moreover, it demonstrates a specifically Haya sense of periodicity, one in which origins are definitively concluded with passing generations. And if origins are explicitly and concretely concluded, it follows that they must be continuously recreated (since all present circumstances do posit their own origin). The ways in which this continuous re-creation is achieved are critical features of Haya temporality and cultural practice. This understanding of periodicity is equally important to other images and processes of generational passage, from landholding and clan migration to mortuary procedures and agricultural cycles.

The hearth is, of course, primarily a place of fires and, for Haya fires at least, this requires wood. Firewood is widely available, increasingly in commoditized forms. Wood is often gathered by girls and women on their way to work in the grassland fields cultivated on the periphery of residential villages, although Kajumolo-Tibaijuka (1985, 17) reports that "traditions require a husband to provide his wife with firewood" and that a wife could refuse to cook for her husband if he failed to do so. In addition to the dry branches gathered largely for use as kindling, stands of trees—especially *Mcalytus* (i.e., eucalyptus introduced by the White Fathers' missions earlier in the century)—are owned by individuals, and villagers often purchase whole trees from their forest-owning neighbors. If firewood is purchased in this way, it is generally the younger men of a household who will fell the trees and chop up the wood into manageable pieces, although I have seen many women chopping off an evening's supply of firewood from their purchased tree trunk. In my experience, a two months' supply of wood could be purchased for 200 Tsh or so (approximately $1), which, while by no means inexpensive, is within the means of most households.

There are, however, some significant political economic dimensions to the provision of firewood, which have critical implications for the meanings of domestic production. To begin with, although Haya men were "traditionally" charged with providing firewood for cooking (a masculine view of tradition that undoubtedly overlooks the practices of women who might even have seen *themselves* as "going to the fields" as opposed to "gathering wood," even when they were clearly doing both), in contemporary Kagera there is a clear division between firewood that is purchased (largely, but not exclusively, by men) and firewood that is freely gathered (almost exclusively by women). The gendered nature of this commoditization process is especially crucial to political economic control over the cultivation of firewood. Firewood has not only become commoditized, its production has become controlled by an increasingly exclusive class of landholders. According to Kajumolo-Tibaijuka, over two-thirds of the forests grown for sale as firewood are owned by less than 15 percent of the households in Kagera (1985, 13–14). Moreover, commoditization of firewood—especially in the case of eucalyptus, which Haya told me drains the fertility from the soil—is marked by a shift from the intercropping of firewood trees with the agricultural products of the family farm (*ekibanja*) to the use of grasslands (*orweya*) to grow separate forests intended to be sold for use as firewood.

The cultivation of wood as a separate cash crop brings about important transformations in the tenure status of such lands as well. Grasslands that are adjacent to or surround Haya villages are frequently unowned. Such open land is commonly worked by women in small fields that are fallowed from year to year. However, when such lands are planted with permanent tree crops, they come under clan-based tenure, a transformation that more or less fixes control over this land in the hands of an agnatic line. In spite of the radical nature of this transformation, in the past only the payment of a nominal fee to the king's administration was required to plant a few trees and establish a woodlot (*ekishembo*). In contemporary socialist Tanzania, where the land is legally "owned" by "the people," planting trees in open grasslands requires only that the land be "un-owned" by another landholder and be suitable for growing trees. Although such woodlots were once planted as a means of gaining clan ownership over grasslands in the hopes of turning it into farm land that could sustain a household (an extremely difficult project in view of the enormous inputs that would be required to render grasslands arable for banana plants), in the contemporary situation, where wood can be cultivated as a cash crop, the land is more readily converted into forest and is still recognized as clan-held "farm" land. As a consequence of these transformations, women's access to the open grassland that is available for planting fields is increasingly threatened by the growth of "commercial" forests that cannot be intercropped with agricultural produce and which are held exclusively under permanent tenure by a relatively small class of agnatic households. The provision of firewood, the most rudimentary and yet essential feature of the cooking process, reveals the complexity of transformations entailed in commoditization. Cultivating firewood as a cash crop has not only resulted in a consolidation of control over the supply of this critical resource, but in the particular context of Haya sociocultural practices, it has had specific differential effects on the ongoing and long-term potential of men and women to productively engage with particular cultural activities on distinct kinds of land.

Yes, We Have Smoked Bananas

The fires built in a hearth serve a number of purposes, most but not all of which have to do with cooking. Moreover, the category of "cooking" is itself complex, there being a wide variety of ways that the Haya use the hearth to prepare raw food for consumption. It is important to recognize, then, that the hearth is not simply a source of generic "fire" or even "heat." These phenomena and qualities are created in the course of carrying out specific actions and using the hearth in order to achieve particular transformations.

The various qualities embedded in the cooking styles that I detail below, their spatial and temporal forms, and their gendered dimensions recall in certain respects some of Lévi-Strauss's discussions of cuisine. To spell out what I have found useful in his account and precisely how my analyses differ from his, let me offer a synopsis of his formulation of food-related issues. Lévi-Strauss describes a "culinary triangle" (1966, 587), a "semantic field" that he postulates underlies all cooking activities. Underlying the three categories of this triangle—the raw, the cooked, and the rotted—are a pair of contrasts: between culture and nature and between the elaborated and the unelaborated. For Lévi-Strauss, these oppositions describe a total system, within which he locates a critical contrast between boiling and roasting and a third category—smoking—which lies halfway between these.

One of the strengths of Lévi-Strauss's discussion is his recognition that these oppositions rest on configurations of space (on configurations of time, see Hugh-Jones 1979, 200ff). Thus, boiling is contrasted with roasting, not just in terms of the cooking medium (i.e., water vs. air) but in terms of their relative enclosure. In turn, this critical spatial contrast has important social implications, the "endo-cuisine" of boiling contrasted with the "exo-cuisine" of roasting not just in terms of the cooking receptacle but also with respect to the commensal group to whom such foods are presented. The boiled is not only enclosed in the pot but also "destined to a small closed group," while the roasted is exposed directly to the fire and also offered to guests and other outsiders (Lévi-Strauss 1966, 589). Further, Lévi-Strauss links these spatial contrasts to certain structures of authority and the relative hierarchical or egalitarian form of society (1966, 590). Thus, his interest is not simply in elaborating a closed culinary system, but in proposing (if not actually demonstrating through a substantiated argument) possible connections to wider principles of sociocultural organization.

On the whole, Lévi-Strauss's way of formulating the issues central to cuisine and his suggestion of the connections between culinary forms and wider sociocultural concerns points to certain intriguing relationships, but it raises as many problems as it illuminates. Of course, the particular empirical *content* of his categories and their configuration in any cultural context could be objected to, as my own ethnography indicates. And, as is typical of his rigorously rationalist structuralism, the culinary triangle Lévi-Strauss proposes seems to create a system *ex nihilo,* one that operates at a strictly conceptual level independent of any human agency or activity which might produce it. In contrast, I explore these various Haya modes of culinary practice in order to address important transformations in their form and meaning over time, transformations that are linked both to the concrete qualities generated through particular ways of cooking as well as to the agency and intentions of those who do the cooking. As Bourdieu's analysis of "the food space" suggests, culinary preferences "cannot be considered independently of the whole life-style" (1984, 185), that is, independently of the social practices that generate specific eating habits. My analysis, though, goes beyond Bourdieu's formulation of "life-style," insofar as I link the particular "conceptual" contrasts in Haya culinary activities not only to a context of integrated social practices but also to the actual *experience* of the foods that these practices produce. The values of these practices are inextricably bound up with the concrete Haya preferences, the tastes and textures that are achieved and experienced in their cuisine.

I begin my discussion of Haya uses of the hearth by looking at smoking, something that, in Haya practice, is not quite cooking. I do this to focus on some of the distinct forms that can be assumed by heat and fire, processing and preparation, etc. In addition, smoking is a means of transformation that expands the focus of the hearth, for it clearly situates the hearth as a particular place that is configured by a broad set of temporal and spatial dimensions.

At the hearth in most Haya kitchens a slatted rack is constructed to stand five or six feet above the hearth stones themselves. This rack (*olutala*) is used on most days as a storage area. Pots and utensils are kept on the rack, and many items are hung from the rack, often tied to the slats by lengths of banana fiber. The *olutala* is also a place for preparing food as well as storing it. Fresh lake fish, most often Nile perch and white bait (*sangala* and *dagaa,* respectively) are laid out over the hearthstones for smoking. This preserves the fish, which later can be cooked by boiling or stewing with other foods. Seasonal foods, especially grasshoppers, are prepared in a similar fashion, as the smoking process allows one to offer these highly prized treats as a snack for guests well past their December harvest. In each of these cases the products are prepared for both eating and preservation. For the Haya, food smoked in this way is said to be well prepared when the smoke and heat rising from the hearth into the *olutala* cause the items to thoroughly "dry out" (*okuota* in Haya, *kukauka* in Swahili).

A major use of the *olutala* rack involves preparing beer bananas for a rather different purpose. Beer bananas (*embiile* in Haya, *ndizi kali* in Swahili) are a distinct variety of bananas that are not eaten in either a raw or cooked form. To make beer, mature but unripened beer bananas are harvested. The stalk of each bunch is split, and the bunches are then ripened (see Carlson 1989, 104–5 for a slightly different discussion of this process). To ripen the bananas, the bunches are carefully loaded into the *olutala* rack above the hearthstones. Sometimes the bananas are then covered with mats to keep them in place. The heat of the cooking fire and smoke from the hearth over the course of many days— upwards of one week in my experience—will then ripen the beer bananas to the point that they are ready for juicing. For beer bananas, then, the effects of the smoke at the hearth are equally transformative, but the bananas are not prepared for long-term storage nor are they "dried out" by this ripening process. Heat in this case works to "ripen" (*okuihya* in Haya, *kuiva* in Swahili) the bananas, a verb that is also used to describe food that has finished "cooking" (e.g., *mpelege zaile* means both "the beans have cooked" and "the beans have ripened").

The process of ripening/cooking is critical to many Haya experiences of produce and food. The hearth is clearly only one of many places in which this process can occur, but this transformation can be usefully explored in order to trace out more of the semantic features of the hearth, both as a source of smoke, fire, and heat and as a place with a definitive shape and form. To do so, we can look more closely at the beer bananas and their ripening process. Ripening beer bananas on the *olutala* rack is a slow process that also hastens the fruit's "natural" ripening. Beer makers say that you have to actively ripen beer bananas once they have matured because otherwise they all ripen at a different pace, making it nearly impossible to procure enough simultaneously ripe bunches to make a worthwhile amount of beer.

To appreciate the paradox of why ripening beer bananas over the hearth is both a *slow* and *hastening* procedure, one has to understand that there is a second common way of ripening beer bananas. Rather than storing them as I have described, some beer makers bury bananas in a pit (*ekiina*), which is connected by a tunnel to a smaller open fire pit. The smoke from the fire pit is fanned into the larger pit, and the bananas prepared in this way will ripen within three or four days, that is, more quickly than they would above the hearth.

The obvious question is why should there be two forms of ripening beer bananas, and more importantly what does this contrast tell us about the meanings of these cooking places? To begin with, most Haya favor the hearth method of ripening on aesthetic grounds. They much prefer the taste of beer made from hearth-ripened bananas. According to *olubisi* (banana beer, literally "fresh") connoisseurs, the slow-ripened bananas are firmer, their sticky starches remain intact, and this allows the brewer to squeeze more and thicker juice from the fruit without overly diluting the mashed banana mixture. Carlson (1989, 104) also reports that around Bukoba his informants enjoyed the *smoky* flavor of beer made from *olutala*-ripened bananas. The advantage of pit-ripened bananas is the speed with which the fruit is readied—but the *significance* of this speed is the monetary gain it brings. When beer is made faster, more beer can be made (and sold). When money is needed quickly, as is often the case, it can be made more quickly with pit-ripened bananas. Many of my friends insisted that pit ripening was a recent innovation, something taken up in "these days" when "people just want money." In this respect, it is important to point out a concomitant innovation (at least in the view of my informants) in forms of beer production, namely the development of banana gin or *enkonyagi*, the Haya term derived from "cognac." Banana gin distilled from fermented banana juice (i.e., *olubisi*, the "fresh" variety of "traditional" banana beer) can generate greater profits, as its much higher alcohol content demands a higher price (Carlson [1989, 287] reports that *enkonyagi* is approximately 40 percent ethanol). All kinds of beer—distilled or fermented, banana, pineapple, honey and millet—are always sold for money, but no beer is more strongly associated with the desire for money and its deleterious consequences than is *enkonyagi*.

The contrast between hearth ripening and pit ripening beer bananas, which is in some ways emblematic of the contrast between *olubisi* and *enkonyagi*, is described by Haya brewers and consumers in terms of the rhythm and pace of production. And the temporal contrasts between these two kinds of beer brewing, the planning involved, the deliberation with which the final product is created and appreciated, extend well beyond these methods of ripening. One of my housemates, Mzee Saidi, was a well-known and highly regarded beer brewer. He claimed that at one time he had brewed both *olubisi* and *enkonyagi*, but in recent years he had abandoned *enkonyagi* production to concentrate solely on finely crafted *olubisi*. And Mzee Saidi was indeed a master craftsman. As we walked through the village, visiting friends or heading to market, Mzee would stop at a neighboring farm and point out a bunch of beer bananas growing on the stalk. Putting a finger to his pursed lips and carefully considering the fruit, he would tell me, almost in a whisper, "These bananas will mature in three or two weeks. Yes, yes. No more than three weeks."

As the weeks passed, Mzee Saidi would contact neighboring farmers, making arrangements to purchase a bunch or two of their finest beer bananas, and consider how many bowls of millet he would need to buy in order to ferment the volume of juice he anticipated this crop could yield. As the day came for ripening the harvested bunches in the hearth rack—*okualika embile*, literally "to welcome the beer bananas" as one "welcomes" a new bride when she is sequestered—neighbors would arrive at the household courtyard with their fruit. The banana bunches were split under the watchful eye of Mzee Saidi, who considered less the total number of bunches than the different levels of maturation, which determines how they are to be stored above the hearth.

During the week before brewing Mzee Saidi would scrupulously monitor the ripening process. He would douse the fires at the hearth after cooking was completed if the bananas were progressing too quickly, or watch a slow, steady fire throughout the day to push their development along. On the day of squeezing the banana juice, Mzee Saidi generally had hired help, one man to actually stomp (*okujunga*) the bananas into juice (*omulamba*) in the beer canoe (*obwato*) and perhaps another to help him roast or grind the millet that will be added to the juices. The juice is tasted as it is extracted; various "grades" of banana juice are recognized depending on how much water has been added to the ripened fruit, and Mzee Saidi prefers not to allow his "weakest" juice to be overly diluted (fig. 5). The beer is assembled in a cleaned out canoe, the roasted ground millet is added to it, and the entire vessel is wrapped and sealed with everything from burlap bags to banana leaf and fiber.

The final product, *olubisi* proper, takes three days to mature—the first day to prepare, the second day to ferment, and the third day to serve (thus, three days,

Figure 5. A beer brewer strains banana juices from a canoe. The juices have been extracted from the mass of grass and bananas in the canoe.

as Haya describe them, can, in fact, take less than forty-eight hours). But, after the first day of fermenting, the mixture is tasted to see how it's coming along. The beer at this point is *omulala,* "one that has slept" (i.e., been fermenting overnight). It is or should be an especially sweet libation, as the millet has begun to extract the sugars from the banana juice without yet converting them into alcohol. The merits of this *omulala* are often judged collectively; Mzee Saidi would ask a neighbor or the man who helped him squeeze the bananas to evaluate its taste and texture. The following morning, Mzee Saidi was as often as not confronted by the entire village awaiting the unveiling of the *olubisi.*

Just down the path from our house were two young brothers, Seve and Kapemba, who often distilled banana gin. Their *enkonyagi* was generally well thought of; they never watered down their gin, and they were not contentious hosts. But the process of creating their beer was quite different from the one characteristic of *olubisi* brewing. When one of the brothers was distilling gin, he alone was responsible for the entire process. Seve would haul by himself four or five bunches of bananas at a time from the various farmers from whom he had made purchases. He dug the pit in which the bananas were ripened, and he stomped the juice himself. Regardless of who was producing the beer, much less

concern was shown for the various stages of its development. Bananas buried in
a pit for four days cannot be scrutinized and regulated as those over the hearth
are. Moreover, I never saw Seve or Kapemba differentiate between different
grades of juice as they extracted it. They might well offer guests a glass or two of
omulamba as they worked, but they didn't explicitly distinguish the weak from
the strong, as Mzee Saidi and other *olubisi* brewers would. On the third day,
when *olubisi* would be ready to serve, the *enkonyagi* was now ready to be
distilled. Behind their house, the "raw" fermented juice was loaded into five-
gallon well-blackened cans (*madebe*) that were tilted over a small fire. Tightly
fastened into the tops of the cans were bamboo "pipes" that fed into large
ceramic pots, resting in a basin of water. The vapor from the boiling cans of
juice drained through the bamboo to be cooled in the pots, from which the
enkonyagi was poured.

The contrast between Mzee Saidi's *olubisi* and Seve and Kapemba's *enkonyagi*
is typical of the difference between these two styles of production. At every
point in *olubisi* production—from the bananas before they are even ready to be
harvested to the sweetened juices all but ready to be served as beer—the contents of the process are scrutinized and assessed. Mzee Saidi is probably more
conscientious than most, but the larger point is that there are recognized
moments in the production process of *olubisi*—moments that allow for refine-
ment and regulation, for the process to be elongated or contracted—that clearly
distinguish *olubisi* from *enkonyagi* production. This production process suggests that the contrast between hearth ripening and pit ripening is only one
(crucial) dimension of a much wider pattern of temporal relations. Each process unfolds according to a distinctive rhythm that allows for different degrees
of intervention and evaluation, evaluations which, as I hope to make clear, also
have implications for the kinds of value, commoditized and otherwise, that
inform these different productive practices.

Money and the Hearth

I hope this extended discussion of beer brewing makes us thirsty for a greater
understanding of its significance to the hearth. To begin with, the relation of the
hearth and the *olutala* rack to money is suggested by the contrast of banana
beer and banana gin processing. Money comes more readily from beer that is
ripened outside of the hearth. It should also be noted that coffee is often stored
in the *olutala* rack, and, again, Haya culture recognizes a critical distinction in
varieties of coffee. Coffee is grown as a cash crop and is the principal source of
income in most households. But coffee that is grown to be sold to the marketing

society is *not* stored at the hearth. The Haya also prepare coffee cherries (i.e., entire pods, each of which contains two beans) by boiling them with spices, and then drying them out. This kind of coffee is then chewed and eaten (something like betel nut or kola in other parts of the world), and is routinely offered to guests or at any friendly encounter. This latter kind of coffee, coffee for chewing, not for selling, is stored above the hearth, an ideal space for drying out and preserving a long-term supply of food. For both beer bananas and coffee, then, we find that the hearth is a location for preparing and storing produce that is less strongly oriented toward marketing, that is, toward acquiring money.

I want to make it absolutely clear that this *relative* contrast between production for sale and production for other purposes is precisely that—a *relative* and not absolute contrast. Indeed, all of the items I have described—from beer and gin, to chewing and brewing coffees, or, for that matter, Nile perch and white bait—are for sale. They are commodities by any definition of the term, and there are certainly many, many Haya who attempt to make vital income by selling "fresh" banana beer or cooked coffee berries. The point is that the items that are processed and stored at the hearth are less directly implicated in the exchange of money for the consumable product. As I have indicated, Haya strongly associate banana gin brewing and consumption with the acquisition (as well as rapid depletion) of money. A small glass of "fresh" banana beer is almost always offered to guests at the home of a brewer, even when he is selling the beer. In contrast, only selected, honored guests might be offered banana gin—and even this is rather rare. Indeed, banana gin is sold by the glass as well as by the bottle, while banana beer is sold only by the bottle. Thus, every increment of banana gin can be given a monetary price, while banana beer is less systematically measured in terms of money.

The distinction between varieties of coffee is even more stark. Coffee berries for chewing are routinely offered to friends and guests. Even coffee sellers at weekly markets provide small free samples to demonstrate the quality of their product. In contrast, coffee that is grown for the world market has no other purpose than to be sold (fig. 6). In fact, Arabica coffee—introduced at the turn of the century, unlike "indigenous" Robusta—is grown only for sale; its berries are not suitable for chewing. In each of these cases there is a contrast between products that are intended for, strictly measured in terms of, and acquired by means of monetary transaction as opposed to products which, while also goods for sale, are routinely available and transacted in nonmonetized exchanges. "Fresh" banana beer and cooked coffee cherries are widely sold, but the *experience* of these products is less rigorously grounded in commercial relations than in relations of neighborliness and friendship. This relative contrast is further

Figure 6. A man dries coffee on mats in the courtyard to prepare it for sale at a cooperative.

inscribed in the processing of these products, for it is those items made and stored *in the hearth* that are less commercial, in the terms that I have indicated. The hearth serves not as an enclave from monetary exchanges, since money pervades the circulation of all of these items (albeit in uneven ways), but rather as a recognized place at which degrees of control over the transaction of these items can be exercised (cf. Carsten 1989).

The hearth is a most appropriate place for exerting control of this sort. Not only does the hearth epitomize the contrast between the household and the outside world, but the character of processing at the hearth produces qualities that actually define and shape Haya ideas of control. I noted before that storing beer bananas above the hearth is paradoxically a slow method of hastening their ripening. The bananas and all products that are kept on the *olutala* rack are processed in the course of ongoing, repetitive activities. Daily cooking and heating at the hearth stones has the *indirect* effect of transforming the foods stored in the *olutala*. As the days go by, a cook or brewer, as we have seen, will evaluate changes in the foods that are stored at the hearth, determine whether they are ripening or drying out too slowly or too quickly, and accordingly regulate the amount of heat and cooking that the fires in the hearth should provide. These indirect methods have a slow and rhythmic form whose drawn-out pace allows for continuous adjustment. Along these lines it is pertinent that the very technique of smoking food is designed to *preserve* it, that is to draw out and extend the life of the food. It is tempting to say that the effect of processing at the hearth is to slow down the passage and experience of time.

Certainly the opposite is the case in the experience of banana gin consumption and the activities that surround it. I would venture to say that everything about *enkonyagi* is fast. As we have seen, its bananas are generally ripened faster than banana beer's. Unlike the indirect method of smoking, in which beer bananas ripen as a consequence of heating and cooking other foods, the fire pits of banana gin are intended strictly to ripen beer bananas. Further, the alcohol content of banana gin gets you drunk much faster, a point of much concern to the Haya. The state of drunkenness produced by banana gin is also held to make you more excitable and quicker to anger. Above all, banana gin is associated with the rapid circulation and depletion of money. Even those who distill and sell gin are notorious for drinking all of their profits. Moreover, drinking gin is also strongly associated with other monetized forms of consumption. When a person has had too much to drink, according to many Haya friends, their body will need to have its "fat" replenished, and this generally means eating fried fish.[6] It is not uncommon, therefore, to find pieces of fried fish being sold wherever gin is being distilled. *Enkonyagi* is so thoroughly entwined with monetary circulation and expenditure that purchasing and drinking gin actually produces a bodily experience that is alleviated only by further purchases.[7] Gin is, therefore, a thoroughly commoditized medium, its production techniques motivated by the creation of monetary gain, and the desires it engenders oriented toward other commodity forms. It is not surprising, then, that Haya men and women often describe distilling as a kind of "get rich quick" scheme, in which the pursuit of cash usually results in a loss of the same. As one friend put it, "All of the money from gin just goes from one house to the next," that is, from the house that is distilling gin today to the house that may be distilling it next week.

The contrast in these forms indicate that activities at the hearth are slower and the circulation and use of the products processed at the hearth are also slowed down. This spatial and temporal quality, I am suggesting, is an important means of effecting control over transactions, as well as a way of *defining* a specifically Haya cultural form of control, namely the slow and regular processing (including production and circulation) of objects. This definition of control may seem tautologous or so general that there is nothing culturally significant about it. Yet, we might well contrast this notion and these practices with those of something like the Futures Exchange, where "control" is exercised by those who can move options most quickly and where a rapid turnover means greater value, higher commissions, etc. Or consider the exchanges of *kula,* in which Gawans cast spells (unquestionably a form of exerting control) in certain contexts in order to "excite" their partners into giving "quickly" (Munn 1977, 50). Most Haya would probably say that this pace of activity would lead to animosity or illness. This Haya concern with speed and pace helps to illuminate how hearth-related activities imply a withdrawal from monetized transactions. The pace of hearth activities indicate that the hearth is not *removed from* the world of money (as we have seen repeatedly), but rather that the hearth's ability to "slow down time" is an important means of controlling money. In this respect, these hearth-related activities are similar to certain "symbolic currencies" that resist the universalizing potential of money (especially its capacity to reduce all values to a rational price), thereby controlling and delimiting the flow of money and monetary evaluation.[8] The hearth can, in fact, be integral to money making, but always in a way that allows one to regulate and tinker with the rate and form of money's circulation.

Space, Time, and Gender at the Hearth

Let me focus more directly on the hearth not in opposition to other sites or objects but as a place that is composed of relations in its own right. All of the objects and dimensions that characterize the hearth, from the stones to the heat, have clearly gendered aspects for the Haya. It is especially important to note that all of the produce that is stored in the *olutala* rack is associated with men. Both bananas and coffee are cultivated and harvested exclusively by men. Beer production, especially, is considered the exclusive province of men. Only men can squeeze banana juice for making beer (they do so by stomping on bananas and grasses in large dugout canoes). Interestingly, a woman can be considered "the owner of the beer" (*mwenye pombe* in Swahili), but in every case that I am aware of the beer that women own is *enkonyagi.* Again, this form of beer would tend to relegate women to ripening bananas away from the hearth. Moreover, even in such cases, women do not *make* the beer, they merely pay for the supplies and the labor of men who squeeze, ferment, and distill the banana juices. In addition, men are more markedly identified with the objects that constitute the hearth—from the stones on which cooking pots rest that once were so crucial to men's mortuary rites, to the fire that is initiated in agnatically centered house-opening rites, as well as firewood which, as described above, may be chopped by men or women but usually is cut from trees that are the concern of—if not owned by—men.

Yet, it would be grossly misleading to suggest that the hearth is a masculine preserve. Indeed, the hearth is in the kitchen, which both Haya men and women say is a place for women exclusively. Haya wives resent it when their husbands come into the kitchen while they are cooking. One young bachelor insisted that he would never enter a kitchen again once he had a wife. Haya men clearly do go to the hearth, if only to store their coffee and beer bananas, but what is equally important is that the *work* of ripening, smoking, and preserving these foods through the indirect heat and smoke of the hearth is always carried out by women. Women perform the repetitive tasks of making fires for cooking and heating. And it is this provision of heat, which not only ripens and smokes but gives the hearth its characteristic slow and rhythmic pace, that *makes* the hearth an appropriate place for the controlled processing of food.

What this process and the objects it transforms reveal are the ways in which male features (stones, woods, fire, bananas, and coffee) underlie the space of the hearth, while women's activities transform these items at a *primary level* of the total production process. That is, men's work (brewing beer or making coffee available to guests) builds on and appropriates the primary processes that constitute the daily, routine tasks of women's work. Male products, therefore, *frame* matters of the hearth. They both establish the parameters of the hearth as a place, and control the final transformations that are produced there.

The gendered aspects of the hearth and of food processing more generally are further inscribed in the hearth's concrete spatial dimensions. The particular feature of the hearth most closely identified with men is the *olutala* rack that stands above the hearth stones. Men physically place the coffee and bananas they store on the *olutala*, which often requires them to actually climb up onto the rack. Firewood, generally associated with men, is also stored on this rack. The vertical rise of the *olutala*, like the *ahadari* attic constructed of bamboo (discussed earlier), makes it an area that is almost categorically a male space. Only men should climb. The fact that a contrast of above and below is a *gendered* spatial dimension is instantiated in everything from the ways in which men sit on chairs while women sit on the floor to dance styles in which men jump and kick their feet high in the air (a style called *okusimba,* "to raise up") while women are praised for quickly shifting their hips from side to side (*oku-chunda,* "to churn or shake"). Indeed, one woman once explained the gendered division of agricultural work by saying simply that "men work above and women work below." The vertical contrast of the *olutala* rack is especially marked in contrast both to the banana pit in which bananas are actually ripened beneath the ground, and to the fire at the hearth stones that burns below the *olutala*.

This vertical dimension must also be understood in articulation with an

encompassing spatial order. The hearth is clearly embedded in a contrast between inside and outside, or perhaps more accurately, in a complex *set of
relations* between insides and outsides. However, the relation between inside
and outside has been less clearly essentialized than, for example, the opposition
between above and below. It is certainly not possible to "read" Haya gender
oppositions into *all* contexts in which there is a recognized distinction between
in and out, as one can for above and below. Rather, the significance of these
dimensions can be assessed only within the contexts of specific activities, processes, and concrete spatial forms. With this understanding in mind, the question to ask is not what does the contrast of inside and outside mean to the Haya
hearth, but how does the hearth (and all that goes on within and around it)
construct this contrast?

The hearth is located on the inside of all houses and kitchens. In the traditional beehive style of house, the hearth is at the very center of the house. In
most contemporary houses, a separate kitchen is built behind, or adjacent to
the main house. But in this case as well, the hearth is usually located at the very
center of the kitchen building. Certainly, the contrast of ripening bananas at
that hearth as opposed to in a pit behind the house entails a contrast between
inside and outside, as does the fact that beer bananas at the hearth are often
enclosed in the rack with mats.

Yet in important respects, the hearth, and particularly processing foods on
the *olutala* rack, involves both an inside and an outside dimension. The verb
okutala, from which *olutala* is derived, means "to establish a perimeter" or "to
circumscribe." For example, when building a contemporary house, the acts of
setting out four corner house posts is *okutala.* The rim of a wheel connected by
spokes to its axis is also an *olutala.* Reading the sense of this verbal root through
these different actions and forms suggests the idea of a perimeter that defines
and is a part of an inside region.

The fact that this perimeter *defines* the inside seems especially important. It
indicates that the act *okutala* is a kind of foundation. Indeed, Haya often
translated the verb *okutala* into Swahili as *kupanga,* "to plan," which suggests
both the idea of laying out a basic framework (as in establishing the position of
house posts) as well as developing a program for future actions. This aspect of
the *olutala* rack can be seen in the food processing I have described, for the
hearth is a place that initiates banana ripening, food drying, etc., for some other
future action (e.g., beer making or stewing smoked fish at a later point). Storing
wood (which underlies all heat and, thus, production at the hearth) on this rack
also indicates the temporal significance of the *olutala.* The fact that the *olutala* is
in these respects a foundation suggests that it is a way of *connecting* actions over

time. The significance of the *olutala* rack to these activities further recalls the meanings of the *amaiga* as a locus of origins. Actions at the hearth are not self-contained. Rather, they are the primary steps in overall processes, which must be carried out in continuous actions. As the "first place" in such processes the hearth necessarily points to connections with those "later places" (and times) which are required to complete production.[9]

This temporal aspect of the hearth and its *olutala* rack, the way in which it establishes connections between original and future events or actions helps to illuminate the spatial significance of the inside/outside distinction. For just as ripening, smoking, and drying link up with brewing and boiling so too do the objects processed at the hearth create concrete spatial links. Coffee is dried and stored at the hearth, yet it is the quintessential "food for guests." Bananas are ripened at the hearth, then squeezed outside the house (in a dugout canoe, *obwato,* surely an icon of movement away from the house) in order to brew a libation that is the principal exchange item in all Haya interhousehold relations (see Carlson 1989, 221ff for an examination of banana beer as a symbolic mediator). The spatial and temporal form of these hearth-centered processes and the objects they create demonstrate that the *olutala* rack does more than just smoke foods. It actively configures certain general forms of Haya sociocultural practices and social relations. The hearth is a place that creates interconnections by making links between the household as an inside space with an internal capacity and the household as it is oriented toward an outside community of social relations. As the form and significance of *olutala* suggests, the hearth is a quintessential "center" that intrinsically defines a "perimeter." These interconnections also extend to the dimensions of gender discussed above. As a place that is underpinned by male features yet characterized by female activities, the hearth combines important aspects of gender identities. The hearth, then, provides a further (perhaps more concrete and elegant) instance of the dynamic coordination of spatial and temporal dimensions, which I suggested was characteristic of Haya fires and the practices to which they are central. Like the perimeter of a house, the hearth both defines an internal place and tangibly marks the connection of that place to the wider world.

Summarizing Smoking

I have gone on at some length about the significance of "smoking" because the spatial and temporal configuration of the hearth that is called into play through smoking activities strikes me as an especially good wedge into understanding Haya ways of interacting with each other and the world. For example, the formulation of "foundations" or "origins" that is integral to the hearth is equally crucial to Haya understandings of intergenerational relationships and to the sense in which one's neighbors are (and are *not*) a part of one's life. All of these are processual relationships with meaningful cultural forms that take on their characteristic dimensions over time (and space).

I am also interested in the way in which uses of the hearth seem so neatly to embody shifts in the experience of time. The fact that smoking preserves food, "slows down time," or is the result of repetitive procedures presents an excellent image of practical Haya understandings of control and process. And as I hope I have made clear, my interest in these aspects of temporality is not merely a bit of anthropological exoticism. Quite aside from the fact that these are the very terms in which people collectively construct their lived worlds, these representations of time provide clear evidence of the fact that processes like commoditization and avenues for constructing class and gender identities are directly experienced in such seemingly mundane affairs. How quickly you ripen your bananas may change the taste of your beer, but the historical forces that have configured the multiple implications of qualities like "speed" also make this a political and moral question.

Sweets and Staples

The category of "cooking" is complex for the Haya and involves numerous means of transforming produce into food. The relation between being fully cooked and being ripe, for example, is an instance of two very similar means of transformation (as we have seen, the Haya term for both cooking and ripening is the same). Nonetheless, even two such similar processes involve what the Haya recognize as distinct kinds of cooking, and these processes yield very different kinds of products for consumption. The main Haya staples are bananas and plantain. *Ebitoke* is the term used for all bananas that are prepared to be eaten at a meal. There is no recognized distinction between plantain and bananas, but Haya do point to different categories of bananas as well as to different varieties of bananas within those categories. Thus, there are several kinds of "sweet" bananas, which can either be eaten raw (i.e., without what we would call "cooking," as *ebihise*, literally "those that are fresh") or be eaten when they have become a bit ripe and then fried or roasted to produce a sweet snack. The many kinds of "starchy" bananas, which are eaten for meals and not snacks, are prepared in an entirely different way. The difficulty with making distinctions between these two categories is that *all* bananas (including beer bananas, which form an entirely different category that should properly never be eaten) can become "ripe"—that is, their flesh can ripen on the stalk—and then be prepared and eaten as a snack. The point of discussing these distinctions is to illustrate the fact that unlike our distinction between plantains and bananas, which we construct as a difference in kind, based on certain intrinsic features of the fruit, Haya recognize a much wider range of differences, and these differences are grounded in the way the fruit is *used*.

Bananas can be eaten as a snack or as a meal. Most often snacks are prepared from one of the many varieties of sweeter bananas. Small finger bananas (*obunana*) as well as many other kinds are often eaten raw and are occasionally offered to guests. The varieties of sweet banana that are eaten raw are also frequently available at weekly markets or along the roadside, much like mangoes and passion fruit. These fruits are often sold at a rate of several pieces for a few shillings, and one need not purchase an entire bunch of sweet bananas.

Varieties of sweet banana such as these can also be cooked for eating as snacks. Before the fruit has completely ripened, these bananas can be roasted at the hearth or occasionally fried in a bit of oil, procedures that both soften the bananas and bring out their sweetness. The banana the Haya most prize for eating in this way (i.e., cooked and offered as a sweet snack) is the *enkonjwa*, a long, flat-sided fruit. The *enkonjwa* is recognized not only as a delicious treat, but as a very important offering for privileged guests. My neighbor once made a gift of *enkonjwa* to me, saying "If you get a guest, like your father-in-law comes to visit you, when you have *enkonjwa* you cannot withhold them!" Similarly, one friend, joking with another about the wife he had very recently married, asked, "What is your bride doing? Is she roasting *enkonjwa* at the hearth?" This latter image nicely brings together a number of themes about this kind of food. As a new wife, this woman is supposed to be well fed and cared for by her new husband. The special treat of the *enkonjwa* suggests a sumptuary pleasure beyond the mere sustenance of one's daily meals and the leisure to sit by the fire and wait for a snack to be roasted. At the same time, the bride remains a "guest" in new home, and the *enkonjwa* encodes this sense of distance (i.e., between natal husbands and virilocal wives) as well.

Sweet bananas for snacks, then, have certain distinctive features. They are commonly purchased, usually individually or a few at a time. They are eaten either raw, fried, or roasted, each a form of ripening/cooking that produces sweetness as the preferred taste. And they are frequently given to guests to be eaten between meals, often while other activities (e.g., chopping wood, fetching water, weeding a field) are carried out.

I emphasize these distinctive features, and cite these different aspects of banana "circulation" (i.e., forms of purchase, forms of preparation, and forms of giving) because they contrast so neatly with food that is prepared for a proper meal. Bananas that are eaten at meals are *ebitoke,* a starchy banana that forms a basic food to which gravies, sauces, or stews (all of which are called *mboga,* a Swahili word for "vegetable" that the Haya use for all relishes) can be added. I discuss later in greater detail the arrangements and significance of purchasing *ebitoke* for household consumption.[10] For now, I simply point out that bananas for meals *should* always be available from one's own farm—and in fact the market for *ebitoke* for household consumption is rather small. Moreover, when *ebitoke* are purchased, they are always sold in bunches, either by the cluster (*oluhaga,* the doubled rows of bananas that grow around the stem) or the bunch (*omukungu,* the entire stalk of bananas). It is quite common for sweet bananas to be purchased, and such bananas typically are bought for *individual* and *immediate* consumption. Yet it is not only much less common for Haya to purchase food for meals, it is impossible, at least in *rural* areas, to buy food for one single meal.[11] An individual who needs to purchase food will have to buy an entire bunch of *ebitoke* to be eaten over several days.

There are (at least) two implications of this contrast in degrees of monetary transaction that I want to stress. The first is that individuated consumption lends itself more completely to buying and selling—sweet bananas are sold more widely and in a greater variety of forms than are bananas for meals. The second and more important point is that the *kind* of consumption that can be individuated in Haya communities is not the most important form of consumption, namely eating a meal. Haya are not only less willing to purchase the *ebitoke* for their meals, but, when they must, they mediate this purchase by insisting on its *collective* purpose. An individual may provide his own snacks by whatever means he chooses; but his meals are too important to be left to his own devices.

Further Haya Culinary Qualities

One day while discussing the relative merits of different foods—from sweet potatoes and cassava to tubers less commonly eaten in rural Kagera, like taro and white potatoes—one of my neighbors said, "We Bahaya, we're born and we just see that muck (*akashabo*)!" The "muck" to which he referred, an appellation that drew a good laugh from our friends, was not intended as a denigration of the various "exotic" potatoes we were discussing, but as high praise for his beloved bananas. *Ebitoke* are prepared for a meal by boiling for at least an hour and a half, depending, of course, on the number of bananas in the pot.[12] This intense boiling produces a piping hot, soggy mixture of bananas—the term "muck" is, in fact, quite appropriate.

The soft texture of the final product is the most sought-after quality. The standard reason my informants gave me for using *ebitoke* as opposed to sweet bananas for preparing a meal is that "those sweet bananas can never get soft." As the preceding commentary may have indicated, *ebitoke* are also preferred to the other recognized staples of Tanzania on these aesthetic grounds. *Ugali,* the stiff porridge made of meal (most often corn, millet, or cassava) and water, is widely detested by the Haya primarily because *ugali* cools and becomes dry and hard too easily.[13]

This preference for food that is so soft and hot recalls the importance of ripening/cooking in Haya cuisine. Note, to begin with, the very different processes of transformation involved in preparing food that is cooked for a meal as opposed to food that is smoked. *Ebitoke* are boiled directly on the hearthstones, while smoked foods are dried in the *olutala* rack above the hearth. This spatial contrast has distinct temporal consequences, for bananas that are cooked for meals are meant to be eaten immediately (lest they dry out and harden), while smoked foods are preserved for future processing and consumption. The form of heat involved in boiling is quite different from that of smoking, as well. Recall that excessive heat is an anathema to the slow-paced processes of smoking. The careful control of heat and speed in ripening and smoking activities distinguish beer brewing from gin distillation. Yet properly cooked bananas must be extremely hot in order to produce their soft texture.[14] This soft, watery texture, again, contrasts with the dried out flesh of smoked food products.

The overall production of these foods, including not only preparation in the kitchen but agricultural activities considered as a part of the process, reveals further temporal contrasts. Beer bananas that are prepared over the hearth are harvested when they are fully mature (*okukula,* "to mature"), and perhaps a bit ripe, and are then ripened over the hearth. Sweet bananas must ripen a bit before they can be roasted or fried, and they must be fully ripe before they can be eaten raw. *Ebitoke,* on the other hand, are harvested when they are completely mature but before they have begun to ripen *at all.* Indeed, allowing bananas for meals to ripen before they are harvested is a sure indication that a farmer is not properly tending his farm. Haya friends told me that the taste of ripened bananas after they have cooked is unpleasant because their sweetness (the *preferred* taste of snack bananas, which all their preparation techniques are designed to enhance) is inappropriate for a meal.

Space, Time, Gender, and Cuisine

Ripe and sweet, soft and dry, boiled and smoked—how are we to sort out this array of qualities and experiences about which the Haya have very definite opinions? I want to focus on the fact that all of these qualities are the results of transformations that the Haya bring about through culinary techniques. Sweet bananas, for example, are not just intrinsically sweet, they are *made* sweet through one of many forms of ripening (cf. Hugh-Jones 1979, 217ff). Looking at the organization of the transformational actions (i.e., the working, harvesting, boiling, roasting etc.) will allow us to appreciate the nuances of Haya gastronomic experience. Further, in drawing attention to the connection between specific acts of making certain finished food products and the kinds of qualities through which the Haya evaluate those products, I hope to provide a foundation for my subsequent analyses of evaluation itself as a social process. This attention to concrete substantial forms offers, I suggest, a tangible framework with which to appreciate the kinds of qualitative values that Haya men and women attempt to secure and control in the course of ongoing relationships and engagements with one another.

Ripening and cooking, as we have seen, are very similar processes in Haya cuisine, yet there are clearly different ways of being "ripe," of being a finished food ready to be eaten. Consider the three principle techniques I have discussed in some detail: ripening (which may involve smoking), which produces "raw" sweet bananas; roasting, which prepares a semiripened fruit; and boiling, which transforms unripened *ebitoke* into a fully cooked meal. Sweet bananas eaten raw are ripened either before they are harvested or by storing them over the hearth for a few days. In either case, the ripening procedure is the work of men and takes place in the elevated "space" of men. With roasted bananas, the fruit initially is ripened as it is for raw fruits, either before harvest or above the hearth. These bananas are subsequently processed by *women* right at the hearth. The most common method of roasting sweet bananas is to stand them by the fire, or even very hot embers, against a hearthstone until they have browned a bit, and then bury them in ashes under the fire until they have finished cooking. Boiled bananas are *ripened/cooked* only by women. Fruits *grown* by men are made edible for meals entirely through the work of women.

These different forms of ripening yield different experiences of heat. Raw bananas, although they may be ripened at the hearth, are never considered hot. Roasted or fried bananas are eaten while they are still hot from the hearth, but they are usually held in the hand while eating. Lastly, boiled bananas are served very hot, and must be served on a plate or leaf, which allows them to be handled more easily. These differing intensities of heat reflect the intensity of the cooking heat, as well. Raw bananas are ripened over the hearth, which diffuses the heat of the fire. Roasted bananas rest alongside or under the coals, which is also a less direct source of heat when compared to boiled *ebitoke,* which sit right in the flames of the fire as they cook in boiling water. These contrasting forms of heat reveal a difference in the ways in which heat is diffused or retained in both cooking and presentation along a continuum from diffuse heat leading to a fruit that retains no heat (raw sweet bananas) to direct application of heat, which produces a fruit that retains as much heat as possible (boiled *ebitoke*).

We can further articulate these thermal contrasts with the gendered dimensions of preparation. The ripening of men is always more diffused and less hot (either via pre-harvest or above-hearth ripening) than is women's processing (roasting or boiling). But in roasting, men's ripening tempers women's cooking; the food produced is both sweet and only moderately hot. In boiling, the distinction between ripening and cooking is eliminated, as only women cook (and thus "ripen") matured but necessarily completely unripened *ebitoke*.

There are temporal dimensions to these gendered distinctions in thermal transformations, as well. Food associated with men is prepared slowly and for long-term use. Smoked foods can be preserved for later use, ripened bananas can be eaten over several days, and beer—the ultimate product of men's work—can be kept for about a week. Women's cuisine is both more rapid (*ebitoke* are boiled in a few hours, as opposed to several days of ripening) and intended for more immediate consumption. *Ebitoke* that have been allowed to cool off become hard and unappetizing.

Lastly, these dimensions of heat, gender, and time should be seen in a spatial context. Men's products come from outside the house (the bananas and coffee grown in the farm) are taken into the house for ripening, and are then offered up outside the limits of the household. Not just coffee and beer but raw bananas and sweet bananas at all stages of preparation are marked more for guests. Women, on the other hand, do not participate in the cultivation of bananas, and their cooking is restricted most narrowly to the hearth.[15] *Ebitoke* are prepared by women for consumption in the house. As I discuss in greater detail below, meals are prepared and consumed by and for members of individual households and are not made available to guests and neighbors as are beer, coffee, and snacks.

The Complexities of Cooking

What I have tried to do so far is to flesh out a model of Haya cuisine or culinary practices that begins with certain gastronomic experiences and preferences and then asks how these are produced and what the implications of that productive activity are. By decomposing the unitary category of "cooking," I have indicated that apparently similar forms of action can have vastly different premises and consequences in Haya culture. If we conjoin the various spatial and temporal dimensions of practices that I have detailed—thermal, speed, gendered, vertical, and concentric dimensions—there emerges a pattern of differences that suggests distinct foci or intentions that orient Haya cuisine. In their overall processing, bananas can be directed toward a long-range use with potentially wide distribution, or a short-term use with a more narrow distribution. The agencies that perform these distinctive practices are clearly gendered, men engaged in the former and women the latter activities. Heat is an index of these orientations as well, for the degree and kind of heat (e.g., hard and dry vs. soft and wet) provide concrete representations in experiencing the spatiotemporal (as well as gendered) form of cooking. Thus, bananas eaten raw embody the qualities of slow ripening through exposure to the most diffuse heat—qualities that are experienced as their "sweetness";[16] while boiled bananas incorporate the intense, direct cooking technique, which is experienced as "softness." I am trying to say much more than simply that ripening bananas makes them sweet and boiling them makes them soft. What I am suggesting is that the experienced form of heat replicates the very method used to transform bananas from agricultural products into one of the various forms of consumable foods. The form of heat taken by a specific type of food, whether it is dissipated through ripening or retained internally in an intensive way, models the ripening/cooking process and therefore provides an index of that process's orientations.

By organizing my analysis in this way and focusing on these dimensions of culinary practice, I am suggesting that a close sociocultural reading of these activities can offer much more than a mere disquisition on the structural form of Haya cuisine. The qualities I have elucidated and the concrete forms these actions take are of interest not simply for their aesthetic properties or conceptual logic. Rather they are directly relevant to the most fundamental aspects of Haya sociality. This much is at least suggested by the gendered dimensions of banana processing and by the ways in which men's and women's foods have very different potentials for creating and perpetuating social relations (Battaglia 1990, 48–49). The very form and meaning of Haya social relations, both intra- and interhousehold, are continuously enacted and represented through these totalizing operations upon and with food. Looking at these operations from this perspective provides us with a more complete position from which to address the issues that persist throughout my analysis—namely, the ways in which persons and objects become reciprocally imbued with values in contexts of ongoing transformation.

To address this question of sociality, its construction and representation, I want to focus more closely on all of the activities that surround the provision and preparation of a meal. I have already indicated some of the salient features of a meal: the ways, for example, in which purchasing a meal differs from purchasing a snack, and the distinct gender dimensions and spatial and temporal orientations that are incorporated in *ebitoke* boiled for a meal. A more detailed examination of the overall process of providing a meal will give us a better sense of the meanings of these practices, and, in turn, a deeper understanding of how the Haya construct their social world.

4 MEALTIME: PROVIDING AND
PRESENTING A MEAL

Beyond Cuisine: Constituting a Meal

Haya cooking techniques are quite varied, and I have tried to suggest that the significance of these techniques lies in the distinct qualities that they entail. For example, it is not sufficient to characterize all cooking simply as a form of generating heat, since the specific characteristics of different kinds of heat—the slow, dry heat of smoking or the intense, moist heat of boiling—carry with them quite specific and distinctive spatial and temporal forms (i.e., they concretely embody different configurations of space and time). The different forms or embodiments of space and time that are objectified in ripened sweet bananas, stored beer bananas, or boiled staple plantain are the products of alternative ways of orienting productive activities. Completed foods, in this way, refer back to the creative culinary practices that make them. Such foods, that is, are icons of Haya sociocultural activity. At the same time, Haya experiences of food—the succulence of well-ripened sweet fruits, the full body of properly prepared banana beer, or, less fortunately, the bitterness or hardness of plantains ill suited for boiling—are also created by these distinct techniques, these particular ways of orienting sociocultural (in this case, culinary) actions. In this way the concrete characteristics of the different forms of food that Haya cook establish a connection between the specific, situated activities of cooking and the qualities of experience that accompany their consumption. These kinds of relations, I argue, are crucial to Haya sociocultural constructions of what I have called *processes of engagement,* the relationship between activity and experience and the world in which both are anchored, a relationship that at all levels is saturated with meaning.

The activities described in the previous chapter demonstrate some of the complexities involved in this relationship at the level of culinary practice. They illustrate, for example, the subtleties involved in controlling certain values that are associated with monetary gain, or the careful coordination of gendered activities as these are instantiated by specific cooking techniques. But these descriptions are in no way complete accounts of the place of food in the Haya world. Haya gastronomic experiences clearly are not limited to the tastes and textures of differently prepared foods; nor are their culinary practices restricted to placing pots over a hearth. In order to give a fuller account of Haya meanings of food, and in particular to expand my discussion of the ways in which Haya cuisines objectifies an orientation to the world, I want to situate these experiences and practices in a much wider process. In this chapter I consider a Haya meal, from its preparation and presentation through its consumption and disposal, in order to provide a more totalizing process as a context for the Haya qualities and orientations we have already seen. Examining a meal will further provide us with a specific *place* in which to locate these Haya concerns, and thereby allow us to consider the centrality of food to maintaining sociality both within a household and between households.

My assessment of the hearth rack as a primary locus of orientation in cooking has to be extended in order to characterize the kinds of spatiotemporal possibilities that Haya create through food. But expanding this discussion into the context of a meal poses the same problems of ethnographic description that the category of cooking does—namely, that these are both highly flexible terms that can refer to a wide range of forms, each with distinctive implications and characteristics. In the case of meal, this flexibility exists at a number of levels.

To begin with, there are certain meals or food preparations that are specifically appropriate to certain ceremonial occasions. For example, I found that *pilau,* the rice dish imported to Kagera from the coast (and the equivalent of *pilaf* in western Asian cuisine, or *bilau* in other African or African-American contexts) is most often served in rural Haya communities at weddings that celebrate marriages recognized by both religious and state agencies.[1] The ingredients for this dish—including garlic, cloves, black pepper, and cardamom—are not readily available in rural markets, the *pilau* itself is often prepared by cooks who specialize in making this dish, and the consequent expenses of preparing this dish are seen to be appropriate to a wedding ceremony that itself requires such elaborate preparation. "The Hyena's Pot," *Enyungu y'empisi,* is a dish that is consumed only by mourners. The first food eaten after a corpse has been interred, "The Hyena's Pot" (bananas prepared without relish or flavoring of any kind) represents the hardships of death and mourning and is eaten only sparingly by those who bear these pains. On yet other occasions, the first meal of a newly married couple or the birth of twins, a pot that consists of "a mixture of every kind of banana" along with a particular variety of bean is prepared. In brief, it is hardly novel to point out that ceremony is characterized by the preparation of distinctive meals, as food seems especially suited as an expressive medium for conveying in both immediate bodily experience (through taste, texture, temperature, substance, and the like) as well as through sumptuary display and demonstration (as in the effort and resources required to procure and produce certain kinds of food) the kinds of meanings that are at stake and recognized in ceremonial activity.

The complexity of ceremonial meals is not diminished at the level of mundane, everyday meals. Haya express preferences for certain kinds of food—as should be clear by now, plantain and bananas are the vastly preferred staple. But we have also seen that Haya eat a variety of foods, with less enthusiasm for some than others. The season of *enjala*, "famine/hunger," occurs at the very end of the longer dry season in July and August. But it must be pointed out that what Haya "hunger" for in this season is bananas, which flourish during the heavy rains of March and April but mature much less quickly as the dry season wears on (Rald and Rald 1975, 22; Seitel 1977, 189). During this period many Haya rely more heavily on sweet potatoes (*emfuma*) and especially cassava (*ebigando* or *ebilibwa*), which is renowned as a crop that is easily cultivated even in dry and hot conditions.[2]

A daily meal may be composed of a variety of produce, but two basic categories constitute any meal. The first is a starchy staple, which Haya call simply *ekyakulya* ("food"). Bananas; *ugali* porridge made of maize, cassava, or eleusine (*oburoi*—rare in these days) flour; sweet potatoes; boiled cassava; or rice (for those who can afford it) are commonly available staples. Rice must be purchased, and most flours, especially maize flour, are purchased as well. The staple is eaten with a relish (*omukubi* in Haya, more commonly called *mboga*, from the Swahili), the second essential component of any proper meal. The variety of relishes is also quite wide and is subject to seasonal availability. Perhaps the relish most commonly served with any staple are beans (*mperege*), a wide variety of which are grown on any family farm. Beans are dried and stored after their harvest in January, and should be available throughout the year on a reasonably well-maintained farm. Bambara nuts (*ensholo*) are also an especially prized accompaniment. Tomatoes and onions are generally available at weekly markets throughout the year. Tomatoes are grown locally on family farms and are more widely consumed than onions, which are produced commercially. Other vegetable relishes include tree tomatoes (*entongo*, a variety of eggplant); cabbage; *mboga ya majani* ("leafy vegetables," especially *mchicha*, a variety of spinach, as well as the tender leaves of most squashes, legumes, and tubers); peanuts (*ebinyobwa*); and a variety of small hot peppers.

It should also be pointed out that one of the most important relishes is salt. Salt is a central ingredient to any meal—one Haya friend (himself a cook) remarked that food without salt is "just water!" Salt is added to all prepared foods, and the absence of "even salt" is especially noted in the unsatisfying "Hyena's Pot."[3] Salt can also be used by itself as a simple relish, and, in some senses, it is salt that makes cooked food into an edible meal.

In addition to vegetable produce, meats are widely available, if not always affordable. Beef is readily available in most areas.[4] While goats and chickens are maintained by many but by no means all households, goat meat is generally preferred to and always more costly than beef, while chicken is most prized and expensive. Curdled milk, typically mixed with beans or greens, is most often *remembered* as having once been an important relish by contemporary Haya— it was rarely eaten in my experience.

Fish is widely available in all areas of Kagera, and provides a significant source of income for many households. Young men often seek work in boats that fish for both white bait and Nile perch in Lake Victoria. Such work often requires these men to leave their homes on the escarpments that overlook the lake for extended stays on the lake shore. Many residents of these highland villages make an income by marketing fish, traveling to the shore to purchase the daily catch and returning to sell these fish to their village neighbors. Fish is widely available in local markets, either fresh or dried. Nile perch that is purchased fresh is occasionally cut into twenty to thirty pieces, which are then deep fried in the fish's rendered fat. These fried pieces are then sold (in 1989, for 10 Tsh, approximately 5¢) as a relish for a meal. Fish, then, can provide an income for a number of people, from those who catch it through those who cook it for sale. It is the most available and affordable of all "meat" relishes, but the fish trade provides the widest income as well.

Another ingredient that is important in many dishes is oil (*amajuta; mafuta* in Swahili). *Amajuta*, like *mafuta* in Swahili, can refer to oils or fats of any kind, from kerosene to butter. *Mafuta ya uto*[5] is the generic cooking oil available in Haya markets; tinned margarine or shortening, though expensive, are also used. Oil is considered something of a luxury. Haya like the flavor and richness of oil and fats, but these are by no means typical ingredients in Haya relishes. Butter (*amajuta g'ente,* literally "cow's fat") is churned by the Haya, although it is not, to my knowledge, used in cooking, but rather as an ointment. In the past, butter was used as a prestigious lotion and smeared on the skin in order to create a shiny, smooth appearance.[6] Haya use commercially produced petroleum-based gels, still called *amajuta,* in the same way today.

This is certainly not an exhaustive list of the ingredients that contribute to a

Haya meal, and it is scarcely even a partial list of the foods and fruits that can be eaten at any time of day as a snack. There are also, as I have stated, individual preferences, as well as important regional differences within the Kagera Region, which make describing "a meal" a fundamentally difficult task. Nonetheless, the components I have described, and especially the division between staples and relishes, are basic aspects of Haya cuisine, and the techniques of their preparation are sufficiently widespread and routinized to merit attention as cultural practices. More importantly, Haya perspectives on food—such as the claim that "famine" (*enjala*) ensues when bananas (but not sweet potatoes or cassava) are in short supply—indicate that certain regularities of choices *do* exist, and my contention is that these choices have consequences for the way that Haya live their lives. Given this assertion, let me turn to an exploration of food preparation as a means of assessing what some of these consequences might be.

Wrapping and Pounding: The Perception of Preparation

The techniques for peeling and boiling plantain are certainly different from pounding and whisking *ugali*, yet there are important features of food preparation that are common to all staple foods. Not only are all such foods prepared within the same space (i.e., in the kitchen at the hearth), but some important orientations toward food, ways of conceptualizing its capacity for productivity, and practices that characterize the movement of food into the house and within it, are shared with respect to staples. The first aspect of food preparation that I consider has to do with simply taking food into the house, and the meanings that this involves.

The *ebitoke* meal bananas (discussed in the previous chapter) for a day's meals can be harvested up to a few days prior to being cooked. Once cut down, a banana bunch (*omukungu*) will last two to three days before it begins to "ripen," that is, to become soft and sweet and therefore unfit for cooking. Haya often wrap the harvested bunch in a banana leaf (*olubabi*) in order to take the produce from the farm into the house. Reining was told that a banana bunch is wrapped in this way "lest it cause quarrels in the household" (1967, 154); one neighbor told me that a bunch is wrapped as a form of "respect" (he used the Swahili word *heshima*) because harvested bananas are "already food" (*chakula tayari*). In either case, this fairly common practice suggests a special relationship between food and the household that is going to consume it, one that identifies the potential condition of a household with the condition of its food. More specifically, it suggests a transition in the status of bananas, from a maturing plant to a form of food, that is marked by the movement of the bunch from out in the farm (owned by the same household that harvests and eats the bunch) to inside the house. This inward movement is indicated by wrapping the bunch, an action that extends the enclosure provided by the house. It further suggests that one of the defining features of food, what it is that in effect transforms a crop into food, is this interior position. As my neighbor said, bananas are wrapped in this way because they are "already food," and food is inherently an internal affair.

A similar point can be made about the preparation of *ugali*, the stiff porridge that is widely shunned but probably the most common staple after *ebitoke*. One night after dark, a housemate was shocked to hear our neighbor pounding cassava into flour for the evening's meal. "Pounding *ugali* at this time of the night! Better I should go hungry!" When I asked what was so unusual about this activity he suggested that when people hear pounding during the night they assume that a thief is at work. Anyone who has yet to finish such tasks in the daylight is, at least according to my friend, assumed to have used the cover of darkness to steal food, which must then be (rather audibly) prepared at night. In fact, by this account and others like it, it may not be a good idea to be involved in many aspects of food preparation—even of *ebitoke*—after dark; neighbors who hear wood being chopped or banana bunches being harvested (with their distinctive leaf-slashing sounds as they are felled) might well suspect that the firewood or bananas have been improperly procured.

This concern with preparing food at night is closely correlated with the importance of wrapping banana bunches. In each case, Haya attempt to control the exposure of food, which, if it is in fact meant to be consumed as food, should be concealed within a household. Acts of food preparation that are loud enough to be heard well beyond any one house will disclose a house's use of food to those who are not a part of the household. Avoiding *pounding* at night is therefore of particular importance, as the sounds of *ugali* being prepared might reveal to others your own household's possible hardships, which many Haya would certainly associate with eating this low-prestige food.

It is exposing food preparation at *night*, however, that is especially problem-atic, because the darkness of the night conceals the way in which food has been obtained. This association (or assumption) drawn between the time of food preparation and the form of its possession indicates that what is *revealed* by the different aspects of *preparing* food—including pounding and harvesting, but also wrapping a banana bunch—is the method by which this food has been *acquired*. Enclosing a banana bunch in banana leaf is a visible indication, a sign of sorts, that the crop grown on your farm is being brought inside to be prepared as food; pounding and harvesting during the day are audible (and less markedly visible) evidence of the same transition. But the night's darkness obscures these connections. At the very least, pounding or harvesting at night publicly disclose the fact that you are having difficulty completing the work necessary to provide your family with food during the course of the day, and this in itself makes such nighttime activities especially troubling. At the worst, such preparations invite suspicion that you are incapable of providing for yourself, and have resorted to stealing from others. In any case, the implication is that ill-timed food preparation discloses the larger process of food production and provision, and opens these processes to the scrutiny of others.

I want to consider a counterexample in order to make the connections that I have suggested even clearer. While many of my friends objected to the idea of pounding or harvesting at night, some of them claimed that these practices were commonplace and acceptable in a region called the *oluhita*.[7] The *oluhita* are lowland areas which, according to Haya villagers I spoke with, have only recently become inhabited. Its new residents are those who have been forced to migrate there from villages on the escarpments (*omugongo*, literally "on the back"; cf. Beattie 1957, 317), where land has become scarce. *Oluhita* residents are stereotypically of such dubious moral character (who else would leave their natal village?) that the suggestion that they typically prepare food after dark is essentially a confirmation of the general claim that only thieves would act in this way. But there is a more important point to be made. The *oluhita* is renowned for being an uninviting environment, its climate too hot, and its soils too infertile to cultivate successive generations of bananas successfully.[8] Food provision, therefore, is seen as a perpetual problem in the *oluhita*, and late-night preparations are seen as a necessary consequence of working long, grueling days in order to obtain an adequate food supply.

My point, then, is not that Haya claim that preparing food at night invites suspicion because it is only done by (what are thought of as) suspicious people. Rather, the suggestion that food is routinely prepared at night in a region where access to food is considered somewhat tenuous confirms the observation that Haya consider methods of food preparation to be evidence of a general control over the entire food provision process. The actions of preparing food at night, then, are not only understood as clear signs of insufficient control over this process, they also demonstrate an inability to maintain adequately the distinction between what should be concealed with in a household and what can be disclosed to others. Maintaining this distinction is critical, I will argue, to a Haya household's capacity to process effectively, and thereby secure and control the values of food.

Haya Hydraulics of Gender, or Containing the Source

An essential element in all foods prepared for a meal, regardless of the staple, is water. Recall that Haya gastronomic aesthetics generally favor a texture and substance that is hot and moist; they prefer not to prepare bananas that remain hard when they are boiled, and the coarse, dry texture of most *ugali* is similarly objectionable. Water, then, is a transformative substance in multiple ways. It is not only the basic medium in which all foods are cooked, but by this process it becomes part of the food itself.[9] Good food, to the Haya palate, is food that becomes soggy, food that takes on qualities of the water in which it cooks. This suggests that, in proper cooking, water transforms itself as it transforms food. To say that water is a fluid medium may sound ridiculous, but this is intrinsic to the penetrating and permeable potential of water in the cooking process.

It is also useful to highlight the importance of water in Haya cuisine because water is so strongly associated with women. Women not only prepare food in ways that rely on water, they also contribute to beer making by providing water for the beer banana mixture that men squeeze into juice. Women and occasionally younger children are responsible for fetching water (*okuta'amaizi*) from local rivers whenever it is needed during the day. Water is usually collected in cooking pots (*enyungu*), or plastic buckets if these are available. These are then stored in the kitchen. The strong association of women with water—and especially with fetching water—can be seen further in the fact that the most important rites of passage for women center of safeguarding the act of collecting water for domestic uses. After completing the period of seclusion which follows either marriage or giving birth, a woman demonstrates her successful reintegration into the community, as well as her productive contribution to her own household, by descending to the river (carefully protecting the path of her trip—especially the crossroads—with medicinal preparations) and fetching water at a spring (*enchulo*).

The ways in which women collect water, and the very fact that it is women who do so, suggest the importance of water to cooking processes and, more fundamentally, illustrate the extent to which the Haya cooking process is essential to the construction of (gendered) sociality. Rivers are places of collective gathering. They are usually named places that lie below residential villages, and therefore outside of what is recognized as village space. And, since rivers do not run through villages, but pass beneath and between them, no single village is likely to use any one source of running water. Clothes are soaked and pounded (*okuogy'emyenda*) on the flat banks of the river, and there are recognized bathing spots, as well. These activities are carried out in the river or stream itself. But the principle use for water that is *collected* is cooking and drinking.

The spring or source, *enchulo,* where water is collected is an especially important location, one that reveals certain basic features of Haya social relations. A central spring can become a site of dispute, for example, on occasions when one member of a community draws the collective disapproval of a significant segment of that community. In the accounts that were relayed to me, someone widely suspected of sorcery would be subject to public sanctions in the form of "avoidance" (*okumuzila,* "to avoid him/her"; the same verb is the root of *enzilo,* the "totem" avoided by clansmen). In extreme cases, a person who is being shunned will eventually be driven off their land, their crops completely uprooted, and their house burned down. But the more common form of avoidance refuses to allow the miscreant to engage in public life, and the standardized sanctions described to me were (1) you cannot pasture your cattle with other cattle;[10] (2) you cannot drink beer with others; and, above all, (3) you cannot draw water from the same source as those who shun you.[11] These prohibitions all suggest the centrality of running waters and collecting water to Haya sociality, as these are the focus of proper relations between neighbors, all of whom draw water from the same source. Moreover, beer provision and cattle pasturage also entail collecting water (either to brew beer or water cattle) in order to convert that water into a powerful medium of social value (Taylor 1992, passim). These prohibitions also indicate the degree to which individual households are grounded in these collective forms, since each home is dependent on water that is drawn from a collective, indeed translocal, source, one that can serve a number of villages and which lies outside of any single village. Moreover, the fact that it is women who collect water reveals the extent to which women's activities, even when their primary focus is domestic provision, mediate between collective relations and individual households in ways that concern fundamental dimensions of Haya sociality.

The uses to which collected water is put also indicate the kinds of activities that constitute Haya social relations, as well as the ways in which these are gendered. Water collected from springs is used primarily in cooking, and this suggests that providing food, so essential to household integrity and viability, is actually articulated through interhousehold relations. Other tasks that require water, bathing and laundering in particular, are, as I indicated, usually carried out at the river itself, and so do not require the security of enclosed domesticity.[12]

A second major use of water, again collected primarily by women, is for banana juice (*omulamba*) and beer making. This is further evidence of the importance of water collection to the actual performance of Haya sociality.

Beer processed and almost exclusively "owned" by men (see preceding chapter) is perhaps the quintessential medium of interhousehold relationships, *the* essential element of bridewealth payments, clan fines, and (at one time) noble tribute (see Carlson 1989, passim). Beer is also used to establish a particular network of exchange relations, in which a man who regularly produces beer sets aside a container full of beer for each of his friends or neighbors who also produce beer (all others will pay to drink). Each of these friends, in turn, provides their partners with beer when they decide to make beer. In this way, those who regularly produce beer are said to "never be without beer."

The Haya term for this kind of exchange relationship is *enchulo,* a "source" that is ever renewable, just as the riverine source provides water to a community. These parallel sources also reveal the commonalities of restrictions on beer drinking and water collecting as sanctions taken against those who are "avoided." This equation of sources suggests more than just a parallel, however, as it entails an important transformation. Women's activities draw on a collective source in order to provide for individuated production, whether it be household cooking or beer making. Men's practices proceed in what appears to be an opposite direction, making use of an individual provision of water in order to generate a collective source of beer. However, it is equally evident that women's water collecting *underlies* and so makes possible men's beer making; and the same is true of cooking, which is carried out by women but facilitated by the households (usually, but certainly not exclusively) owned by their husbands and fathers. The larger point, though, is that both processes, cooking and beer making, involve the articulation of collective and singular activities, and reveal the fact that the nature of this articulation is gendered in distinct ways.

An additional point to be made about water pertains to certain qualities that it contributes to the cooking process, which in turn, serve to constitute important attributes of Haya gender. Water is collected primarily for cooking. Moreover, water usually is collected in the largest cooking pots (*esufuria* from the Swahili, or *enyungu*), further suggesting the importance of water to cooking, as well as the fact that cooking is the reason for collecting water. The specific qualities that are made manifest by the act of collecting water are containment and enclosure, qualities (and acts) that require interrupting the dynamic flow of the river's source and containing this for other purposes. I have already suggested the dynamic quality of water as it is experienced in Haya cuisine, the fact that water has the ability to transform food by transforming itself in the cooking process. Collecting water might, therefore, be seen as a way of *enclosing*—understood in these contexts as an active means of *transforming* this dynamic potential that is then deployed in cooking.

Furthermore, the woman's rites of passage that center on collecting water for a household serve to reintegrate a woman and her household into her community, and they do so by demonstrating the fact that a woman who performs these acts has become an able "container," in this dynamic sense of being able to enclose, redirect, and thereby transform a fluid potency. Such rites are carried out after a woman has given birth or after she emerges from bridal seclusion (in the past, the latter was enabled by the former), each of which requires not only that a woman be able to bring forth a child, but also that she be able effectively to contain the initial semen that her husband gives to her following the birth of any child. This initial semen (*ebisisi*, literally "embers") establishes a husband's right to determine the clan membership of the next child to whom his wife gives birth at any point in the future (cf. Reining 1967, 151; Swantz 1985, 72–73). Haya men and women also point out that repeated acts of intercourse are necessary throughout pregnancy in order for the fetus to develop properly.[13] Thus, a woman who successfully gives birth and completes the seclusion period has demonstrated a capacity to control long-term processes of both *giving forth* and *taking in* her husband's progeny. Her body is seen to be more than a secure container, but rather an able and dynamic processor that literally embodies an *internal* control over the flow of reproductive potential. Successfully collecting water for cooking is an act that succinctly reveals this capacity to engage and control similar transformative forces.

The qualities of water, and in particular of collecting cooking water, suggests some critical potentialities that are brought to the cooking process. Collecting water, through its associations with collective resources and female reproductivity, exemplifies the dynamic generativity characteristic of water in the cooking process. At the same time, these actions, through their demonstration of effective containment and enclosure, embody the *inward* orientation that, as I suggested in my discussion of wrapping and pounding, is essential to food provision. Collecting water draws on a collective, dynamic potential and initiates a transformation of this potential by containing and enclosing it.

Work in the Kitchen

In the previous chapter I described the concrete form of the hearth and certain gendered dimensions of it. Let me present a somewhat fuller picture of the surrounding kitchen as a site of women's and men's activities. A Haya kitchen (*omuchumbilo*, from *okuchumba*, "to cook") is occasionally located inside the main house but is more commonly a separate structure, situated behind or to the side of the house. The stones (*amaiga*) and rack (*olutala*) that make up the hearth are only one part of any kitchen. Many kitchens are circular, with the hearth located at its center, thus replicating the plan of the former circular house. Most kitchens, however, are small four-square buildings, with the hearth off to one side, and an area for storage and conversation adjacent to it. Food can be stored in the hearth rack, or anywhere near the hearth. Relishes like tomatoes, meat, fish, and salt are often wrapped in lengths of banana bast (*ebigoye*) and suspended from the rack, which is fairly effective at preventing mice from getting at them.

In the beehive-style house that was once common throughout Kagera, kitchens occupied the very center of the house and were shielded from view of the sitting room at the front of the house by large woven screens. In most houses today, the kitchen is a separate building, and this shift, from inside to outside and from center to periphery, is of some consequence to Haya notions of gender. The shift is also characteristic of what many Haya feel to be the contemporary ongoing dispersal of "social relations" in general (which might be defined as clan, marital, household, or village relations, depending on the matter being discussed). My informants throughout Kagera, including those in urban areas, always described the unique quality of the beehive-style house (fig. 2) as one that had "everything on the inside" (*buli kantu omunda*). Haya frequently cited the *omushonge* house that exhibited such qualities as an example of "authentic Haya culture." One young man even suggested to me that the ability to build a fine house that could contain many things was a unique feature of Haya culture, in contrast to other Tanzanians who shamelessly "dig holes in the ground and call them houses!" From this perspective, locating kitchens outside the house when they once occupied its very center is one of the more concrete instances of dispersal and displacement. Clearly, contemporary Haya houses no longer have "everything on the inside." Some of the significance of such dispersal can be assessed by exploring the kinds of activities that go on in the kitchen, and characteristic Haya accounts of the gendered nature of these acts.

We have already seen a contrast between beer bananas prepared on the inside of the house as opposed to those that are ripened outside, a difference that has certain gendered dimensions, insofar as women are more likely to use the outdoor method. Another significant aspect of this contrast is its relation to money, and the sense in which bananas ripened quickly outside the house are somewhat less palatable but certainly more profitable. In addition, fish pieces that are fried in their own fat for sale are also commonly cooked outside. These fish pieces are often fried in a pot that is set up over a temporary hearth, three stones placed together in the courtyard (*ekibuga*) out in front of the house (see figs. 2 and 3). Neighbors frequently gather in the hours before dinner at a house that is frying fish, chatting, picking out the fish pieces they prefer, and some even eating the fish on the spot. It is also not uncommon to hear people ask their neighbors who are frying fish that night, much as they might ask "*Amaarwa galai?*" ("Where's the beer?"). It is worth bringing up these details because all of this makes fish frying a very public activity and, as I hope to demonstrate, very different from forms of food preparation, presentation, and consumption surrounding a meal, and especially meal staples. Such differences also point to the degree to which fish preparation of this kind is so clearly tied in to generating cash, a project which, like the gin distilling that follows pit ripening, literally "takes place" in a clearly outside, open, and publicly accessible context.

What goes on inside a kitchen for meal preparation is rather different. Bananas must be peeled before being cooked. The tough peel of a plantain that has matured, but not ripened (i.e., that is ready for cooking) must be scraped from the fruit itself. This is usually achieved in a two-stage process of first tearing off the loose outer peel, and then scraping away the fibers that remain. Once peeled, these bananas are placed in a pot of already boiling water. A large portion of bananas are prepared for most Haya meals. Actually counting out the number of bananas to be served at a meal is considered inappropriate (for reasons considered in chapter 5), but by my own estimate, eight to ten average sized bananas (whose volume is equivalent to the bananas found in most Western markets) per person provides a typical meal.

When plantain/banana is the meal's staple, it is not uncommon for the accompanying relish to be prepared in the same pot. Beans are allowed to boil for up to several hours before a meal. I never saw or heard of dried beans being soaked before they were cooked. Fresh beans, in the days just after harvest, are prepared in less time. When beans are harvested, they are typically allowed to dry out in their pods while still on the stem. Whole vines of beans are then gathered in the courtyard and beaten with sticks in order to shell them (*okuhandula*). The beans are then gathered up and sorted by kind (*okulonda*, "to choose, select") and stored in baskets, or any available container. Before they are cooked, the meal's portion of beans are sorted again to remove any twigs, grit, or beans that have rotted while in storage. All of these activities—harvesting, hulling, and sorting beans—are usually performed by a mother and the children of her household. Sorting different varieties of beans is considered tedious, but exacting work (different sizes of beans mixed together would not cook uniformly). I found that sorting was often carried out by groups of young women, not children, sitting and talking together in the "back of the house" (*omukisika*; see chapter 2).

In addition to beans, meats when they are available (especially beef and goat that have been drying at the hearth for a day or two) can be added to the pot along with the bananas. This reconstitutes the meat, and lends some flavor to the pot, as well. Tomatoes and other vegetables usually are added to the pot as the bananas near completion. Often, delicate foods like fried fish or leafy greens are wrapped in a supple section of banana leaf and placed over the bananas, which steams the contents while the bananas boil. A smaller cooking pot can serve as a lid when inverted; more commonly, a large section of banana leaf is carefully tucked around the edges of the pot in order to seal it while it cooks.

Cooking pots today are hammered tin and are available at most local markets. They come in a variety of sizes; none have handles, only an extended lip around the circumference of the pot. After a very few months of use cooking pots build up an extremely blackened heavy carbon deposit. By most accounts, tin pots have been readily available only since World War II. Prior to that, earthenware vessels, some of which are still produced today and are occasionally available in markets, were used for cooking.

When bananas are prepared by themselves, or whenever *ugali* or rice is prepared, a relish is prepared separately from the staple. If oil is available, it might be used to fry onion or tomato as a base for additional ingredients. More commonly, beans are boiled separately, and vegetables can be added to the broth created. Bits of meat or fish can also be used to create a thin soup to which either peanuts, tomatoes, greens, or peppers, as well as the necessary salt can be added. Haya relishes when prepared separately in this way are rarely very complex. They usually can be assembled in a few minutes, as the preferred consistency is thin and rather watery, instead of the density and thickness which prolonged cooking would produce. This is especially the case when *ugali* is eaten, since it is considered to be particularly dry and requires the wateriness of a good relish or gravy (*mchuzi* from the Swahili is used by Haya speakers).

Flavor, Heat, and Sexuality

Before discussing how the food prepared in this way is served, let me point out some of the aesthetic, tactile, and sensory properties implicated in the foods already described. In the previous chapter I discussed different forms of heat in the processing of food in terms of their spatiotemporal qualities, contrasting in particular the slow, desiccating heat of drying and smoking with the intense, direct heat of boiling. I will draw on these properties here, and further point out certain gastronomic experiences that these forms of heat and cooking create.

On the whole, Haya cuisine is rather bland. Haya tend to speak of the pleasures of satiation more often than the toothsome in matters of food. Salt is a necessary ingredient, one that makes cooked produce into consumable food, but "saltiness" as a flavor is little remarked upon by Haya. The most common attribute of well prepared food is that it is "sweet," a quality that is expressed as a verbal form, with the verb *okunula*, "to be sweet." This sweetness is the central feature of *okunula*,[14] as evidenced, for example, by the fact that the augmentative form—*okunulilila*—is used to describe things that are sugary sweet, such as overly ripened fruit, commercial candies, or sugar itself. However, *okunula* is not used exclusively for sweetness but for good-tasting, agreeable qualities in general. In fact, bananas that are cooked properly are said to be "sweet" (*ebitoke byanula*), while bananas that have *ripened* prior to being cooked and therefore become sugary sweet would never be described in this way.

Moreover, the sense of taste, or flavor of any kind is described using the abstract noun *obunula*, derived from the verb *okunula*. This suggests that to have taste of any kind is to be good tasting, much as in (American) English something good to eat is "tasty," or something generally pleasing can be "tasteful." It is also critical to point out that the desirable qualities suggested by *okunula* are not limited to food. Any enjoyable event or activity can be said to be "sweet" or "tasty." All of this suggests that the qualities of taste and flavor are highly flexible attributes in Haya experience. "Sweetness" is a central feature of taste with reference to food, but taste can also be used at an abstract level, as well as to describe experiences that are not even related to food.

While sweetness is a core value of taste, bitterness is both the opposite of sweetness, while still a variety of taste itself—that is, it is a recognized "flavor" within the abstract category of taste (*obunula*). Like sweetness, bitterness is expressed in a verbal form, *okushalila*. Foods that are acrid or sour, like lemons or pineapple, as well as those that are pungent and piquant, typically hot peppers or very strong banana gin, are all described as "bitter foods," *ebyakula ebyashalila*. Like sweetness, bitterness can be used to describe experiences that are unrelated to food. *Obushasi*, the abstract noun for bitterness, can be used to describe stinging or penetrating pain. It is also the Haya term for grief, much as English expresses the affect of loss as "bitter." Again, bitterness is a generalizable, almost diffuse quality, with both abstract and concrete properties.[15]

I want to explore one of the more concrete instantiations of bitterness in order to trace through its particular relevance to the experience of food. In Haya experience, bitterness and especially piquancy imply a thermal dimension as well; that is, bitter, acrid foods are considered to be markedly hot, just as in English we speak of hot peppers, the burn of sour flavors, or strong drinks. One of the critical meanings of this kind of heat is seen in the association of piquant foods with sexuality. Hot peppers, *pilipili*, are not a necessary addition in Haya cuisine. When peppers are used, they are rarely incorporated into a relish, and so do not permeate the flavor of a meal. Rather, peppers are typically steamed whole like other fragile vegetables on top of boiling bananas, and are then served like a condiment that each person can add in varying degrees to their meal. Hot peppers are often passed, like salt, among people eating together. When I shared meals with Haya friends, especially in the company of men, they almost never failed to mention the sexually stimulating effects of eating hot peppers. "Now you need a woman!" was a common suggestion, since "those peppers give you a 'charge' [the English word used]."

The association of heat with sexuality is not terribly surprising, but I would further suggest that the heat of sharp bitterness is particularly constitutive of Haya masculine sexuality. This can best be illustrated by working through its contrast with feminine sexuality or, to be more specific, with Haya men's experience of women's bodies' sexual possibilities. I have previously described the importance of water to feminine forms of agency and identity, and female sexuality has significant watery components as well. This association is implied in the rites of water collecting, which accompany a woman's return to sexual activity following the birth of a child. Water, of course, need not be cooling. Boiling water is essential to productive cooking, and boiling—*okutagata*—is a common way of referring to both men's and women's sexual excitement. Haya men also frequently speak of the moisture and wetness of women's sexual secretions as essential to the pleasures of sexual activity.[16] Many men were able to provide me with what amounted to a sexualized anatomical index of a woman's body, a listing of physical features—from the space between a woman's toes to the glistening skin on the back of her knees—that they saw as a certain indication of, as they put it, "how much water she gives out" during sex.

A common simile on this matter was that a desirable woman "gives out water like a banana stem!" ("*Yaihya maizi nk'omugogo!*"). This is a felicitous phrase, not only because it makes certain connections between sexuality and food but, I would argue, because it reveals important complementarities in men's and women's sexualities. The banana stem referred to (*omugogo*) is the tall "trunk" of the plant from which the banana stalk and bunch grow. In order to harvest the mature fruit, men slash through the banana stem, bringing down the banana bunch and leaving the sticky, wet banana stem.[17] This suggests, again, a relationship between men's actions and the kind of wetness they produce and enjoy (through either women or banana plants) but do not possess themselves. There is also a more critical aspect of male sexuality implied here, and one that links back up with Haya gustatory experience. The Haya verb "to cut" is *okushala,* which is the root for "to be bitter," *okushalila* (the augmentative form of *okushala*); given this derivation, it might be appropriate to think of bitterness as sharpness. This, then, suggests a connection between hot peppers or other bitter foods and masculinity, for bitter, hot foods impart a form of "heat" whose *sharpness* is especially characteristic of men's productive activities. Another exclusively men's action is "spearing" (*okuchumita*). Spears are presented to men by their fathers upon their marriage, and the action of spearing is also basic to planting and uprooting banana shoots. In addition to these explicit associations of spearing with the achievement of affinal relations and ongoing agricultural reproduction, "spearing" is also a standard euphemism for sexual intercourse. The taste of sharpness in bitter foods for men is therefore an immediate and heightened experience of their own creative capacity, an experience that they characterize as more than just "hot"—as intrinsically physically and sexually "charged."

Heat is a quality that is pervasive in Haya sexuality, both men's and women's. But it is configured in distinct ways, ways that reveal men's and women's distinct orientation to the world and to each other. Men's sexuality and the experiences of bitterness and sharpness that typify it, have an intense, sudden quality. The form of heat they embody is also spatially delimited, the sharpness of pepper is implosive and restricted, like the swift chopping motion that fells the banana plant. The heat that represents Haya women's sexual experiences, on the other hand, is much more fluid and diffuse. The expansive heat of boiling or the particularly feminine capacity for a continual flow of sexual fluids are clearly opposed to the restricted, "sharp" heat of Haya men's experience. As Kenny indicates in his discussion of cosmology in and around Lake Victoria,

> the sexual symbolism of the Interlacustrine area gives diffuse capacities to women, and "sharp" authoritarian capacities to men; this is represented in the contrasting symbols of the cooking-pot and the spear. (1977, 720)

Haya sociocultural practices also suggest that women's capacity for and control of heat in general, from kindling a cooking fire to the regular flow of menstrual blood, is much more pervasive than is men's. Women have the ability to regulate and transform heat, to cool down or heat up within a continuum of thermal conditions, and this, too, may account for men's insistence that the sudden burst, or "charge" of bitter, "sharp" heat brought on by pepper requires a woman to satisfy or temper it. I would suggest, then, that while the heat of Haya men's sexual experience has a penetrating orientation, one that is explicitly "sharp" and "stabbing," women's heat permeates and fluctuates during sexual activity and experience.

This contrast between penetration and permeation might be a useful device for bringing together many of the points about Haya cuisine that I have thus far described. The contrast between beer and meal bananas, for example, turns on the periodic nature of men's activities, the occasional preparation of beer to be served to a larger community, vs. the ongoing activities of women, the practices of everyday meal production, which not only *complement* men's beer making but (through the smoking process) actually *enable* its success. Similarly, it is a woman's continuous control over the medium of water that not only characterizes her own transformative agency but also facilitates the extension of her male kin's reputation for beer making within that larger community. In general, then, I would argue that the creation of Haya space and time turns on questions of the successful integration of these differently oriented forces (cf. Hugh-Jones 1979, 200ff), forces which I have tried to suggest are objectified and experienced in the overall processing (provision, production, consumption, etc.) of food.

Concentric Farming

As my discussion of the gendered dimensions of the hearth as well as this analysis of sexuality indicate, the orientation, control, and creation of very specific forms of heat is essential to Haya productivity. Heat is a pervasive quality that is elaborated in a number of domains. Bodily heat can be sexual or feverish. Sexual heat can itself be intense and sudden or more encompassing and expansive. In cooking practices, heat can be intense or diffuse. It has the potential to both desiccate and moisten. It can make coffee berries last indefinitely or render *ebitoke* highly perishable.

Heat is also an important means of orienting agricultural space, especially the agricultural space of the *ekibanja,* or family farm. To begin with, the family farm can be contrasted with the grassland fields of the *orweya,* savanna that surrounds a residential village. These fields (*emisili,* singular *omusili*) are cultivated by women on a seasonal basis. When a new plot of *orweya* land is selected for cultivation, it is generally burned off in order to concentrate the nutrients of the grasses into the soil. Land on a family farm is never intentionally burned, and it would be difficult to do so, given the high moisture content of the banana plants (*engemu*) that are its principal crop. In addition to this contrast in agricultural technique, the *orweya* itself is generally considered to be hotter than *ekibanja* land. It lacks the tree-cover and shade of family farms, as well as their moisture (figs. 7 and 8).

Yet a properly run household and *ekibanja* is also considered a warm place. While a farm may not and should not experience the searing heat of direct

Figure 7. Ta Gregory's well constructed house in the midst of its farm. The large *engumu zanyineka* (banana plant of the head of the household) grows on the small elevation closest to the house.

sunlight, the very productivity of a farm should generate heat. Moreover, this heat is in turn itself generative. On a well-maintained *ekibanja,* according to the many Haya farmers I knew, the heat of a household and of the house itself add to the productivity of banana trees. One neighbor pointed to the fact that the bananas grown nearest to the house are always the largest and most fertile,[18] and he attributed this productivity to the fact that these plants absorb all of the garbage, the urine, and the cooking heat and smoke that are created by the members of a household. All of these materials add to the fertility of a farm, and all of them embody the heat that is created *by* and creative *of* a productive household.

Within the agricultural and residential space of a family farm, certain forms of heat are associated with establishing centers. The house itself is a focus of hot activities. I often heard that the new, square houses that had come to replace the round *omushonge* may have been easier to build and more durable, but they lacked the warmth of the *omushonge*. While the *omushonge* was a place of totalizing enclosure, a structure that could house multiple generations as well as husbanded livestock, the *ekibanda* homes have less room inside, and the inter-

Figure 8. Looking out from Ta Gregory's house, a long, well-maintained courtyard leads to village paths. Grasses that will be cut to use as floor coverings in the house line the fringe of the courtyard. The farm itself has banana plants at various stages of maturity and a flourishing bean crop.

nal space of a household is usually distributed between a house and a separate kitchen building. A certain kind of heat, therefore, would seem to be characteristic of a more inclusive enclosure.

Moreover, the thermal dimensions of the dynamic relation between interior and exterior can be seen in the organization of agricultural space on the farm. Nearest the house, as we have seen, grow the largest and most productive bananas. These plants are always meal bananas (*ebitoke*) that will be boiled for a meal. Farther off from the house lie other types of bananas: *obunana* sweet bananas, which are eaten as a snack, and varieties like the prized *enkonjwa*, which is roasted and served to guests. At the edges of a farm, *embiile* beer bananas are usually found. Interspersed throughout the *ekibanja*, but almost always a good distance from the house itself, are coffee trees.[19]

If we consider this concentric arrangement of crops in terms of the various cooking techniques described in the previous chapter, we can see that it presents a set of spatial and temporal relations with distinct thermal characteristics. The crops at a distance from a house are prepared and stored above the hearth. Coffee berries for chewing are dried and stored above the hearth; beer bananas typically are ripened over the hearth for several days. Closer to the house, the sweeter bananas are occasionally ripened above the hearth and are most often prepared for guests by being roasted at the fire in the hearthstones. Finally, the meal bananas closest to the house are prepared by boiling in pots. As crops are grown closer to the house they are made progressively interior, not just in terms of their spatial position on the farm, but in relation to the techniques of preparation—with smoking, drying, and ripening being the most exterior, and enclosed boiling being the most interior form of cooking. The construction of agricultural space, then, replicates the spatial form of the hearth. Proximity to the hearth during preparation parallels proximity to the house in planting. Moreover, the thermal qualities of these spatial patterns is identical, as the intensity of heat increases as crops and food are moved toward the interior of the house. The hearth (*amaiga*) in the *omushonge* house condenses and articulates all of these thermal and spatial qualities. Constructed at the very center of the house, the fire at the interior hearth determines both the tangible properties of cooked food (i.e., boiling, roasting, and drying are created through their relative proximity to the hearth), as well as the qualities of growing plants, for the heat produced at the hearth has consequences for agricultural productivity.

There is still another quality embedded in the organization of agricultural space on the *ekibanja* that should be assessed. I once commented to a neighbor (before this concentric scheme of planting had been explained to me) that he had some very large beer bananas growing right outside his door. My mistake was quickly pointed out to me; "Those aren't beer bananas! Why would you plant beer bananas so close to the house? They're not food!" This response suggests an important distinction between bananas, not just in terms of their preparation technique, but in terms of their status as *ekyakulya*—"food." My neighbor made clear to me that not all edible products, even the well-loved roasting bananas, can be considered food.[20] And this distinction between "food" and (edible) "nonfood" further displays the spatial orientations of household production and consumption. The category of "food," and not merely "edible substance," is associated with the interior position. It is also important that, in addition to meal bananas, greens and peppers, which are common relishes and flavorings for a meal, are grown very near the house. In contrast, beer and coffee, edible products that will be consumed by nonhousehold members and household members alike, are produced from plants grown at a distance from the house. The spatial configuration of the *ekibanja* therefore objectifies a pattern of consumption (meals vs. nonmeals) that is simultaneously an order of *social relations* (household vs. nonhousehold). It should not be surprising to find that this spatial contrast also incorporates a relative distinction between commoditized and noncommoditized products. Even when beer is brewed for ceremonial exchange or coffee is prepared to give to guests (and my neighbors made it clear that these strictly nonmonetized processes are extremely rare), some quantity of the finished product will be sold. Meal bananas, however, are marketed with much less frequency.[21] Again, the significance of commoditization in Haya sociocultural activities is concretized in a meaningful pattern of agricultural orientations. This spatial form further indicates that an interior orientation is intrinsic to specifically Haya understandings of food. As the importance of pounding and wrapping suggests, and as the total preparation, presentation, and consumption of a meal will make clear, interior enclosure is part of what makes the merely edible actually food.

Sitting Down to Dinner: Placing a Meal

Food that has been prepared for a meal is taken from the pot and can be served up in a number of ways. *Ugali* is scooped into individual servings, and each person is given their portion on a plate or a section of banana leaf. *Ugali* is always served with a separate relish, which is served in a small bowl. The way in which bananas are served depends to a degree on how they have been prepared but, more importantly, on the context in which they are served (and, accordingly, the resources of those who provide the meal).

With the exception of the ceremonial meals that accompany weddings and funerals, it is rare for guests to come for dinner in a Haya household.[22] In fact, a friend of mine was quite surprised to find that some (British) doctors from the local hospital whom I had invited for lunch actually *came*. In any case, in my experience I found that it was most common for a meal to be served in individual bowls when guests were present. In houses that can afford them, plastic-covered serving dishes are a common item. The pot of cooked bananas is drained and poured into this dish, and then presented to those who are eating, each of whom then serves themselves a portion of bananas. If a separate relish has been prepared, this too is served in individual bowls.

As I suggested, the presence of guests at a meal is rare. More commonly, bananas are served in a collective fashion. The cooking pot containing bananas and the relishes that have been cooked with them is swiftly tipped onto the serving surface—in some cases this is a large round tin platter, in others (perhaps, more commonly) a large unbroken banana leaf fulfills this purpose. A banana leaf is always placed under the platter of food, and this provides a surface on which to spread out the piping hot banana mixture, and allow it to cool sufficiently to be handled and eaten. When a separate relish has been

Table 1. Haya Staples: Their Sources and Uses

Food	Source	Preparing	Serving
Ebitoke (meal bananas)	Family farm (interior)	Peeled and boiled	Collective meals
Obunana and *enkonjwa* (sweet bananas)	Family farm (periphery) or market	Ripened and eaten "raw," some roasted	Snacks for guests
Embiile (beer bananas)	Family farm (periphery), purchase from neighbors	Ripened, juiced, fermented	For guests, gifts, and for sale
Ebigando (cassava)	*Orweya* fields; some grown on family farms	Peeled and boiled, or roasted	Some meals, some snacks
Ugali (corn and cassava flour porridge)	Purchased; some cassava grown in *orweya* fields	Pounded and mixed with water	Meals, individual portions

prepared, this can be served in individual bowls or poured over or around the platter of bananas. It is also common to cover food that has been served on a platter with another large banana leaf when presenting it to those who are eating, a practice that has its equivalent in the covered plastic serving dishes that are a popular "luxury" item.

A few points can be made about these rather simple matters. To begin with, there is clearly a contrast between the way in which bananas are served within a household and the way in which *ugali* is served. The individuation of each portion of porridge and relish indicates the association of *ugali* with money by the fact that each is partible and enumerable.[23] The uncertain, if not undesired, status of guests at a meal might also be signified by the similar service of individuated food portions.[24] In both instances, the unity of the collective meal is fragmented either by the qualities of the food that is eaten, or the relations of those who share the meal (table 1).

The practice of covering cooked food for presentation is also worth noting. Plastic lids and banana leafs do have the explicitly stated practical effect of retaining heat, but they have additional semantic—and equally explicit—effects. The use of these coverings recalls the banana leaf in which the harvested banana bunch is wrapped. In each case, the covering is said to be a form of "respect" for the food, as well as for those who eat it. The cooked food, therefore, concretely instantiates the form of enclosure that is central to the successful production of food, and the viability of the household that provides it. Food presented in this way, then, demonstrates the form of its own provision and preparation by iconically presenting the values characteristic of those processes.

The placement of a meal, the position of the cooked food and those who eat it, provides a critical representation of the values at issue in domestic productivity. In houses with a separate kitchen, food is taken from the hearth and placed in the back room of the main house. In some cases, food is eaten in the kitchen itself, in an area separated from the hearth. In houses without a separate kitchen, where the hearth lies at the back of the house, food is eaten in the front room. In all cases, however, there is a recognized location that is set aside for eating a meal. This location has consequences for how one is supposed to sit whether or not food is present. At mealtime, if only a small group of people are eating together, as is usually the case, it is inappropriate to sit in a position facing the front door while eating. A large group of people will form a circle around the meal, and thereby prevent the person facing towards the door from looking outward. People should face their food while eating—this is a common instruction to children and thus an explicit feature of socialization, which makes it and the related practices described here a matter of current discussion and interpretation, being more than merely "customary" or a reified rule for behavior (see Bourdieu 1977, 10ff, on "rules" and "norms"). Looking toward the door not only diverts attention from the food being eaten, but makes one appear greedy and suspicious that outsiders are seeking to gain access to your food.

Forming a circle around the meal, facing the food, and not looking outward while eating are all means of ensuring what I have suggested is the enclosure that is so important to Haya control of food provision. Above all looking outward, even if sitting off to the side, is avoided because this establishes a clear connection between the inside of the house and the outside, while eating and (I would argue) the entire process of food provision has an interior orientation. Turning away from the outside, therefore, establishes a bodily and collective enclosure that complements the architectural enclosure of the hearth and house, and the enclosed form that the food itself assumes when it is presented on a covered platter.

The position of the food during a meal is equally important to these orientations. Food is placed in a privileged point within the room, the *akabanga*. This may be the very center of the room or it may be a central place just in front of a passage leading to the back of the house; but in any event the *akabanga* is a recognized position in each house. Even when food is not being served, people do not sit in the *akabanga* but sit off to the side along a wall—as one man put it, "out of respect for food," which has its own place in any household.

The significance of this *akabanga* can be explored in order to specify the spatial situation of food in a household. *Akabanga* is a diminutive noun, whose root, *-banga* denotes "elevated things"; thus *eibanga* ("mountain") and *aha-banga* ("heaven/sky"). The *akabanga* might then be thought of as a small mound, and, indeed, an additional pile of the grasses that line the floors of a Haya house are usually placed under the platter of food served at a meal. As suggested in my analyses of the hearth rack, verticality is associated with masculinity, but it is also a spatial form characteristic of authority more generally. The Haya class of nobility, Abalangila, were recognized for their tall stature, as suggested by the honorific terms *oluyonge* ("loose-limbed one") and *oluk-winamile* ("thin, bowing one") (Seitel 1986, 8). The central house post that is raised to initiate house building establishes a place that is reserved for the household head, indicating the strong associations of authority with verticality and centrality—both of which are characteristic of the *akabanga* and the spatial orientations of eating—at the household and architectural levels as well.

Positions such as the hearth rack or the major house posts, which conjoin elevation and centrality, are Haya points of focus, loci which continuously attract persons and activities to them and disperse them in transformed ways. I have discussed this process with regard to beer brewing and the hearth rack. The principal house post—known alternatively as *Enyomyo y'omukama w'enju* ("Post of the Household Head"; Cesard 1937, 94) or *Engambilo* ("The Speaking Place")—is, as the latter name suggests, a position from which a household head greets and engages in conversation with his neighbors. These verbal exchanges are as critical to the constitution of mature masculine identity as beer brewing.[25] Each communicates and extends personal identity among a community, and each is characterized by a similar form of spatial orientation—that is, coming and going around an elevated, central position. Moreover, this house post and the central hearth share a common "biography" with the household head. This main post is treated with the same medicines that secure the house opening fire during "binding rites," and when household authority is deconstructed at the death of the household head, this main post and a single hearth stone are removed from the house and destroyed. Horizontal and vertical spatial orientations, centripetal and centrifugal movements, elevation and descent—all are condensed in these positions and the objects that occupy them, and the potentialities latent in such a configuration are shared by the position of meals (*akabanga*) as well.

The conjunction of these spatial orientations with Haya forms of authority, particularly as this is realized in mortuary performance, suggests another critical connection to Haya meals. The *akabanga* is not only the position for a meal, it is the very place that a corpse is laid out in the house prior to burial. The connection between a meal and a corpse is also made explicit by the parallel drawn between the banana leaf that serves as the collective eating surface, which must be placed with its tip pointing toward the front of the house, and the corpse, which is laid out in a similar fashion, with the deceased's head pointing forward. This important parallel between a meal and a corpse, far from having grisly cannibalistic implications, reveals further significant dimensions and qualities that are integral to what I am calling Haya focal positions.

The activities surrounding death and burial are central to the Haya constitution of social reproduction.[26] By securing the proper burial of a household head on his own farm a Haya family also asserts its continuous claim to residence on and access to this farmland. Mortuary rites, therefore, serves to establish a connection between past and future generations, providing a memorial (a remembered location, the grave) that, in effect, moves forward in time, influencing, if not strictly determining, the ways in which successive generations will hold and work the land they inhabit. The parallel position of the corpse and a meal within a house, I suggest, reveals a similar set of attachments between the members of a household and their land. Eating a meal, like burying a corpse, is a means of confirming a household's attachments to and, indeed, dependence on the preceding generations, who secured the land that provides their food. A meal is a daily, routinized acknowledgment of the structure of authority embedded in the spatial form of the domestic landscape.

The spatial dimensions created when a meal is consumed therefore have important temporal implications. The focal position instantiated in the *akabanga* not only conjoins horizontal and vertical space but, as the meanings of both food and death illustrate, also connects ongoing activities with the past that made them possible. The meal consumed here further projects these relations into the future, a fact made evident by typical Haya comments about the necessity of eating well to ensure healthy sexuality and reproduction, as well as the insistence that the very purpose of maintaining a farm is to provide food for one's children. Meals provide the occasion for the immediate bodily experience of sexual and reproductive potential, as well as a means of determining a future by nourishing the products of that potential, that is, children. This multidimensional condensation of space and time made possible at positions like the *akabanga*—the links of horizontal and vertical as well as past, present, and future—is a concrete realization of what I suggested earlier is the way in which such focal points may be both spaces of origin and finality, the places from which persons and things originate (as in house opening rites or the sexual potential of eating well), and to which they ultimately return (most vividly embodied by the corpse and the dismantled objects that accompany it).

Earlier I indicated that the activities surrounding fish frying provide a useful point of contrast to meal provision and consumption. Let me highlight these contrasts in order to illuminate the central features of Haya meal presentation and consumption. To begin with, the most important distinction is that between preparing and eating fish outside the house vs. the activities of a meal, which are internally focused. Those who eat a meal avoid even the suggestion of contact between inside the house and the outside, turning their backs to the front door and directing their attention toward their food. Fried fish is occasionally consumed outside, where it is cooked, but in this case it is only as a snack, and could never be considered a meal in itself. This contrast of a proper meal with a snack, invokes the distinction between staples—which are the critical element in a meal—and relishes, which is how such fish typically is eaten. Staples are agricultural products, the most prized of which, bananas, are grown right on the farm of the household that consumes them. Fish, on the other hand, are the products of a circuit of long-distance travel and marketing, passing through multiple hands before the final cooked product is procured.

This contrast between local origins vs. a high degree of movement is also signified in the very space of fish frying, the courtyard in front of the house called *ekibuga. Okubuga,* the verb from which this term is derived, means "to move about, or drive"—for example, "to ride a bicycle" is *Okubuga ebaisikeli.* Thus, the Haya courtyard is an essential place of movement, and this is not only characteristic of the fish trade at all levels, it also contrasts nicely with the kind of centralized focus that characterizes the spatial organization of eating a meal inside the house.

Lastly, the contrast in mobility of both the media (staples/bananas vs. fish) as well as the practices through which they are processed connote a monetary contrast as well. Fish constitute an industry that produces cash through a variety of practices, from fishing to transport to frying. Frying fish in this way is only the "final stage" of all possible methods of generating cash from fish, and the spatial arrangement of this activity—the fact that it is open, outside, and in the household's place of movement—demonstrates the fact that it is implicated in monetary transaction.

Enclosure Evaluated

Enclosure and a general inward orientation is characteristic of food provision and processing at a number of levels. This quality was first discussed in connection with beer banana ripening, which takes place at the hearth and hearth rack, interior positions which are contrasted with outdoor pits. The values of this contrast are reproduced in the practices surrounding fish frying, another outside activity associated with monetary gain. I have further discussed the importance of enclosure in terms of food preparation techniques, such as wrapping banana bunches and avoiding pounding during the night. The significance of collecting water to creating the productivity of cooking also depends on establishing interiorized control. Lastly, the entire process of serving a meal is one that is thoroughly enclosed. People eating a meal never direct their attention or even position themselves to face toward the outside of the house. Indeed, the house is always enclosed during meals. Doors and windows are closed when meals are being eaten, and visitors turn themselves away when they see doors closed, lest they disturb those who are eating. In the past, large screens were raised during meal times to enclose a household (Reining 1972; Seitel 1977, 190–91). Meals were taken "behind the screen" (*omukisika*) just as a newly married bride (*omugole*) is sequestered there. Evidently, eating and the initial stages of marital relations were similarly delicate and intimate matters.

If by chance visitors should let themselves into a house while people are eating (e.g., if a family is eating in a back room closed off from the front sitting room into which guests might enter unaware), then rather than excuse themselves and leave, visitors will remain in the house until everyone has finished eating. Similarly, those who eat together all remain inside and wait until everyone has finished eating before leaving a house. For example, on one of the last days I spent in Buhaya, I went to visit some very good friends. They were an older couple who had once allowed me to live in their home with them for a brief period. Having finished my lunch, I walked to the next village, and knocked on their back door when I arrived. The couple were, in fact, in the middle of lunch. The husband opened the door to the interior room in their kitchen where they were sitting, and invited me to join them: "*Tulye!*" ("Let's eat!") I told them I had just eaten, and politely (I hoped) declined their generous offer. The door to the interior room was then carefully shut once again, so that the couple could not see me, and I could not see them. But we continued our conversation while they ate, and when their meal was finished, the door was opened and we all sat together and chatted. The spatial form of such "table manners" have a clearly centripetal effect. These practices indicate that a meal must not only be properly enclosed and contained, but that it should take place in a clearly fixed situation. People do not come and go at a Haya meal. Once they have been included in it, even in a peripheral or unintended way, they are obliged to "respect" its integrity, an integrity that has a determinant spatial and temporal form.

The enclosed and interior position of food-related activities, especially meal preparation and consumption, is clearly a pervasive feature of these Haya practices. The ability to control food as well as show your competence in basic social graces are demonstrated by internalizing these activities, placing them out of view of a larger community (unlike, for example, beer consumption, which has an expressly public reception), and isolating them within a household. The question that should be asked, however, is why should this spatial form be necessary? What motivates Haya food practices so as to determine this particular set of spatial and temporal orientations? This is not merely a question of "custom" nor is it strictly a matter of the conceptual logic of eating. Many Haya, for example, suggested to me that "those Sukuma" across the lake always ate their meals out in front of their houses, and anyone who passed by could see what was being eaten and help themselves (I have no idea whether this is in fact the case, but the practice is not unheard of in other parts of Africa). The point, however, is that this way of eating, for the Haya who described it to me, was not merely evidence of cultural diversity in Tanzania, and it was certainly not an indication of the open-handed hospitality of the Sukuma. Rather, it was undeniable proof of their utter barbarity, and the difficulties the Sukuma must have with providing food for themselves if they are so abject as to eat in this way. Such practices, in other words, are *evaluative* expressions. They are means not only of encoding the world in meaningful ways, but of asserting *preferences* with respect to those meanings, as well as creating and demonstrating the *authority* to control these preferences.

What, then, motivates this interest in enclosure? My Haya informants indicated that keeping doors and windows closed during meal times was a way of safeguarding yourself from trouble. "If neighbors can see what you are eating they may become jealous"; this kind of concern recalls the claim that bananas are wrapped when they are harvested to prevent quarrels within the house. An even greater concern is that you will be disgraced when others see your meager food; one neighbor talked about the burdens of having a relative in the hospital, and the "disgrace" (in Haya, *enshoni;* in Swahili, *aibu*) that comes when everyone sees the food you bring to feed your kin.

Moreover, the concerns with jealousy and disgrace may not simply be a response to the quality of the food one eats; they may, in the view of many Haya, be the *cause* of these qualities. That is, keeping food enclosed within the house is also understood as a means of preventing hunger.[27] This concern with the relation between food provision and the situation of a household within its wider community recalls the concern with pounding flour at night, an action that, I suggested, indicates an inability to maintain the separation of the internal household from a wider social field. The interests and feelings of this external community, then, can actually transform a household, undermining its ability to provide food for itself.

Household sufficiency and viability, therefore, are clearly dependent on the ability to maintain an enclosable, interior position. My discussion of Haya house entering rites indicated that such rites enact a basic set of spatial relations and thereby attempt to establish precisely such an interior position, one intrinsically distinguishable as a *place* differentiated from the places around it and integrated as a totality unto itself, while also intrinsically connected and oriented to an encompassing context. Haya food provision and consumption practices further inscribe the concrete orientations of these spatial relations, routinizing them in the course of ongoing activity as well as perpetuating them through the motivations they engender.

It is equally important, then, to point out that the differentiated but connected situation of these food-related activities makes them avenues for transformation as well. The internalizing focus of Haya eating and the attempt to secure enclosure as an integral aspect of controlling food provision, is persistently challenged by any number of elements of this process itself. For example, I detailed the symbolic dimensions of fish production and noted their contrast to meal provision. These contrasts turn on the open, public, mobile, and thoroughly monetized methods through which fish "operate" in the region, as opposed to the encircled, focused provision of a household meal. The contradictory challenge of this contrast, and what makes these spatial orientations inherently transformative, is the fact that fish typically are produced for and consumed as a *part* of a meal. The distinct modes of organizing food production, characterized by household meals and frying fish, are in fact conjoined in many instances. The same is true of *ugali* provision, or the purchase of other forms of relish, like milk, tomatoes, and even salt. These components are basic elements in most meals, yet they can be acquired only in ways that challenge the sense of enclosure and interiority that is central to a Haya sense of household sufficiency. It may well be possible for a household to make meals of only bananas and beans grown on the family farm, and for fish and other marketed foods to be eaten only for snacks. A much more likely scenario, however, is that a family will grow much of its produce, perhaps sell a few tomatoes in the market, and purchase other relishes with cash remittances provided by sons who work in the fish trade. All of these practices are articulated into the *single* (although complex) process of providing and consuming a meal. And it is this articulation that gives Haya food-related practices their transformational possibilities.

The complexity of these various practices and elements, all of which may comprise a single meal, indicate that the Haya processes of enclosure I have described are relative ones. As I suggested in my discussion of house opening rites, the interior position of a house—or, indeed, of any recognizable *place*—is constituted by a coordination of directional orientations. Any enclosed place therefore is necessarily defined through a *relation* between an inside and an outside. Thus, an inside position is defined by a form of encompassment that is simultaneously inclusive and exclusive. This cultural model, and these practices surrounding Haya meals suggest that food processing and household sufficiency, which is realized by the capacity to control the inward direction of food, both require the *exclusion* of what lies beyond the enclosure of a meal. This much is indicated by Haya claims that the neighbors' intrusion on a household meal may bring about hunger, or the fact that neighbors *avoid* entering the houses of those who are eating meals. A household's attempt to conceal and enclose food preparation, presentation, meals, and the like, is equally recognized outside the household by the actions of those who exclude themselves from these activities.

My point in specifying the relational character of these processes is twofold. First of all, these relations must be understood because they are readily apparent in the actual Haya practices of food provision. A Haya household can define itself as a *place* only through its ability to control the relation of what is inside with what lies outside, and the passage that must take place between these positions. And since all households must necessarily participate in processes that are external to it (like marketing, the fish trade, etc.), it is the degree of control over the relative coordination of these forces (e.g., how much and what kinds of foods or supplies must be acquired outside the household or its farm— or who knows about or participates in this provision) that determines a household's viability. The self-sufficiency that enclosure seeks to create is at best a *relative* independence, and it is the shifting boundaries of this enclosure that allow for its transformation.

The second reason for drawing attention to the relational character of Haya household enclosure is to make clear that the set of spatial (and temporal) relations this entails is not merely applicable to food provision activities but is in fact a much more general feature of Haya sociality. The dynamic, symbolic character of enclosure can tell us as much about Haya *inter*domestic relations processes as it does about activities within a given household. Let me turn now to a consideration of these relationships, again mediated and constituted to a significant degree by practices surrounding food, in order to address the question of sociality at a wider level.

Bewitching Refuse

The characteristic Haya forms of enclosure create a relationship between inclusion and exclusion, between inward and outward movements. This set of orientations, I would argue, is a general feature of Haya sociality. Moreover, the interdomestic aspects of this spatial and temporal form are actually incorporated into the order of intradomestic activities. The fact that a concern for other households and outsiders of all kinds is embedded in the processes that make any household productive and viable is especially apparent in Haya views of sorcery (in Haya, *oburoga;* in Swahili, *uchawi*). Sorcery, according to the explanations of my Haya neighbors, arises from the problematic intrusion of any person into the lives of their fellows. "He doesn't like to see that you exceed him" (in Swahili, *Hataki kuona kwamba wewe unamzidi*) is a common way for Haya to describe a sorcerer's motivations. A sorcerer, therefore, is usually someone who is excessively preoccupied with others' well-being. He or she may make unwelcome comments on the good fortunes of their neighbors. One friend was shocked to hear that someone had said "Your baby has gotten so fat! What are you feeding him?" Such a comment is disturbing because it indicates an unwarranted interest in the *comparative* success of one person or one household against another.

Given the centrality of food provision to domestic success and independence, it should not be surprising to find that concerns about sorcery are important to the preparation and presentation of a meal. Moreover, it is clear that food, a highly malleable substance that can become infused with the properties of other persons and things and whose consumption establishes tangible, bodily social connections, presents an ideal vehicle for sorcerers who seek to impose themselves on others. This is perhaps especially so in a cultural context like the Haya, where sorcery is predicated on the manipulation of substances or "medicines" (plural, *emibazi;* singular, *omubazi*). While certain precautions are taken to secure a household's meals against sorcery,[28] the techniques of sorcery are usually more subtle and indirect than simply placing medicines in the foods their victims will eat.[29] Haya efforts to thwart these techniques are integrated into everyday activities, and an examination of these techniques and the daily attempts to counter them will reveal the extent to which sorcery is grounded in the tensions of interhousehold relations.

Haya concerns about sorcery are well illustrated by the way the final products of a meal are treated. The final products to which I refer are not, however, cooked foods, but garbage. The waste products of cooking and eating are always returned to the farm. Banana peelings from an evening's meal are gathered as they are cut away, and will be dumped behind the house. In my experience, there is no fixed spot that is a garbage dump on a farm. Rather, as my discussion of the centripetal movement of heat on a farm indicated, agricultural waste products are distributed throughout the area surrounding the kitchen and back of the house. When an entire bunch of bananas has been completed (which may take several days if it is a large bunch), the stem (*omukungu*) on which the bananas grow and on which they are stored over the course of their use is disposed of in a specific way. The stem is first split lengthwise down the center, and each half of the stem is then cut into smaller pieces before being dispersed into the farm.

I was struck by the uniformity of this practice, and asked many people why stems were always split down the middle when they were finished. Many people suggested that this was simply to speed the breakdown of the stem, and hasten its transition to fertilizer. Indeed, when a banana stalk (i.e., the "trunk" and leaves of the banana plant) is harvested, the large section above the stump is always hacked into small pieces. As many neighbors told me, the stalk becomes "immediate fertilizer" (in Swahili, *mbolea tayari*). But others told me that while it was certainly true that a banana stem would become fertilizer once chopped up and returned to the soil, it was especially important to split the stem first in order to prevent sorcerers from making use of it. A sorcerer, according to many Haya, could use your unbroken stem to bewitch your farm, which would diminish the productivity of your future banana plants, and bring hunger to your household. Such purely destructive actions are typical of sorcerers who want to ruin their successful neighbors.

Clearly the claim that properly destroying and disposing of agricultural wastes enhances the fertility and productivity of a farm and the contention that these practices also prevent sorcery are complementary perspectives. Sorcery threatens not only the reproductive dimensions of the agricultural cycle, but especially its *recursive* form—that is, the serial connection between previous generations and future generations. And it is precisely this recursive, periodic cycle, so crucial to Haya agricultural practice, that is concretely realized in the decomposition of "old" plant materials for the purpose of nurturing future "new" generations. Yet it is also especially important that sorcery is felt to be a threat to this recursive cycle at a particular *moment* in the cycle. It is less likely for the initial stage of the productive process to be manipulated by sorcery—it's not the new shoots of a banana plant or the flowering fruit of a mature stalk that are most vulnerable—than it is for the final stage to be at risk. As is the case with so many productive Haya processes,[30] it is the proper *completion* of an action that assures the continued success of ongoing processes in the future.

Sorcery threatens the temporal form of an agricultural cycle, as well as a comestible cycle. And as the finished products of any Haya cycle hold the promise of perpetual and continuous nurturance and growth, it is these completed objects that are especially vulnerable. It is this characteristic temporal pattern that accounts for Haya attention to garbage. For not only are the completed objects of the agricultural process carefully destroyed and disposed of, so too is the garbage at the end of a meal.[31] All of the disposable elements of a meal not only become garbage, but they are finished off, like the split banana stem, in a careful and deliberate fashion. If a small section of banana leaf is used as a spoon (*endosho*) at a meal, this piece of leaf will be shredded into even smaller pieces. The large leaf on which a meal is usually served is folded up and broken before it is thrown away. A banana leaf that has been folded into a cup (*ekitegala*) for drinking beer is similarly torn to pieces when it is finished. All of these actions delineate and ensure the thorough conclusion of a process.

Moreover, this stage of completion is particularly vulnerable to the attacks of sorcerers. I discovered this inadvertently one evening after dinner. I gathered together the remnants of a typically robust meal and folded them into the banana leaf plate from which I had eaten. Tucking the leaf into a small packet, I got up and went to open the front door in order to toss the garbage onto the decomposing dump behind the house. My housemate looked up and stopped me: "Place that over here," he said motioning to a corner of the kitchen. "You can't throw away your garbage at night!" As my friend and others explained to me, when an evening meal is finished, the accumulated garbage is never taken outside to be disposed of immediately. Indeed, not just the unfinished food that remains after one has finished eating but all of the garbage left after preparing the meal—the banana peelings, the withered banana leaf that covers the steaming pots, perhaps even the spent embers and ashes from the hearth—are kept tucked away in the safety of the kitchen until morning. Disposing of garbage after nightfall[32] would expose a household to sorcerers who use the cover of darkness to their advantage. Again, these completed, finished objects are the focus of sorcery. The dangers of night and darkness are a topic of unending Haya discussions; but while most Haya worry about thieves illicitly harvesting their uneaten bananas during the night, they worry about sorcerers attacking their already finished food. Like the finished banana stem and the garbage from an evening meal, many Haya friends told me that the hulls of coffee cherries, which are discarded after the coffee has been chewed, are an especially potent vehicle for bewitching. All of these materials are thought of as finished, and one usually "tosses" (*okunaga*) them away. But garbage that is carelessly left aside can be used against you.

These Haya domestic activities and images of sorcery confirm the fact that productive processes have a characteristic temporal form, and indicate that the moment of completion is particularly marked as a vulnerable point. Finalized products provide a link to future cycles of production and growth, and sorcery seeks to impose itself at this instance of transition and continuity. It is also crucial to point out a second set of tensions, in the passage from enclosure to disclosure and in the relation of inclusion to exclusion, that is also seized on by sorcery. Haya may attempt to conceal and enclose productive activities in order to control them, but these very activities are always grounded in a wider social and *public* set of relations. The spatial movement of garbage, banana stems, and the like from inside the house to outside not only discloses what was carefully enclosed, it allows for general access to what were a restricted set of relations. This is graphically demonstrated by the bewitching of coffee hulls, as these are publicly accessible materials that provide evidence of intimate exchanges. Sorcery, it seems, is feared much less at those stages of "production" that are carefully concealed and restricted (i.e., even such "productive" stages as "consuming" a meal) than at those moments when productive activity must disclose the fact that it is tied into a wider set of social relations.

Looking at the threat of sorcery in relation to food provision and production in this way, with an eye to its situation with respect to the specific temporal (and spatial) form of productive processes, also allows us to consider the threat of sorcery more generally. The sorcerer's techniques, according to my Haya informants, involve the manipulation of "finished" products of many kinds. A footprint may be used to bewitch the person who left it (see also Comaroff 1985b, 128), or the grasses on which he or she was sitting may be secreted away for malevolent purposes. The technique, therefore, is not necessarily to cause someone to come in contact with dangerous substances (i.e., a sorcerer need not make someone step over, sit on, or eat medicines), but to bewitch the things with which they have already been in contact. Most of these substances do involve close bodily identifications. They are things that have been touched, held, broken, or spit out. But just as importantly, they involve aspects of bodily experience that become *accessible* to others. Garbage, these bits of detritus and waste that are tossed aside, provides concrete traces to *completed* actions that are no longer *present*. I am arguing that control and viability are predicated on enclosure and exclusion; yet these very processes are always situated in a social context from which a household tries to close itself off. Sorcery, then, is able to strike at precisely this point of interpenetration. The very items that publicly demonstrate a household's ability to provide for itself are potential vehicles for its undoing. I want to explore this aspect of Haya sociality, the tensions entailed in creating and demonstrating intrahousehold productivity at an interhousehold level, by considering some of the activities and objects that typify Haya exchanges.

Food To Go: Collective Presents and Private Exchanges

Growing food for oneself or purchasing it through marketing or other monetized contexts are only two of the many means that Haya commonly engage in to acquire food. For example, produce can also be acquired as a form of rent on certain categories of land. In lean times, men often agree to work in their neighbors' farms or field in exchange for food. There are also important exchange relationships which, while not necessarily pursued as a means of acquiring food, have food as their fundamental exchange medium. I want to examine certain aspects of these kinds of exchanges because, unlike the activities described above in which households attempt with varying degrees of success (whether through agricultural practices, purchase, usufruct, or labor), to supply *themselves* with food, such exchanges are explicit acknowledgments of a household's being supplied with food from others.

Gifts of food are commonly forthcoming in the Haya practices called *okuzilima,* perhaps best translated as "celebrating." More than just the recognition of a special occasion, *okuzilima* are the acts in which guests, usually kin, bring baskets of food to a household. The preparation and delivery of these offerings are a fairly common occurrence in rural Haya communities and can demand considerable resources. In this assessment of the *okuzilima,* I want to consider what kinds of occasions in particular call for offerings of this kind, who especially is responsible for and engages in these exchanges, and what concrete form these presentations take. Exploring the meanings represented in these offerings will allow us further to examine the implications of enclosure and food provision, not just for a household but for the values of Haya relatedness more generally.

Going "to celebrate" and making a present of small baskets (*entukulu*) filled with food almost always surrounds occasions relating to affinal relations. A wedding celebration is a common scene of people arriving *okuzilima.* The birth of a child will bring the bride's natal family from their home or homes, offering foods for the mother and child. Similarly, a woman who returns home from her husband's household for the first time subsequent to her marriage will be greeted by those who have come with similar presents. When this woman returns to her husband's home, she will frequently bring a retinue from her natal home to celebrate. Indeed, each time a woman leaves her parent's home to return to her husband's home, she might be expected to bring a few gift baskets, and this too is considered a form of *okuzilima*.

All of these situations in some way recognize the success of affinal relations. Presenting food in this way, often as a consequence of marriage patterns, also involves travel between villages. Unlike the beer exchange relationships (*enchulo*) described earlier, it is rare for one's local neighbors to offer foods in this way in order to celebrate. *Okuzilima* is not only about the gift of food from outsiders, it is about the distance traveled and mobility entailed by these gifts.

Like the movement of married women between their natal and marital homes, the celebratory foods offered in this fashion travel between villages and are means of enacting and recognizing affinal relations. It should not be surprising, then, that it is women who provide and control these celebrations and gifts. When coming *okuzilima*, women travel collectively from various homes to the home of the person being feted (usually a woman herself, as the occasions indicate). The fact that women provide these gifts further adds to the mobile nature of this food, since sisters of a single natal home may come from an array of marital homes in order to "celebrate" their matrikin. Haya women also organize parties (*ekyama*, from the Swahili *chama*) that are self-help associations, in which women collectively contribute to help each other in a variety of projects, from paying school fees to planting peanut fields. The composition of these parties is extraordinarily varied, from a group of immediate neighbors to women of several villages from all throughout the district. These women's parties are also one of the primary agents of *okuzilima* practices and so extend the diversity of sources from which food gifts of this kind can originate.

The organization of these kinds of gifting practices, the fact that they make food available from outside a household—indeed, in many cases from beyond the local community of the household—seems quite different from the practices of Haya household food provision described above. If the daily orientation to food attempts to thoroughly internalize and enclose the process of food provision within the household, the effects of *okuzilima* would seem to test severely the limits of that enclosure. However, like the potentially fractious affinal attachments these practices tend to recognize, the gifts offered on these occasions can have contradictory implications. The tensions inherent in these gifts, tensions that suggest once again the complex character of food as a medium of Haya social relations, can be seen when we look at the concrete form of the food gifts themselves.

The foods offered when one goes *okuzilima* are not only presented by women, they are usually women's foods as well. While no food (except perhaps

Figure 9. A group of women going *okuzilima* ("to celebrate"). They carry baskets carefully wrapped in banana leaves and tied with white papyrus decorations. Even the bunch of bananas has been wrapped in banana bast to "conceal" its contents.

ugali) would be considered an inappropriate gift on these occasions, it is most commonly the relishes grown by women that are provided. Peanuts and beans are standard gifts, and prized Bambara nuts can be expected during the season of their harvest. Cassava, according to my Haya informants, is a common gift as well, one that usually can be counted on to provide an abundant staple as is generally needed on the occasions when many people might be expected to gather to celebrate. All of these are women's crops, grown in the seasonal fields tilled exclusively by women and typically in cooperation with the other women who are members of one self-help party. These collective associations of women are, thus, thoroughly identified with their gifts, as both the producers and presenters of these foods.

Moreover, some of the most important concrete qualities of these gifts are not their contents but the form of their presentation (fig. 9). Women present these foods in baskets (*entukulu*) woven from spliced reeds. These stiff, vertical baskets are carried on the head. The filled baskets are always carefully wrapped, as well. Large banana leaves are smoked over the fire until they become pliable, and are then wrapped so as to enclose the entire basket. The packaged basket is then bound with lengths of papyrus fiber that have been torn into long strings. The strands of this papyrus (*ekishisha*) are tied together to create a decorative top knot for the gift basket.

This style of presentation reveals some of the distinctive spatial implications of *okuzilima* practices. While food is provided to a household by distant, outside sources, we also see that the form of this presentation is one of careful enclosure. The baskets of food are always wrapped in banana leaf, a gesture that not only conceals the foods being provided but also recalls the banana leaf, which is used both to wrap a banana bunch after harvest and to cover the household meal when it is served. Further, the decorative knot of papyrus fiber that ties up the wrapped gift is called an *ekishembo*, from the verb *okushemba*, "to hide, to conceal." These elements confirm the importance of concealing food; as a friend explained, "You don't want everybody looking at your relishes!" Foods offered by *okuzilima*, therefore, extend the enclosure of food processing beyond the household to potentially long-distance exchanges. The distinctive spatial configuration of these presentations, then, lies in the fact that these are gifts of food that are highly mobile, come from multiple sources, and are the products of distant relations, yet the presents themselves instantiate the spatial characteristics of food provided by and consumed within the household. The distinguishing features of these baskets mark their enclosure, so that even when they travel over great distances *okuzilima* gifts retain the intimacy associated with food provision.

The properties of these gift baskets are suggestive of the ways in which Haya forms of organizing the provision and presentation of food are also means of establishing relations that go beyond individual households. We also see that certain qualitative features of food provision within the household can be extended to these extra-household contexts as well. Food enclosure is not something limited to a particular place, since, as these *okuzilima* practices demonstrate, it is a form that can circulate within and throughout a community. This is important because it indicates not only that food is a critical medium of social relations, and not only that the orientations of food (e.g., its inward movement, its marketing, its presentation as a gift) are revealed by certain spatial indices (e.g., being wrapped up, being sold outdoors, being hidden), but that these specific qualities of food are also attributes of more general and generalizable conditions of social relations. I am arguing, then, that Haya food mobility and exchanges are able to represent a given state in social relations because food, or an agent's means of *engagement* with food, reveal the fundamental qualities that define the character of sociality itself. This crucial capacity can be explored by looking again at the significance of enclosure, the basic spatial form whose multidimensional configuration I have detailed at some length, as a perceptual as well as practical, objectified feature of Haya social life.

To See and Be Seen

Haya gift baskets are wrapped and tied with a decorative covering, the *ekishembo,* that literally "hides" the contents of the gift. Hiding of this kind is essential to the intimacy of these gifts, a feature that indicates both the kind of relationship these baskets enact and the kind of goods presented. The fiber that makes this covering, *ekishisha,* has other qualities and uses that suggest further dimensions to the significance of such "hiding" and why it should be so pervasive to Haya attempts to control food more generally. *Ekishisha* is used to create decorations of many kinds, from simple household wall hangings to wedding regalia. Thin strands of papyrus are carefully separated and twisted and tied together to create these decorations, a labor intensive procedure that is carried out by women, usually older women. One of the most important and common uses of *ekishisha* is as an "accessory" in coffee presentations. Most Haya households offer coffee berries to their guests in a small woven plate which is covered by some twisted strands of *ekishisha*. Guests take the *ekishisha* and stroke their fingers with it prior to picking up coffee berries. This is called "washing," *okunaba,* the same verb used for cleaning one's hands prior to taking a meal. Haya also told me that they liked "to touch" (*okukwata*) the *ekishisha* strands, which have a soft texture, prior to chewing coffee.

This use of *ekishisha* demonstrates additional aspects of the place of food and food presentation in constituting Haya social life. These fibers are used for guests, and they are provided only with coffee, an offering that, as we have seen, is the "food" *par excellence* of guests. Presenting *ekishisha* provides a pleasant immediate sensory and bodily experience for one's guests, an act that is intimate and welcoming. At the same time, "washing" with *ekishisha* indicates that offering coffee is both like and unlike a meal. Coffee presentations "represent" a Haya meal, but their very similarities (the use of the same term for washing, the way in which both food and coffee are covered for presentation) also point to the fact that these activities are different. As Haya friends told me, you offer guests coffee because coffee can never fill them up—it is, thus, unmistakably distinct from good food. The point, then, is that *ekishisha* can establish both connections and separations in social relationships, just as the *ekishembo* made from these fibers "hides" the gift basket, simultaneously marking the intimacy of enclosure while also displaying the distance of a gift from diverse donors. In effect, the use of *ekishisha* in all of these instances works to transform outsiders into *guests,* a gesture that asserts a relationship but also insists on a *distinction* between those who give and receive. My formulation of this transaction and its characteristic social relational contexts has certain similarities with Strathern's account of Melanesian personhood and sociality, especially her suggestion that "in the activation of relations people make explicit what differentiates them" (Strathern 1991, 588). While I would not go so far as to argue that "the Haya person" should be so defined, I would suggest that these attempts to establish, concretize, and demonstrate differentiation in the course of ongoing relationships (some of which involve such exchanges) is a characteristic concern for Haya sociality. It is a telling point, for example, that Haya most frequently cite one's father-in-law as the stereotypical recipient of coffee offered in this formalized manner. The fact that one's father-in-law is the preferred recipient of coffee, on the one hand, clearly distinguishes a gift of coffee from sharing a meal, for while a father-in-law should always be offered coffee, one should *never* eat a meal (or other foods) with a spouse's parent. At the same time, the fact that a father-in-law is the most appropriate recipient of this offering of "food" is indicative of the ways in which such offerings can generate a form of social connectedness that necessarily entails (as Haya affinal relations do) clearly defined differentiations.

There is, then, a dialectic of intimacy and distance, relatedness and separation, that can be embedded in Haya forms of food presentation, and is characteristic of the affinal contexts in which food (especially coffee) is offered as a gift and *ekishisha* is present as a decoration. Just as the interiority of food provision and preparation in a meal demonstrates a household's control of food sufficiency as well as the intimacy of household relations, the spatiotemporal form of Haya food *gifts* concretely embodies the qualitative aspects of a wider social situation that is often fraught with ambivalence and tension—and perhaps never more so than in highly fractious Haya marital relations, which, as we have seen, provide the principle occasion for "celebrating" with precisely such gifts.

Another part of the experience of *ekishisha* is critical to this dialectic, and also indicates the larger semantic and pragmatic implications of the Haya concern with enclosure and interiority. The papyrus fibers that are shredded for *ekishisha* are aesthetically pleasing not only for their supple texture but because they are exceptionally white. The use of *ekishisha* as a decoration at weddings is explained in terms of this whiteness, which is seen as auspicious as well as beautiful. Whiteness, like other perceptual categories I have described, is expressed as a verb in the Haya language. *Okwela,* "to be white, clean, shining, brilliant," as an attribute of an object refers not just to color, but to a more general condition and to a form of perception as well. Whiteness is "clarity"; in Haya, as in English, something that is "clear" is both visually transparent (e.g., clear water) as well as unblemished—as in an open clearing. This sense of being unblemished or unsullied makes whiteness an especially auspicious condition. The New Moon (*Omwezi Kwema*, or *Kwela*) was once the critical calendrical referent for Haya ceremonies. It was auspicious both for its visual clarity as well as for its "newness," the fact that it is a phenomenon that initiates a process and is therefore unsullied by the passage of time. As one neighbor put it, "It is a period that has made no mistakes." Indeed, the Holy Spirit for (Protestant) Haya Christians is *Omwoyo Gulikwela*. This purified condition is also important to Haya gastronomic aesthetics. White beans are especially favored as relishes. When they are sold, white beans always fetch the highest price at market, and this was never explained to me in terms of their taste but in terms of their color. If *ugali* must be eaten, I often heard Haya express a preference for the whitest possible flour, which would be free from impurities of any kind.

As these preferences might indicate, whiteness is particularly associated with visual acuity for the Haya (cf. Turner 1967, 60–90). Plants that secrete white fluids, for example, are widely used as eye medicine. Something white, *ekintu kilikwela,* is visually attractive, its shininess actually emanates and draws the eye to it. This brilliant quality suggests that part of the value of whiteness, of clarity and purity, is the way in which it is perceived and the way in which it creates an appearance that draws attention. These capacities become important when we return to the example of *ekishisha,* as they point to the ways in which this form embodies contradictory orientations at yet another level. The *ekishembo* wrapped as a decoration around gift baskets is literally "that which hides." This hiding, I have suggested, is integral to the enclosure that a gift of food objectifies. However, the fact that "that which hides" is made out of brilliant, white *ekishisha* conveys quite a different message. This decoration may hide the gift, but its own form is explicitly attractive, in a way that accentuates its visibility. Thus, the visual attractiveness of a decoration that attempts to conceal establishes a tension, one between the visible and invisible, that is a restatement at this perceptual level of the dialectic between intimacy and distance, relatedness and separation equally embodied by these packaged gifts.

The importance of clarity and visibility in Haya social practices is not, of course, restricted to the display of fiber decorations or the exchange of food gifts. Rather, visibility is a central dimension of "social" relations, including the relations between person and objects as well as interpersonal relationships, and this is especially apparent in consideration of the Haya concern with interiority and enclosure. As has already been discussed, much Haya discussion and exegesis of practices like wrapping food, closing doors at meals, or taking provisions to relatives in hospital focuses on the issue of the ability of "others" to see the food you are providing. Indeed, this possibility is an active threat, one that has the potential for seriously disrupting household productivity. If neighbors can see what you eat or watch you while you eat, it will certainly shame you and might even bring hunger to your home. The spatial form of enclosure is, therefore, clearly integral to the perceptual character of vision. Enclosure restricts the range of visibility, while making something visible is to *dis*close it. I would further argue that just as enclosure is a relational position, one that is situated at the interconnection of inward and outward orientations, so too is vision configured in a relative way. Visibility, from this perspective, sets up a relationship between seeing and being seen, the dynamics of which are fundamental to a Haya lived world.

Visual clarity not only connotes well-being and auspiciousness in Haya experience, as the New Moon and *ekishisha* demonstrate, it is also a concrete instantiation of relative power. Being able to see something is to engage it in a profoundly powerful way, to act as a subject with respect to what is being seen but also, possibly, to be subjected to it. This might seem a trivial assertion that is universally typical of sensory perceptions more generally. While this might be true, I would suggest that there is something particular about Haya constructions of the ability to see that make it especially central to the sociocultural processes under discussion. For example, Haya construct both hearing and seeing as forms of understanding and being receptive to authority. Narrated reports are often equally punctuated with *Wabona?* ("Do you see?") or *Wahulila?* ("Do you hear?"). The verb *okuhulila* means "to hear," but like its Swahili equivalent, *kusikia*, also means "to feel, or sense" in a more general way, as in *Wahulila izoba?* (in Swahili, *Unasikia jua kali?*; "Do you feel the sun?"). However, "seeing" is a form of perception that encompasses these perhaps more immediate tactile kinds of sensation. Thus, storytelling is framed by the audience's request to the teller *Bona tulole!*, "See so that we may see!" It is the storyteller's ability to "see" a story that can be communicated to an audience and actually enable the audience to see the story as well (Seitel 1980, 27–28). Seeing, therefore, can provide a means of recreating a complex, perceptually organized context, a lived world that includes within it an entire range of experience—visual, auditory, and otherwise. Similarly, *Olabona!* "You will see!" is a most deadly personal threat, especially stated as a threat of sorcery (Beattie 1963, 34), which implies that the totality of one's very existence can be apprehended through and encompassed by the act of seeing. Indeed, the Haya verb *okulola* means both "to see" and "to have life." The ability to see, then, is both a form of perception and a means of control that can entail a breadth of abilities for formulating subjectivities and engaging with the world.

Given this encompassing potential of seeing, it is not surprising to find that concerns with controlling access to the visible pervade Haya practices. While the capacity to see is a form of power as well as perception, making things visible is essential to Haya constructions of authority. The right to see and be seen are central means of demonstrating relative rank, position, and privilege in Haya social relations. This feature of authority is evident, for example, in practices relating to "unveiling," *omweshululo*. Unveiling is especially associated with marriage ceremonies, but it is also a feature of bridal seclusion and of birth. At a wedding, the bride, accompanied by her matrikin (father's sisters as well as sisters), will be covered with a wrapper as she approaches her groom's home. Before she enters his home, the groom must make payments to her entourage in order to have his bride unveiled to him. At larger weddings, the bride is often presented at the bridewealth meetings in the days preceding the actual wedding ceremony, and many members of the groom's party will make payments in order to unveil her. A bride kept in seclusion will also receive payments from guests in order to be shown to them, as will a newborn infant. In all of these cases called *omweshululo*, unveiling establishes a hierarchical relationship, as the ability to see is constructed as an esteemed position that must be paid for. Those who look upon others are asserting an encompassing control over them, and must earn the authority that accompanies the privilege of this gaze.

The authoritative position of those who see others or those who can make others visible can also be seen in the contrast of the bride who is unveiled with the groom and his attendants who look upon her. A bride must demonstrate her restraint and modesty (*obugole*) during her wedding and while she is in seclusion. In effect, a bride must make a presentable appearance. One word for a wedding is *olusigilo*, a term that derives from the practice of smearing (*okusiga*) the bride with fat, an application that is meant to give a bride an especially gleaming, clear skin complexion. Indeed, the Haya would say such acts are designed *okweza* (from *ukwela*), "to whiten" the bride. Given the associations of gleaming clarity with visual acuity discussed above, it is appropriate to note the sense in which a bride makes "an appearance," a visible display that is intended for others to behold. Furthermore, the modesty of the bride is demonstrated most vividly by the way that she always averts her eyes from all others, for to look directly at anyone else would be remarkably shameful. The bride, therefore, is meant to be looked at, but never to look at others. She is controlled by the gaze of others, and in turn demonstrates that control through restraining her own ability to see.

The ways in which authority is constituted by the power of seeing and being seen are ramified throughout Haya sociocultural processes. Not only is the ability to see an assertion of a certain kind of authority, but the power and privilege to make visible is similarly central to Haya forms of hierarchy. Under royal rule, Haya commoners met passing nobility with the greeting *Kaboneka waitu!*, (*very* roughly translated as "Visible our lord" or "At your disposal"); this is still the response that juniors give when they are summoned by elders. To be visible (*okuboneka;* from *okubona,* "to see") is to be available, as well as to be dependent on and subjected to the authority that sees your presence. Reflexively, Haya forms of propitiation, making offerings at important shrines or dispersing coffee (as described in my account of binding rites), are called *okubonekya* (the causative form of *okuboneka*), "to make visible." Through providing offerings to ancestors and others, Haya households acknowledge their dependence upon as well as the privilege of these greater powers, and these acts literally "make visible" the capacity of those who propitiate. The practice described above of covering meals with banana leaf before they are served is a similar kind of acknowledgment, one that indicates that those who are gathered for a meal are not only welcome to eat it, but have had the esteemed exclusive privilege of uncovering and looking at the meal reserved for them. In this way the respect of the food signified by its covering accrues to those who are allowed to disclose it for themselves.

To see and be seen are clearly reflexive abilities and conditions that are intrinsically empowered positions in Haya sociocultural processes. The ability to see is a form of perception that can encompass the very possibility of perception as well as life itself. It is also a means of power, a specific form of asserting subjectivity. The control of this kind of power, the right to have access to the *appearance* of others, or the acknowledgment of dependence on those who have such rights, is realized through the interplay of the visible and concealed. Hierarchy in social relations is constituted by the ability to make visible, and thereby accessible, the power of others.

The Creativity of Comestibility

In this discussion of food provision and preparation I have demonstrated the significance of enclosure at a number of levels. From properly wrapping staple food products to consuming meals behind closed doors, Haya practice has an inward-looking orientation. I have suggested that this concern with the spatial restriction of food and food-related processes is a means of ensuring household integrity and sufficiency, and the cultural construction of enclosure is, further, a fundamental feature of Haya sociality. Thus, the particular enclosed form of gifts objectifies both the intimacy of givers and receivers as well as the degree of separation that is necessary to establishing a *relation* between them. Enclosure, then, attempts to assure that sufficiency is specifically located as a quality that is *internal* to the social relations (households, matrikin, neighbors, etc.) that engage in food processing.

This relation between enclosure and sufficiency is clarified in Haya constructions of visibility, a perceptual quality that explicitly entails relations of power. To be seen is to be accessible and dependent on those to whom one is visible. This is evident in the acts of "making visible," which are means of acknowledging dependence—the dependence of commoners on royals, children on adults, or the living on the dead. Therefore, the dimensions of value, power, and authority embedded in visual perception indicate that food sufficiency and integrity have an emphatically interior orientation, because exposure intrinsically leaves one "open" to the possibility of dependence, if not outright subjugation. Enclosure, that is, assures internal control by turning away from a reliance on outside authority, which visual perception concretizes. In this way, enclosure is not merely a productive practice with respect to food, it is a basic orientation that maintains the proper differentiation and interrelation of social agents. The interiority of Haya food processing is in this way iconic of Haya sociality more generally. Establishing an interior location, and inscribing its focal orientations in the persistent course of daily activities *simultaneously* orients a household to itself *and* to its encompassing sociospatial context.

At the beginning of this chapter I highlighted a process of objectification in which concrete objects, namely cooked foods, are considered as embodiments of social practices, whose specific form and properties (e.g., their gendered dimensions, their temporal unfolding, their centrality or peripherality) can be recognized and interpreted through the *experience* of these foods. This is most apparent in the tactile, aesthetic, and gustatory features of food—its temperature, texture, and taste. By working through Haya food production at a broader level, I have further demonstrated that the spatial and temporal organization of this process entails a theory of perception and knowledge that is intrinsically a theory of society as well. Embedded in Haya means of preparing and presenting food is an understanding of the ways in which these activities are received as a part of a social situation. Such practices explicitly configure a set of spatial and temporal arrangements—they create Haya domestic space and time—in a way that reveals the inextricable connection of spatiality and temporality to Haya modes of perception. In Haya culinary practice, then, just as there is a reciprocal relation between the (objective) concrete products of this practice (i.e., cooked foods) and the (subjective) sensations of taste and texture, so too is there a reciprocal construction of the objective form of enclosing or *dis*closing the acts of cooking and eating and the perceptual qualities of visibility and the kinds of agency and subjectivity they connote. Thus, at all levels of their food provision and production processes, Haya construct critical dimensions of themselves and the objective world they inhabit.

5 A MORAL GASTRONOMY: VALUE AND ACTION IN THE EXPERIENCE OF FOOD

"Food Is Our Wealth"

In my initial encounters during field research I was often asked what people eat where I come from. It quickly became apparent that this was more than idle conversation on the part of my interlocutors, as I was often pressed for detailed answers and asked specifically to compare my own indigenous diet with the cuisine that could be procured and prepared in the temperate local environs. Moreover, when I traveled with friends from my immediate home to neighboring villages or districts within the region, our discussion often turned to the quality of the land in these distant areas and (inevitably) their inability to provide food as well as the farms at home. Regional differences, from one kingdom to the next within the region and from one region to the next within the nation, are often talked about in terms of the kind and qualities of food available there. The extent to which food is implicated in collective and personal identity is suggested by a moment of such "idle conversation"; the following is a characterization once offered to me and repeated in similar forms on many occasions: "What do you think of the life here? You see that we are not wealthy. We don't have things. But, we don't have any trouble with food. Food, we do have. Food is our wealth" (in Swahili, *Chakula ni utajiri wetu:* on other occasions I heard the same expression in Haya, *Ekyakulya n'eitunga lyaitu*).

The claim "food is our wealth" is a routine assessment of local priorities, but it provides us with a rich starting point from which to examine a wide range of finely nuanced understandings and activities. Food, as I have argued at length and this assertion makes clear, has a very general and pervasive significance and value in Haya communities. It is highly significant insofar as food is commonly the vehicle of elaborately coded practices, as evidenced by its capacity to orient domestic practices, the symbolic construction of its preparation and consumption, and its centrality to problems of power, agency, and personhood. But food is also a medium and source of value—it is worth something. This value is not merely the price that food can bring, or requires—although this is often *one* means of measuring the value of food. Nor is the value of food to be understood in terms of its caloric content—yet, again, the importance of "eating well" and being sated are often integral to food's value. The importance of value here, and that which is implied in the assertion that "food is our wealth," is as a feature of the particular forms and qualities of food itself; and of the potential that food and access to food has to bring about certain conditions or to enable people and communities to enhance their lives. In this sense, food is meaningful and valuable because it *motivates* action in a number of ways. It is an object to be pursued both for itself and as a means to the encompassing actions, relations, processes, etc. of which it is a part. Food becomes an objectification of value in a process that is generated through culturally specific forms of action. Food thereby becomes desired for its own sake as well as its wider potential.

The Haya word for "wealth" used here, *eitunga*, is derived from the verb *okutunga*, "to bestow or endow." The meaning of bestowal is more complex than simply giving (*okuha*, to give). A Muhaya who is a member of the local royal family and thus very familiar with (to say nothing of interested in) the nuances that distinguish giving and endowing, once explained their differences to me in this way:

> If I give you something, maybe a hoe or a bucket, on any day I can say to you, "Return that thing to me that I gave you." But if I say, "I endow you!" [*Nakutunga!*], that is yours completely. I can't say, "Return it to me." And you, if it is your wealth, you can take it and endow another [*nomutunga ondijo*].

This kind of wealth and the act of endowing is also commonly used—by royals and commoners, men and women alike—to describe the passage of land from seniors to juniors as well as the presentation and provision of a wife for a husband. This connection of affinity to processes of land devolution as well as the relation between receiving and endowing that is indicated by the verb *okutunga* suggest that wealth and wealth production are generative dimensions of social relations. That is, wealth is an objectification that embodies the reciprocal relation between the act of bestowal that creates it and the future acts of bestowal that wealth makes possible. The form of the act of being endowed and the act of endowing others are conjoined in wealth.

In this chapter I examine the significance of food and food-related practices and conditions (e.g., eating, feeding, plenty, hunger, fatness, thinness) in relation to other kinds of objects used and commented on in everyday experience.

In particular, I explore the issue of food as a form of "wealth" in the terms just described. This will require us to consider food as a commodity and as a noncommodity. Haya men and women recognize important contrasts between food that is purchased and sold and food that is acquired by cultivation or other forms of nonmonetized production and exchange. This issue will also allow us to consider the differences and similarities between food and money, a contrast that is expressed in a number of activities and commentaries. Again, this contrast will take us beyond the strictly defined context of food as a functional resource and open onto the kinds of divergent processes and potentials intrinsic to food and money as media for generating meaning and value.

This assessment of the potential commodity forms of food will also allow us to link this section to the more general concern of this work—that is, the changing processes of signification entailed in the contemporary and ongoing transformation of a local political economy. As I have argued in my discussions of the hearth and food preparation generally, food in the Haya community provides a means of commenting on, interpreting, and in some ways challenging the forces of this wider transformation. At the same time, the very nature of food—its potential for making and extending aspects of personal identity and collective relationships, for properly feeding some and being fed to others—is actively engaged in these changing orders of signification and politics. Food, then, may serve as a critical condensation of history. The implications of this history are revealed in the community's interest in food, as surely as this concern with food configures the course of their history.

In order to assess the historical process worked out in the shifting potential for creating "wealth" with food or money, it will be useful to consider a set of "key practices" in which these media routinely figure as sources and transformations of value (cf. Rappaport 1985, 31ff). Eating and feeding, growing fat and wasting away, being sated and going hungry may all be taken-for-granted aspects of everyday life. But they are also *activities* that have consequences for the way in which that everydayness is put together. For example, the power dimensions embedded in relations of feeding, the implications for health and status signified by growing fat, and the motivational force of going hungry all confirm that such mundane affairs are actually constitutive practices. They represent cultural values and simultaneously create the cultural order through which such value is made.

I emphasize the fact that eating, feeding, and related acts are all simultaneously meaningful and material activities rather than, for example, signs or cosmological principles, in order to assert precisely this constitutive character of food and its attendant processes. Indeed, the very category of food itself suggests this connection to activity; the word for food in both Haya and Swahili (the cognates *ekyakulya/chakula*) means literally "for eating." That is, while food may be an object, it is inherently oriented toward an action. It *is* food because it is *for* eating.

Counting Food and Spending Money

The assertion that "food is our wealth" is a testament to food's potential. But for the Haya who characterize it this way, this potential is raised as a point of *contrast.* In this instance, the wealth of food is opposed to the wealth of "things" (*ebintu/vitu*). This notion of "things" is commonly referred to in complaints about the local economy. "*Sisi hatuna vitu!*" (in Swahili, "We don't have any things!") is a remark even more devastating than complaints about runaway inflation. There are vivid memories in Muleba of the early 1980s when "You couldn't buy even salt in the market!" or when soap was available only in Mwanza—a town across Lake Victoria, where most villagers had never been. Today, the unavailability of things remains a point of frustration for most Haya villagers and is often used by them to characterize their local predicament as well as the condition of the Tanzanian state and Africa as a whole. The experience and memories embedded in such "things" are concretely *about* history and about the Haya sense of their place in its creation (Comaroff and Comaroff 1987).

Certain theorists of modernity and its global systems of economy might attempt to account for this opposition in terms of the complex arguments about "gifts" and "commodities" I discussed in my introduction. Accordingly, the world of food might be contrasted to the world of things, as the world of gifts is contrasted to the world of commodities. Thus, this Haya discussion of things might be said to refer to the alienability of things, as opposed to the intimate associations of food (or other gifts). While I do think a contrast is being invoked in the Haya statements, I am not suggesting that this can be accounted for in terms of such essentialist typifications (cf. Carrier 1992). "Things" can be gifts—indeed, very important gifts. For example, the most common way for Haya to describe bridewealth objects cumulatively is as *ebintu*—things. Moreover, there are things about *food* that give it the potential to be appropriated as alienable wealth—indeed, as we shall see, certain qualities of food make it *the* most appropriate vehicle for describing alienation.

The world of things, as it is referred to in such assertions, is clearly a powerful means of evoking and uniting collective identities and memories. In important respects, these "things" are a kind of evidence whose absence demonstrates not only the particular poverty of the local community, but also the marginality of that community from the world that possesses such wealth in the form of "things." At this point, therefore, I want to focus on the significance of the value of things in contrast to the value of food. To begin, let me point out that this contrast between food and things implies a contrast of food to money and the "things" money can procure. And the implications of money for the values of food have a long history in Kagera. Mukurasi notes that during the banana weevil infestations of the 1930s the local farmers "suspected the colonial rulers of having introduced the banana weevil in Bukoba so that the subsequent shortage of food would make the Bahaya work for a wage to buy 'Ugali' [maize flour to cook porridge]" (quoted in Rald & Rald 1975, 55–56). This suspicion, again, suggests a contrast of money with food, in terms of food that can be cultivated vs. food that must be purchased. And, more importantly, it recognizes the effects of encompassing transformations in political economy (colonialism, wage labor, commoditization, and the like) as having their greatest and gravest consequences on food. It is interesting to note that this understanding of colonial policy is expressed (at least in Mukurasi's account) not as an attempt simply to starve the Bahaya or wantonly destroy their way of life. Rather, the point of these policies is seen to change the very experience of food itself. The social location of food as an object that is produced and transacted, desired and consumed, is seen to shift as a consequence of the colonial encounter. The substance of food changes (from bananas to *ugali*) as the ways in which it is acquired also change. This understanding, then, further indicates that this historical process is not one in which food and money are easily separable into icons of distinct spheres of exchange, regimes of value, or other orders of signification. Indeed, the problem illuminated by the explicit contrast of food to money is the very fact that even food can (and on occasion must) be purchased.

In the contemporary situation, purchasing food remains a frequent and troublesome source of discussion. Villagers think of life in the city as especially difficult because of the daily costs of food. Again, the construction of contrasting, although not separate, worlds turns on the relation between food and money. Further, when detailing the escalating costs of travel within Tanzania, Haya people I know are likely to add up the costs of transport from one stop to the next and the number of days in transit and then conclude by adding; "*Na hujaweka chakula!*" (in Swahili, "And you haven't even included food!"). The point of this additional category seems twofold. It suggests not only that food costs something that has to be taken into account as a separate and distinctive expense (i.e., that food costs are especially marked); but also that the cost of things is most tangibly realized in terms of food. Food has a price, but price becomes most meaningful (and menacing) when it measures food.

Mukurasi's comment about colonialism and banana weevils has another significance, for this meaningful evaluation of expenses and budgets in relation to food is epitomized, for most rural Haya, by *ugali,* the food objected to by local farmers. To this day, *ugali* is a despised food that is eaten only in times of desperation. The significance of *ugali,* and the reason for its low status, extend well beyond its association with wage labor and colonialism.[1] *Ugali,* as we have seen, is a porridge that is made with either corn flour or cassava flour. I have discussed many of the semantic values embedded in *ugali,* from the consequences of pounding during preparation to the less than pleasant taste and texture of the finished food staple. At this point, I am primarily interested in elucidating the significance of *ugali* in relation to the meanings of commodity forms, and the strong associations between *ugali* and purchasing food.

Corn is grown in Kagera, but the local produce is usually eaten roasted or boiled. Only a small volume of the local produce is milled into flour. Furthermore, the local corn that is milled is done so almost exclusively on a commercial basis. Corn flour that is used to make *ugali* is therefore almost always purchased in a store or at a weekly market. Moreover, it is widely recognized as the quintessential food of Tanzanians who live outside of Kagera. This makes corn flour a product that is not commonly associated with local production and preparation. The fact that it is available almost exclusively in a commodity form adds to this association of nonlocal foods with the demands of purchase.

Cassava is grown locally in two forms. Regular cassava can be eaten roasted, boiled, or even (and perhaps most often) raw. Bitter cassava must be soaked, drained, and dried to extract its toxins before being pounded into flour. The cassava that is used to make *ugali* is grown locally. However, most families do not grow it in sufficient quantity to provide for the needs of a household. Thus, as with corn flour, cassava to be pounded for flour (*makopa*)[2] is usually purchased.

At the level of agricultural production, most Haya see cassava as a crop of hot weather and periods of hunger. Many Haya from the northern Kagera region recall the war with Uganda in the early 1980s as a time when cassava had to be imported from Mozambique due to shortages of other food staples. The history of cassava in Africa more generally, as a crop that was introduced into Mozambique by Portuguese colonial administrations from Brazil, further suggests its association with severe hardships brought about by transformations in the control of local forms of labor and production. In Kagera, many Haya farmers also told me that the local government agricultural extension policy mandated that each family farm plant some (unspecified quantity of) cassava, as it was a hardy plant capable of providing sustenance in case of drought. Most Haya agreed that cassava could grow under any ecological circumstances, but they resisted planting it in their farms because of the fear that its roots would "sap the moisture" (*okuonka amaizi*) from their banana plants. Cassava, then, is not only a plant of hot weather, it is experienced as especially desiccating. Given the connotations of extreme heat for commoditized forms and practices, which we have already seen in discussions of beer brewing and gin making, as well as the significance of moisture to the aesthetics of food, it is not surprising to find that cassava is not highly regarded as a staple food.

I have gone into some detail about these aspects of *ugali* in order to indicate the extent to which it is tangibly experienced as a commodity form. But this simple condition, the fact that flour of any kind is usually acquired with money, is not enough to account for the particularly unpleasant demands of purchasing food. Nor, more importantly, can this commodity form account for the low status of *ugali* as a food. Indeed, rice, which is produced entirely outside of Kagera and can only be purchased, is recognized as a prestige food that is virtually necessary to ceremonial meals, such as wedding receptions and Christmas dinners. Yet, bananas, which do not *have* to be purchased,[3] remain the most highly regarded staple. If they are available, then, they "cost" nothing. The low prestige of *ugali* is, therefore, not reducible to its low price. As these disparities between high prestige and no price vs. low prestige and low price make clear, value is *not* equivalent to cost. I would argue, instead, that the values of *ugali*, its status as a food of "hunger" (*enjala*) and "trouble" (*ebyemba/shida*, the Swahili term more commonly used), arise not just from the fact that it is an expense, but from the fact that it is an expense that must be incurred when bananas are *lacking*. This combination of factors, the lack of bananas and the low cost of *ugali*, mean that acquiring this sort of food has become an act of *economizing*. In purchasing flour, one allows the logic of money and the market to determine one's relation to food and all that it entails. In this regard, as Haya suspicions in the 1930s indicate, *ugali* epitomizes the capacity of money to transform food. If food is wealth, then *ugali*—a food that is purchased when there is, paradoxically, a *lack* of food—is a counterfeit form of value.

The fact that certain kinds of food can only be purchased and (generally) only under certain conditions has important implications for the ongoing (re)evaluation of nonmonetized means of acquiring food. These implications are often realized in local understandings of the importance of domestic food provision. On one occasion, for example, I made the slightly insulting mistake of apologizing to my hostess about being full. I was afraid that I had been served "very many" bananas and told her that I was sorry that I could not finish them. Her response was abrupt: "Don't say anything about it. Do you see these bananas? We don't buy them. We don't pay money. We grow them right here.

We have enough food. If you're full, just leave them. That's all." Similarly, food is not counted or measured when it is prepared. The bananas that are harvested for a meal are never counted "unless you are going to take them to the market." On another occasion, friends of mine were unfortunate to have one of their otherwise healthy heads of cattle fall off a ledge and break its neck while at pasture. The carcass of the cow was butchered, and divided into packets that could be distributed to the neighbors. I asked one of the men butchering the animal how many packets of meat would be distributed. "Ah, many!" he said. Could he be more specific, I asked. "*Huwezi kuhesabu*" ("You cannot count"), he answered. At first, I took this innumerability as an indication of there being "so many" bundles of meat. But the meat that was butchered for *sale* in the shops every day was readily counted. It is food that is being provided for friends and neighbors without monetary transaction that, literally, cannot be counted. It would seem, then, that measuring, quantifying, or even commenting on the sheer quantity of food within the household is inappropriate. Indeed, it is considered "greedy" and petty to scrutinize a household's food in this way. Simply entering a kitchen to have a look around can prove to be a daunting experience.

At the same time, these contrasts make it clear that such quantification is possible—perhaps even necessary—when food is to be sold or purchased. This confirms, once again, that the relationship between food and money is reciprocally transforming. The potential for monetized transactions creates different categories of food (e.g., that which can or cannot be counted); and, as we have seen in the case of *ugali*, which has become metonymic of market transactions and wage labor relations, different kinds of food have different consequences for money. This articulation of commoditized with noncommoditized forms of food reveal distinct ways of relating to and controlling wealth. It is particularly interesting to consider the objection to observing that there is "too much" food in terms of cultural forms of controlling wealth. This suggestion, as we have seen, connotes excessive scrutiny and a parsimonious attitude inappropriate to eating food from one's own farm. The implication is that eating the *proper kind of food* will be unrestrained and satisfying. Purchase, on the other hand, opens eating up to the possibility of food's limited availability. The fact that such food is actually countable thus transforms eating from a process in which you are well satisfied and indifferent to an amount of food to one in which you are dependent on a fixed, limited quantity. Counting and quantification, so clearly associated with money, indicate the capacity to fix value in a determinate form. However, if, as Haya claim, "food is our wealth," then the very logic of counting and quantifying, which necessarily entails *delimiting* a specific amount, may allow one to concretely experience a lack of food as poverty. This fixity, then, implicitly undermines the sense of plenitude and abundance that should be experienced when eating.

I want to expand this consideration of eating (*okulya*) because it is a key action, critical to the construction of wider dimensions of experience and practice. Eating is an activity that comes into play at many levels of sociality. It is realized in the ways in which people relate to each other and to objects. A great deal of attention is paid to the ways in which people can and do eat; and not just to the food they consume, but to the very capacity for providing and properly controlling the availability of food. Eating must be carefully controlled in collective contexts, and yet it extends to a vast range of phenomena in Haya communities. Moreover, eating as a constitutive practice illuminates many of the tensions that have arisen as a part of the commoditization of food and other forms of wealth and power. Indeed, the centrality of eating to these historical projects is indicated by the fact that one can even eat money (*okulya amahera*).

Eating as "Finishing"

As President Mwinyi gave a radio address in his low rumbling voice (markedly contrasted with the higher pitch of Julius Nyerere), my friend jokingly commented, "Ah! You hear, he has had his soda today!" The stomachs of state officials are the object of some scrutiny in Tanzania. This scrutiny, and the wry and ironic commentary that accompany it, is more than attention to how much food these bureaucrats receive. The jokes also express something other than jealousy on the part of the poor who wish they could eat so well, for precisely what does matter is *how* these officials eat. On innumerable occasions I heard men and women complain that someone who had been paid in advance for a good or service had simply "eaten the money." Any money that is quickly disposed of—due to the sudden demands of sickness, school fees, or similar crises—is just as likely to have been eaten. Similarly, the Haya speak of "eating debts" (*okulya amabanja*). This expression applies to those who are continuously in debt and acquiring new debts. Such an understanding, then, stands in contrast to the American expression "eat your losses." For the Haya, the eating is done by the person who assumes the debt, not by those who are owed. Yet, to eat money is not just theft. Thieves, who are certainly a subject of tremendous concern to all, are not said to eat money. Eating money is instead a particularly deceitful form of consumption. You may quite openly and intentionally pay for something, but only later realize that your money has been eaten.

Money that is eaten gets used in ways that are unfathomable. It is made off with (by others) by means that cannot be known to those who lose it. Such money is not taken by "force," but your ability to control its flow is undermined either by the unscrupulous practices of those you have trusted or by the force of circumstances that create overwhelming demands. Concerns about eating money thus underscore the illusive nature of money itself.

I am not suggesting that, in popular commentaries, Tanzanian officials "grow fat" simply because they are "eating money." While they may be accused of eating money at times, what is more general is the understanding of deception that is expressed in eating money, and its application to the practices of bureaucrats. Like those who eat money, such imagined officials act in ways that conceal their actual intentions. The importance of concealment, and its implied secrecy and deception, is further suggested by the expression "to eat inside" (*okulya omunda*). "Eating inside" is aptly translated by the English expression "going behind your back." It suggests not merely getting away with something, but actually doing it at the expense of one to whom you appear to be an ally. The "inside" aspect of this kind of action is especially significant. On the one hand, it implies being concealed and unseen. That which is on the inside is not open to public scrutiny—much as food that is oriented toward the "inside" cannot be subject to the close inspection of enumeration and quantification of "outside" (i.e., marketed) food. But "eating inside" also connotes the inside as a familiar and intimate location. As suggested in my discussion of the phenomenal form of gifts and the ways in which this constructs sociality in the relations of hosts to guests and strangers as well as in my analysis of the spatial and temporal dimensions of food preparation and consumption, the interiority and the intimacy it suggests are always fraught with tension. In these respects, "eating inside" is a threat from within. It is a most unscrupulous form of undoing, because it attacks that with which victims are themselves identified. It is this dynamic ambiguity—the sense of both concealment and deception, of intimacy and subversion—that makes "eating inside" (and the deception of "eating money") so pernicious.

Eating is an act of appropriation. The notions of "eating money" and "eating inside" and the ways in which they are realized in practice make it clear that this kind of appropriation is often an alienating action. These forms of appropriation entail not only deception but also a sense of the unruly and capricious flow of wealth, power, and, indeed, *being* away from those who attempt to possess or control them (and toward those who "eat"). This capricious aspect of appropriation often came up in discussions of land tenure. As one of my neighbors explained to me, one who sells a farm "doesn't have anything to eat. This is the foolishness (*upumbavu*) of money. You think you've got a profit (*faida*), but it just finishes! Even 100,000 shillings, after a while you just eat it and it is gone." This exegesis recalls Boddy's characterization of "eating" in the Northern Sudan: In "Hofriyat, eating describes situations in which things formerly under control and regulated by concepts of harmony, balance, and closeness have gone awry" (Boddy 1989, 99). This lack of control associated with the appropriation of aspects of personhood (e.g., health, social standing, or material wealth) is typical of certain Haya understandings of eating. Further, the temporal form or pace of this kind of eating is markedly fast, and terminal. This contrasts with proper and satisfying consumption, which should be slow and deliberate in order to be satisfying—proverbially, *Mpola mpola ekalya ebya muno* ("Going slowly eats a lot") or *Egenda mpola enywage* ("Go slow, drink well").[4] Eating money not only rapidly diminishes apparent values, but it does not renew them. The spatial and temporal forms of food production and household organization and their relation to land holding, as discussed above, are centrally concerned with the land's capacity to sustain the household members who live on and work it—members who in turn secure the continuity of the land as a recognizable location. Here, then, we can see that eating money is pointedly unlike eating *food,* especially food grown on your own farm, as eating food does allow you to perpetuate your ties to the land and so to renew its value. When food is eaten, the value of the land (and of the ongoing processes of inheritance, transmission, devolution, etc.) is confirmed by its capacity to provide for those who hold it. The productivity of long-term landholding activities is realized recurrently, at each meal. Food is an icon of the process of endowing, *okutunga,* a form of wealth that objectifies the past's provisions for the sustenance of the future. When one eats money, on the other hand, its value cannot be sustained; as Haya say, money is quickly "finished" (*amahela gawile*).

Eating and Feeding: The Ambiguities of Intimacy

Eating provides a flexible conceptual and practical activity for interpreting a complex series of processes and transformations. As I have shown, the implications of money for the broad purview of experiences that are associated with eating are realized in a variety of forms. These effects can be seen in the contrast between monetized and nonmonetized access to food as well as in the difference between eating food and eating money. I argue that what is intrinsic to each of these constructions of difference, and what makes eating a privileged practice for the discourse that expresses these differences, is the sense of intimacy and interiority that is at stake in eating. As we have seen, part of the contrast between nonmonetized and monetized food turns on the distinction between internal production and external observation. Further, eating money is seen as an invasion into or violation of intimate relations. Money that gets consumed by crises, or by wasteful spending—and that very process of consumption itself—is similarly concealed from those who lose it.

The productivity of eating, as well as these alienating aspects, also depends upon the power of intimacy and interiority. Sexuality, for example, is widely characterized as a kind of eating. Not only is eating food considered essential to pleasurable and productive sexual ability, but sexual activity itself is likened to eating. This direct association is made in the ribald puns (Seitel [1977, 203–4]) of adolescent boys (who kid each other that they have "had a taste," *walosa!*) as well as in formal wedding songs, where the bride's matrikin sing: *Akanana, akanana kaile / Akaile, kaile nikaehogola* (Sweet banana, sweet banana is ripe / It is ripe, it is ripe and I plucked it). The equation of eating and sexual activity can also be seen in the prohibitions on eating together that must be respected by affines. A husband never eats with his wife's mother, and Haya exegeses of these restrictions explicitly indicate that such an association would be tantamount to a sexual advance. The form of food itself suggests that it is a means of opening the body to the substance of others, and the strong connection of such commensality with sexuality confirms this. Again, the implication is that eating is essentially an act of intimacy.

The ambiguity of intimacy—the ways in which it can represent and create closeness and lasting relations but also (as the spatial qualities of "eating money" and "eating inside" make clear) provide the opportunity to conceal aspects of yourself and so to undo these relations where they are most vulnerable—can be seen in a humorous exchange. It was well known that a young friend of mine had been seen quite often with a young girl who was a neighbor of ours. When I asked him if he might be thinking of marrying her, he replied, "I can't take that girl home! With her I just eat, I relax!" This equation of eating and sexuality, like the forms of "eating money" and "eating inside," suggests alternative dimensions of intimacy. Sex requires a certain familiarity, but the ramifications of this familiarity are not self-evident, and its consequences may in fact result in a loss of control over the most intimate aspects of personal identity. It is not fortuitous, then, that my friend should refer to this kind of sexual encounter as eating, an act of appropriation that has the capacity to enhance, transform, or undermine the close personal bonds in which it is grounded.

The dynamic potential that is integral to eating as a constitutive action is focused on the meanings of its intimate, often concealed character. It should not be surprising, therefore, to find that actions that are related to eating but are less concealed—indeed, they are often quite revealing—should be especially problematic. Feeding (*okulisa,* the causative form of the verb "to eat," *okulya*) is such an action. While eating has the potential for individualistic and selfish action, feeding requires a collective setting. To be fed by another is to acknowledge one's dependence on them. The acknowledgment associated with being fed and feeding is especially laden with power: *Akulisa niwe akutwala,* "He who feeds you is he who rules you," goes the Haya aphorism (Seitel 1977, 202). While the power inherent to feeding is occasionally cited with reference to "political" authority—at one time to royal control over nonroyal clans or, currently, in the form of juniors' dependence on seniors—the kind of feeding I more commonly heard discussed was men's ability to feed their wives. Men provide food for their wives, and through this kind of feeding they establish their identities as responsible husbands. Furthermore, they secure their attachments to children born to a wife by providing special nurturance during and after her pregnancy, as well as by providing food for the child itself. I often heard men disparaging their neighbors for sending their wives out to purchase or work for food at other homes in the village. Worse yet, in the view of many locals, children who are sent out to look for food will eventually steal food for themselves. As one neighbor put it, while looking in scorn and disbelief at a woman returning from the neighbors with her family's evening meal, "When I brought my wife, I brought her here to do work (*okumukoza*—literally, to put her to work) and to feed her (*okumulisa*)."

I placed "political" in quotes because such domestic arrangements and the capacities and authorities they enact are of course always political. To begin with, women consider themselves the "feeders" of their families as much as do men. Women do work their own fields and, as we have seen, provide a substantial amount of food through marketing, the exchange relationships of gifting in *okuzilima* celebrations, and their own agricultural activities. Moreover, women are acknowledged to be the exclusive *preparers* of food, and in this absolutely critical respect they also feed their families. We have seen that the specific meanings entailed in the cultural construction of agricultural and culinary activities, from the relations of center and periphery established by men's and women's agricultural locations, to the spatiotemporal forms of smoking and boiling, have consequences for the gendered nature of Haya productive practices. What is important to note for the purposes of the present argument is that "feeding" as an action with political consequences can be constructed in very different ways, even within a single household. In this respect, an example cited above is instructive. Note that in the young bride's song, her female relations sing that the "banana is ripe" and "*I* plucked it" (*nikaehogola*). As we have seen, the verb "to ripen" is the same as "to become cooked" in both Haya and Swahili languages (*okuiya/kuiva*). The implication is that women are responsible for preparing the bride (and in effect, for marriage itself) through actions—like cooking—that they alone control. These women also assume the role of "plucking" for themselves, which suggests that it is they who will determine the timing of these marriage practices. If men think of and refer to their own sexual actions as "eating"—and if they marry women in order to "feed" them—these are possible, these matrikin seem to suggest, only because men are "fed" by women.

The links of feeding and eating to affinity—as seen in the examples of affinal sumptuary restrictions as well as in men's claims that they marry their wives in order to feed them—seem especially important. For if, as I have asserted, the significance of eating is bound up with the creation and potential of intimacy within the household, the clear associations of feeding (which at some level *enables* eating) with marriage requires that the activities of eating be placed in the context of a wider order of relations within which that intimacy and enclosure are defined. Intimacy, insofar as it emerges out of this encompassing context of sociality must not, therefore, be equated with "privacy" or (worse) "individuality," as though each household were the independent and self-evident source of its own intimate relations. Moreover, as the following discussion makes clear, the fact that feeding situates eating within an encompassing context lends it its particular *political* value. But in order to assess the meanings of the political power at stake in feeding we need to understand exactly *how* Haya men and women go about the processes of *feeding*.

Consider, for example, the conflict between husband and wife that is raised by husbands' insistence that it is they who must feed their wives. On the one hand, a wife who procures food for her family's meals from her neighbors' farms is said to shame or scorn (*okugaya*) her husband; however, families often rely on the crops that are grown in a wife's fields. In part, this conflict can be accounted for in terms of the differences between men's farms (*ebibanja*) and women's fields on the surrounding savanna (*orweya*), a contrast central to Haya spatial and temporal constructions. A husband may go to his neighbors in time of need and seek food from their farms. "To look for food" (*okushaka*) in this way—by making arrangements to weed, prune, or garden in another man's farm in exchange for a bunch of plantain—is seen as unpleasant, but is recognized as occasionally necessary by most household heads. A woman who seeks food from her neighbors' *farms* is therefore specifically commenting on her husband's capacity to provide food from the lands that he works and with which he is most strongly identified.

The political significance of "feeding," this example would imply, is manifold. A husband's claim to feed his wife, at one level, is an assertion of his exclusive control over her relation to other men. A wife may be able to provide food from her own fields, but her attempts to get food from another's *farm* associate her with the locales and activities through which other men assert their authority as husbands. By feeding his wife, a man is excluding her from the resources of other men. At another level, this insistence on the importance of feeding a wife restricts the meanings of feeding to the relation of a *husband* to his *farm*. By specifying this particular form of feeding localized within the family farm, men are not only asserting the importance of their ability to provide for their wives, they are systematically *devaluing* the work that women do to provide food. A husband who asserts that he has "brought (his) wife to feed her" and who is outraged when a wife seeks food from others is simultaneously claiming that the places that men cultivate, the agricultural work that men do, and the foods that men provide are what *really* count toward the process of "feeding."

Feeding is clearly charged with power within the household. It provides a means of asserting control and an avenue for commenting on the capacity to assure that control. The political nature of feeding can also be seen in the way it is used for evaluating the relative significance of different contributions to the household. Some kinds of feeding can be said (by some) to count for more than others. But the power of feeding also has a more general significance, one that extends to the relations *between* households as well. Thus, male heads of households see feeding their wives and families as means of restricting their relations to other households. This restriction also applies within households between generations. Men of all ages always speak of how "difficult" it is to bring a new wife into one's father's house. Sons prefer to build a house for themselves upon marriage. One of the often cited reasons for the hardship of new husbands living with their fathers is that "a new wife will not be able to fill up" in the father's house. A father will control the distribution of food within a single house and will use this ability to restrict his son's capacity to feed his wife, thereby asserting control over his son's relationship to his wife as well as to both of their reproductive abilities, which is so intimately connected to the son's capacity to feed his wife. Thus, in order to demonstrate his ability to feed a wife properly, a son must move out of his father's house and establish himself as a household head. If feeding makes one dependent on those who feed you, then these restrictions on sons and wives serves to focus this dependence *within* the house in relation to the houses of neighboring household heads, and one's own ascendant generations. Through this focus on internalization, the restrictions of feeding sustain the values of eating. These reflexive actions, feeding and eating, are dialectically related, for the very intimacy and enclosure that is both generative and threatening in eating is grounded in the cultural construction of feeding as an activity that should arise within the household. Eating can be intimate only when the relationship between those who feed and are fed is properly internalized.

These critical practices centered on food clearly suggest that food is integral to the cultural formulation of the tension between relatedness and exclusion. Close (re)productive relationships exemplified by sexuality and affinity must be worked out as dimensions of encompassing orders of sociality. We have seen this tension throughout our discussion of food and food-related practices. From the creation of domestic viability by the articulation of "inside, here" with "elsewhere," through the presentation of gifts in baskets, to the practices surrounding bridal seclusion, enclosure is always constructed in Haya socio-cultural practice as a *relative* position from which to engage the wider world. The activities of eating and feeding further embody the dynamics of this process. Eating, as a constitutive action, gives relative weight to the qualities of intimacy and enclosure as they are experienced in these relationships; feeding situates these qualities with respect to the wider social world and attempts to ground them internally. That is, feeding orients the intimacy of eating to the wider world, while simultaneously making the prerogatives of power in that world an aspect of intimate relations.

However, as much as Haya attempt to restrict the scope of eating and feeding to an enclosed and internally delimited position, there is always an equal risk that they will be opened up and exposed. This much is demonstrated by the concern with "eating money," which exploits internal relationships, as well as by the threat that is posed to male household heads by wives and children who search for food and so expose their husband's or father's inability to feed them. And it can also be seen in the less remarkable statements that all villagers make as they simply walk through a village and comment on the quality of their neighbors' farms. Here, too, the ways in which food is controlled—how well one eats or one's ability to feed a family—are open to others' evaluations.

Growing Fat and Wasting Away

More important, still, is the fact that although eating and feeding may be considered properly grounded in internal settings and relationships, the *consequences* of these actions are *always* revealed. This is especially true of the bodily signs that accompany eating. Growing fat (*okugomoka*) and wasting away (*okuteba* in Haya; more commonly, *kukonda* in Swahili) are seen as conditions that give evidence of the efficacy of eating and feeding. Growing fat or thin demonstrate not only that one has eaten, or been fed well or poorly, they are conditions that embody—as this discussion of the implications of food for an entire cultural system would suggest—a much more encompassing set of qualities and values with which they are associated. One who grows fat does not simply eat a lot. To grow fat is, literally, to be healthy. The claim "*Wagomoka,*" "You have grown fat," is used to say that one looks healthy after an illness or other hardship. Similarly, the first and most certain indication of illness is losing weight, a sign that neighbors' gossip seems endlessly to interpret. A fat person is "*omuhango,*" a "big person," one who tangibly occupies space and extends his or her person into the world. Growing fat and wasting away, then, do not merely reflect the fact that one has or has not eaten a certain quantity of food. Rather, they are processes that index the quality of one's relation to food, and in so doing they constitute and demonstrate a general state of well-being (cf. Comaroff 1985a; Popenoe n.d.).

These processes of growing fat and thin are, I am suggesting, forms of well-being, as well as means of demonstrating and evaluating one's condition. And just as the actions of eating and feeding become acutely charged with a range of meanings and values through the variety of phenomena in which they are embedded and by contestation over the agency of these actions so too are growing fat and thin (which are both the products and representations of these activities) ambiguous and nontransparent conditions. The ambiguities of these bodily processes and the meanings they signify are suggested, once again, through their association with money. We have already seen that the ways in which state officials grow fat is often made note of in popular commentaries. But the implications of money for growing fat or thin are not restricted to the importance of "eating money" or other covert forms of consumption. For example, on one occasion, a group of friends were discussing a visitor who had come earlier in the day. One young man asked me if I had noticed how this man "had already grown a belly" (in Swahili, *ameshaota kitambi;* from *kuota,* Swahili for "sprouting"). The others in the group then remarked that you could always tell when a man got a bit of money because he would immediately grow a belly. I did not think much of the assertion at first and suggested, rather prosaically, that it was not surprising that a person with money should grow fat, because he or she undoubtedly would be eating a lot more. Everyone present disagreed! "A person with money doesn't need to eat a lot. He just eats a little bit and he is full. He doesn't even want to eat a lot, and he just gets fat!" When I asked how this could be the case, I was told that a person with "a bit of money in his pocket" is able to get fat because "he has no worries"—*Taina ebitekelezo* (literally "he has no thoughts/preoccupations," from *okutekeleza*, "to think about, be concerned with"). In contrast, a poor person always has "many worries" about where he is going to get money next. As a result, he, or she can eat a great deal but will never get full and will continue to lose weight.

I heard similar comments about the significance of growing fat and thin in a variety of other situations. A young man once told me that "a new wife can't get fat if you beat her or mistreat her," an assertion that no doubt reflected the concerns of a man preparing to marry, the burdens of "feeding" a wife, as well as the respect that a fattened bride would bring to himself and his household. A woman pointed out, with a mixture of concern and contempt, how one of our neighbors had gone into decline during her years away from the village; "Her skin used to shine, and her buttocks, big like this." In this instance, the loss of weight was linked, or so my interlocutor implied, to the probable contraction of AIDS or (significantly) "Slim." In another case, my friend suggested that the reason that an acquaintance of ours was losing a lot of weight was not because he was sick, but because he was a wealthy man who was losing money. "A rich person who is used to having money in his pocket," it was suggested, "one day if he doesn't have money, he loses weight very quickly. He starts to get a lot of worries, he must lose weight!"

All of these commentaries indicate that gaining or losing weight is clearly a representation of one's self that is available for others to evaluate. It is equally evident that the values entailed in these conditions and representations relate to a far wider range of processes and activities than the mere consumption of calories. These values embody a more general sense of well-being. They confirm a person's establishment of built and sustained growth and generativity. Social fields as diverse as marriage and gender relations, sexuality and somatic illness, as well as rising and declining economic fortunes are all encoded in these bodily conditions (note, again, that "growing fat" and "wasting away" are conditions that imply forms of *action*) and transformations. Yet this process of encoding is not merely referential or transparent. The young bride who fails to grow fat is not simply demonstrating that she has not eaten enough. Indeed, she may eat quite a bit and still waste away. The final example of the rich man down on his luck, cited above, is especially intriguing because it adds still a further dimension to the subtly shifting and unstable relationship between food and money. This case recalls the idea that those who do not have money, no matter how much they eat, will never get fat because of their incessant "worries." It adds the understanding that a loss of money is experienced as particularly difficult by those who are used to money, and that this loss is expressed most directly by losing weight. The exegesis of this position further suggests that the control of money heightens or exacerbates one's experience of eating—that small increases or losses in money will have clear and demonstrable consequences for the visible signs of weight gain or loss. In these situations, it seems, fluctuations in weight can be "read" (or, I think more correctly, interpreted) as accurate and direct representations of even the most subtle transformations in a person's more global condition. What remains to be explained, however, is why this should be the case. Why, that is, should the appearance of growing fat or wasting away be only an indirect expression of the actual quantity of food one eats, and how is this indirection complicated by its associations with money? Put in another way, we might try to account for the apparent paradox of the undereater who grows fat and the glutton who wastes away.

This ambiguous relationship between eating and growing fat or thin, I have been arguing, seems to turn on the relationship between processes that are intimate and concealed and the openly demonstrated consequences of those processes. One who grows fat or wastes away allows others to make evaluations of the concealed, internalized processes, namely eating, that created this condition. But the concealed process is always situated within particular circumstances, which will determine its outward expression—circumstances such as one's relation to money or to a wider order of social relations. The apparent paradox of growing fat or wasting away in relation to undereating or gluttony can be resolved in terms of the nature of these circumstances (e.g., being a well-cared-for bride or a rich man), which configure the particular quality of one's ability to eat.

Hunger

Eating well means "filling up" (*okueguta* in Haya, *kushiba* in Swahili), and not being able to get full is to have hunger (*enjala* in Haya, *njaa* in Swahili). Hunger is often cited as a motive, perhaps *the* motive, for a range of activities. When I asked one of the founders and current chairman of my village association (which provides support during times of crises, especially funerals) why the villagers had formed the association, he replied, simply, "*Enjala.*" Brothers fight over plots of land as small as a few square feet because of "hunger"; the prohibitions on counting food and similar forms of scrutiny referred to above are also necessary to prevent hunger; as we have seen, an array of amulets and medicated preparations are incorporated into houses and fields in order to "keep off" or "drive away" hunger; even in the epic royal narrative of Lugomola ("The Provider," literally "One who fattens"; from *okugomola*, the benefactive of *oku-*

gomoka), the founding of his capital and ascending to the throne is motivated by the season of hunger (Schmidt 1978, 305ff).

To a degree, of course, this concern with hunger is an expression of the extent to which food is central to the local organization of practice. However, hunger is a specific experience within this complex of practices. If, as I have argued, the significance of food cannot be restricted to the provision of calories, then hunger is not simply a lack of food resources. Hunger is a form of evaluation. The season of hunger, for example, refers to that time of year when bananas and plantain are relatively less available and the daily staple often consists of cassava or sweet potatoes. The fact that the latter two are largely women's crops suggests that, like husbands' claims to "feeding" their wives, the assertion that this is a time of hunger is a way of devaluing certain food-related activities and (more importantly) the agents of these activities. Moreover, the ways in which hunger can and cannot be expressed are critical to its formulation of value. *Enda mbi ekugambisa ebyolile* ("The bad stomach tells what it has eaten") is a Haya proverb that suggests some of the subtle interpretations that can be given to hunger. The statement indicates that troubles cause one to reveal the sources of one's difficulty. It further implies that those who do not have "bad stomachs," those who eat well, do not reveal themselves. To admit to being hungry, then, is to reveal information which one would prefer not to disclose. In interpersonal relations, hunger is generally discussed in an impersonal, almost abstract sense. For example, when there are changes in the weather, a sudden decrease in rainfall or an ill-timed excess of rain, people will often talk about the hunger that is likely to ensue. But it is rare to hear anyone describe themselves or others as hungry, even during those times of crisis that everyone acknowledges have brought hunger. More importantly, it is extremely insulting to ask neighbors or guests *"Oina njala?"* "Are you hungry?" when small snacks or beer are being served. If you were to ask this, it would be thoroughly demeaning to your guest, as it places you in a position so far above your guest that it forces him to admit an inability to provide for himself in order to accept your hospitality. Guests should simply be offered food informally and without comment in such situations. Similarly, at meal times neighbors who have been visiting into the evening will often be invited to eat; but they are *always* expected to excuse themselves and leave the household to its meal. As one of my neighbors put it, "We say, 'Stay! Let's eat!' (*Oikale! Tulye!*) in order to drive people away!"

Each of these situations tell us that hunger should not be acknowledged, and one should not be put in the position of having to make such an acknowledgment. They also suggest that hunger can be a kind of intrusion on social relations and that even simple norms of etiquette encourage restraint on such matters. In this respect, the assertion that one is hungry is not simply an admission that one is abject. Hunger, in this situation, becomes an extension of one's self that overreaches one's capacity to depend on (or feed) one's self. It is as though hunger, which imposes itself on the person, might cause that person to impose his or herself on others.

This potential for the unrestrained extension of one's self, and its disruptive effects on interpersonal relations, is well expressed by the notion of insatiable hunger—*obulusha*—a ravenous desire to consume food that is often cited as a reason for the failure of marriage. *Enjala bugumba: Tibushelekwa* ("Hunger [is like] sterility: They are not hidden") is another proverb that deepens this association between interpersonal relations, hunger, and restraint. It suggests that hunger is a form of incapacity with respect to food that is tantamount to social impotence. By conjoining the failure of affinal productivity (i.e., sterility) with hunger, this understanding confirms, once again, the links between intimacy in social relationships, marital relations above all, and eating. And what concretizes this connection from a Haya perspective is the way in which each of these conditions forces a disclosure of these aspects of one's self. The demands of hunger are such that they seriously challenge one's ability to maintain proper personal restraint. They truly cannot be hidden.

Hunger of this sort is a potentially threatening extension of one's self in relation to others, as well as in relation to food. Claiming to be hungry suggests that you are not able to properly distance yourself from food. "You want to eat every little thing!" (*buli kantu kona!*) when you have hunger. *Tibagusibwe!* ("They are never full!") is a common insult. This is more directly disparaging than the subtle question "Are you hungry?" but both play on the notion that those who demonstrate hunger reveal a lack of self control. If hunger makes itself known as an unwarranted exposure and imposition of one's self (as in the extreme case of *obulusha*, a ravenous desire to consume everything), then eating well—filling up and avoiding hunger—requires an ability to distance one's self from the demands of food and the desire to consume (cf. Devisch 1983, 26; Hutchinson 1980, 371–73). To be filled up and sated, one must show appropriate decorum. As we have seen in the contrast to "eating money," eating food should properly be slow and deliberate in order to be satisfying. Those who eat well are able to control themselves and to avoid the unbridled extensions of the person with respect to their food that extreme hunger entails. Therefore, one can eat well while consuming only a small bit of food, while those who eat poorly, ravenously, consume everything in sight yet remain hungry. Growing fat follows as a consequence of eating well *in this way*. Gains or losses in weight reveal, not the sheer mass that has been consumed, but the control and restraint with which it has been eaten.

This relative capacity for control and restraint is what I am characterizing as well-being, a degree of distance from others and the world of objects (like food) that restricts excessive extensions or undue impositions of one's self on others. Indeed, Haya recognize such well-being as the specific ability to be properly restrained—*okwekomya*, literally "to make one's self bound" (Dauer 1984, 276ff). Reciprocally, such control restricts "the world" of subjects and objects from imposing itself on the person. Thus, hunger and worries will plague those who are not in a position to restrain themselves. A rich man may grow fat while eating little or a wife may waste away from abuse despite eating a great deal because these conditions (i.e., growing fat and wasting away) represent relative states of well-being in relation to others and the world.

Food, Productivity, and Value

Let me close this section by reiterating the main points of my argument and by suggesting some of the ways in which these analyses will be extended to a wider series of activities. I have attempted to trace the sense of the meanings and values that are entailed in an experience of food in a particular local cultural order. To do so, I have focused on certain critical actions, actions that generate the "objective," tangible, givenness of the world, while simultaneously situating the agents of these actions in that world, thereby producing the qualitative aspects of "subjective" experience. This is a process that I have described as central to Haya culinary practices, in which the acts of cooking and ripening are concretized in the form of food produced and experienced in its taste and texture, as well as to the dimensions of food preparation and presentation, which configure specific cultural forms of perception. Eating and feeding, growing fat, and wasting away, similarly are ways of making and representing a concrete, historical order of relations between persons and the world. In the course of this analysis, I have attempted to demonstrate that these critical actions have a determinate form that orients agents to actions which are grounded in (but also productive *of*) a structured field of personal and physical relationships. Thus, eating and feeding are practices that are situated in contexts of intimacy and enclosure; and they also are necessary for creating the very contexts in which they are situated. They produce intimacy as much as they are produced through it. I have further tried to suggest the ways in which this concern with intimacy orients a far wider array of practices. The flow of persons and objects within and between households, villages, and clans is configured by the tensions inherent in establishing degrees of relatedness, in the relation between inclusion and exclusion. The implications of these orientations can also be seen as essential to a model of representation. So, if eating and feeding embody and produce concrete forms of relationships, growing fat and wasting away represent their consequences as conditions that *demonstrate* the quality of these actions and the relationships of which they are a part. These critical actions, then, orient agents to action in the world, and to the *consequences* of that action. This model of practice, therefore, insists on the transformative potential of sociocultural action, for the consequences of action cannot be foreseen and often offer highly ambiguous representations, whose interpretation must figure in the course of ongoing actions.

This ambiguity is important, for it points us to the fact that the world that is generated through Haya domestic activities is not simply a neutral order of cultural principles or a nifty set of cosmological preconceptions that form a backdrop to "the real" forces of economy and society. The actions that constitute the social world in this way are intrinsically *evaluative* processes. The relationship between food and money confirms this. Transformations brought about by the possibility of sale and purchase are clearly implicated in the construction of eating or having hunger. Images of "eating money" and the effects of money on growing fat tell us that commoditization is articulated with and not simply imposed upon local orders of value production.

The ways in which evaluation is intrinsic to feeding a family or being hungry further indicate that the actions I have described are not meant to essentialize an abstracted form of practice or culture. Indeed, these are critical actions precisely because they are condensations of meanings and therefore incorporate a proliferation of concretely situated positions. Eating may seem to offer social prominence for some and result in alienation for others. Those who feed may have power over those who are fed; but if you feed *ugali*, this power may be seen as hunger. This suggests that the humble pot of plantain is a site of struggle. The ability to control food in this local context is not only engaged in an ongoing global process of historical transformation, but the critical actions I have described are, for the agents of these actions, forms of *engagement* itself.

II THE WORLD UNMADE

In the chapters of part 1 I have described the spatial and temporal form and qualities of Haya lived experience as these are generated through a unified, if broadly configured, process: the control of food. Before turning to part 2, I want to draw together some of the important themes and conclusions of these first chapters and to suggest how they are relevant to my subsequent analyses. My discussions of Haya activities have focused on the construction of interiority as a critical feature of domestic productivity and viability. This analysis of the specific Haya meanings of interiority was developed through an exploration of directional orientations, inward and outward, as fundamental dimensions of place. I then detailed the implications of these orientations as they are grounded in both a specific physical location, the hearth, and the particular cooking techniques that are organized around the hearth. I then traced the spatial and temporal form of productive process located at and objectified in the hearth through a much wider range of activities (from agriculture and cooking to sorcery and gift exchange), and my analyses closely linked Haya experiences of food production, provision, and consumption to the qualitative dimensions of these activities. I also attempted to demonstrate that the Haya concern with interiority as embodied in the control of food is a more general feature of Haya sociality, that is, of the meaningful character of Haya persons' experiences of themselves in relation to others. Through these analyses, I have argued that Haya sociocultural activities, and intra- and interhousehold relations attempt to establish interiority as a qualitative form that assures the mutual acknowledgment of *each* household's self-sufficiency. In matters of the household, as demonstrated by conditions of hunger and acts of sorcery that are the most prevalent threats to domestic viability and self-sufficiency, "insiders" attempt to keep their neighbors out, just as "outsiders" make certain to acknowledge their independence from their neighbors. Interiority is constructed and demonstrated in the reciprocal relation between these alternative orientations.

My treatment of interiority in Haya lived experience suggests important similarities to Boddy's account of enclosure in the Northern Sudan (1989). In Boddy's detailed analyses, Hofriyat understandings of enclosure serve as a central motive for a broad range of actions, from female circumcision to labor migration. She also draws connections between these activities and the spatial and temporal form of sexuality, architectural and homestead spatial relations, and bodily processes (such as breathing, bleeding, and digesting) more generally. I have also addressed the relevance of enclosure to many of these fields of practice—sexuality and cooking, binding rites and beer exchange.

Moreover, I have always examined interiority as a set of *relative* orientations in space and time. Haya forms of enclosure, in my view, are never merely set positions, they are means of focusing practices and experiences through the interrelation of opposed directions. Thus, any inside position in space is always configured as a dynamic location, one that is defined through inward orientations that simultaneously turn away from, exclude, or forcibly remove external elements. This dynamic dialectic, and the consequent tensions it engenders, are of particular significance to the processes of commoditization in Haya communities. The production, control, and consumption of marketed commodities (such as fried fish, or *ugali*), as well as the potential conversion of *any* product into a commodity (as seen in Haya efforts to enclave meal bananas from marketing contexts) takes a particular spatial and temporal form in Haya activities. Commoditization continues to redefine the contours of Haya space and time, just as the lineaments of this lived world construct the values of specific commodities. This process of commoditization also makes it clear that Haya forms of "enclosure" are always realized in relation to "disclosure." Interiority is always a relative position, and this means that the efforts of Haya men and women to control the processes of domestic viability, processes such as growing a series of banana plants, purchasing flour at the market, or simply eating and feeding, have important *political* dimensions as well.

In part 2 the relation of enclosure and interiority to Haya understandings of productivity and viability are examined in light of some recent phenomena that are seen as especially threatening. In particular, Haya concerns about bodily integrity and physical well-being are explored. I trace Haya experiences of health and affliction to encompassing processes in the Haya political economy and demonstrate the semantic load implicit in both of these material dimensions of Haya society and culture. To do so, I draw attention to a set of particular qualities that are characteristic of Haya spatial and temporal orientations. As

I demonstrated in part 1, interiority and enclosure are qualities that are culturally specific configurations of space and time. I also described the importance
of thermal qualities in Haya sociocultural practices. The relative heat of a given
practice, object, or experience, as well as distinct forms of heat (dry vs. wet,
diffuse vs. intense, indirect vs. direct) are qualities that reveal important dimensions of Haya agency and capacity. Thus, the rapid, enclosed heat of boiling is
characteristic of cooking a meal, which, in turn, embodies the capacity of a
household to establish its focal position. Or the intense, sharp heat of peppers
condenses (and stimulates) the actions typical of male agency. Qualities like
heat or speed (e.g., the relative pace of different cooking techniques, beer
preparation activities, or eating) can objectify and thereby represent the sociocultural processes that create them. My arguments here follow Munn's discussion (which follows Pierce 1931–1935) of "qualisigns," embodied qualities
that signify the transformations in time or space, that is, the *values* produced by
activities (Munn 1986, 16–17). This focus on embodied qualities as objectifications of transformations of space and time also allows me to examine these
qualities as *historical* products. For example, the kind of heat produced in
preparing beer or in residing in a brick house shifts as the set of activities
involved in this process are transformed. In the second part of this study we will
pay particular attention to changes of this sort and to the specific qualities
intrinsic to Haya experiences of them.

6 PLASTIC TEETH EXTRACTION: AN ICONOGRAPHY OF HAYA GASTROSEXUAL AFFLICTION

Body Parts: Totality and Dismemberment

The rapid and devastating spread of AIDS in Africa is well known today, and the Haya villagers in Kagera are all too familiar with its effects. But a considerable number of them are equally concerned with yet another new, deadly disease, one whose symptoms and prognosis relate to and may lend insight into Haya understandings of the AIDS epidemic. The victims of this disease are infants and children who suffer severe disorders brought on by the growth of plastic teeth and who will die if they do not have them removed.

This chapter explores the contemporary appearance of this dental affliction by tracing the symbolic valences of its symptoms. I then relate this symbolism and symptomology to a wider range of sociocultural transformations in Kagera. Such an analysis grounds these particular symptoms, symbols, and transformations in Haya understandings of their bodies and their bodies' significance to social action and the world. Mindful of Jackson's objections to studies in which the body "is dismembered so that the symbolic value of its various parts in indigenous discourse can be enumerated" (1989, 124), I would nevertheless argue that the experience of disease and therapy frequently entails a condensation of meanings in discrete forms. Indeed, dismemberment in this situation is less a faulty analytic perspective than it is a tangible concern for Haya parents and children. It therefore seems more fruitful to insist that segmentation and totalization presuppose one another—wholes are always and necessarily a relation of parts, and can be understood only in terms of the significance that derives from their dynamic organization. Further, Haya notions of totality, and especially bodily wholeness, entail an understanding of this relation between parts. Physical disorder and well-being can be assessed through attention to various discrete symptoms or conditions that can be interpreted as expressions of more general states of being. It is certainly important to recognize that bodily experience is not reducible to the resultant of separate physiological units; but the relationship between certain "various parts" of the body *is* at issue here precisely because of the *problematic* nature of the body's relation to the world that, as we shall see, is characteristic of the Haya experience of plastic teeth. Thus, while the body may allow us to remember (see especially Battaglia 1992; Bourdieu 1977; Casey 1987; Connerton 1989; Jackson 1989; Munn 1986; Schieffelin 1976), this is often achieved by dismembering procedures. The processes through which such singular parts come to acquire more general and diffused meanings therefore demand our analytic attention.

My intention, however, is not to break down the practical unity of the body in order to assess its conceptual organization. Rather, I will examine Haya processes of embodiment by "thinking through" their construction of teeth and other bodily and symbolic forms. In this way I hope to capture the dynamics of an encompassing order of sociocultural practices in and through which bodily experience is constituted; and to address the symbolic processes through which particular, concrete, and occasionally discrete (even dismembered?) phenomena become the objectified forms or iconic expressions of these practices.

An assessment of the body's ability to remember will also alert us to other culturally significant forms of memory. Such forms of affliction as these plastic teeth clearly concern not only the dynamic of local sociocultural orders as they orient the body, they also give evidence of the historical nature of these orders as they experience rapid and sweeping transformation. The juxtaposition of the body with tokens of this social transformation, such as plastic and other commodity forms, affords us a privileged position from which to assess the particular Haya experience of history and to recognize this experience as part of more global processes.

While these local accounts and actions clearly demonstrate important connections to such global processes, they also pose a challenge to much of contemporary theorizing on "the global economy" and its purportedly inevitable alienation. Indeed, Haya concerns tell us that what is essential to any process of social transformation are the experiential and meaningful aspects through which it is realized. Rather than focus on the alienating effects of commodity flows, these accounts remind us that commodities flow into situations in which they transform experience, and in this same process are themselves transformed (cf. Sahlins 1985, viii).

This challenge to social scientific paradigms thus suggests another form of re-membering, of properly situating local orders in encompassing relations. Analytic attention to such enigmatic forms of experience as affliction may allow us to get at the ways in which the "world system" becomes what it is through its actualization in *particular,* local forms.

In what follows, I begin by examining Haya constructions of bodily process as well as dynamic forms of growth more generally. I then explore the ways in which disease and disorder, especially as they are related to the particular forms of affliction presented by plastic teeth, are articulated with these processes. The grounding of these sociocultural meanings in a concrete order of social relations and practices ultimately allow us to consider the material, historical transformations of commoditization as aspects of a creative, semantic reconfiguration of everyday life. The experience of these material and semantic transformations are embodied in these forms of affliction.

Symptoms, Signs, and Therapy

Plastic teeth (in Swahili, *meno ya plasta,* from the English "plastic"; in Haya, *ebiino,* literally "bad teeth") is said to be a new illness, one that has arrived in Kagera only in the last two or three years. But its effects are already pervasive; according to most of my Haya friends, all children are now born with or are susceptible to developing plastic teeth. These teeth are said to be made of plastic, *nko nylon,* "like nylon" (the English word used).

Children who develop plastic teeth present a range of symptoms.[1] The most commonly cited are diarrhea, vomiting, and fever, as well as a refusal to nurse, and wasting. The proper treatment in such cases is to have the plastic teeth removed; in most cases, two to four canines or incisors are extracted by a local dentist. Children up to the age of three or four (according to my data and press reports), but more typically younger children are thought to be susceptible to the growth of plastic teeth. Plastic teeth are often removed before the child, in many cases a neonate, has begun to teethe. In such cases the teeth are removed from below the surface of the child's gums.

Different accounts of the origins of plastic teeth are offered. All Haya that I spoke with agreed that this disease had come to the region from somewhere else; some held that it came from Uganda, while others claimed that milk from the cattle brought by Rwandan migrants was responsible. While there is a widespread familiarity with the symptoms described, certain people, usually women whose own children have had their teeth removed, are sought out in order to make a preliminary diagnosis. The women with whom I talked about diagnosing plastic teeth said that the gums of the afflicted child were often runny with water and "soft."[2]

Once a specialist confirms the preliminary diagnosis of plastic teeth, the teeth must be removed. This is always the task of a specialist, although locals claimed that anyone could learn how to remove plastic teeth simply by watching other dentists, much as the local women had learned to diagnose them through their children's experiences. According to those who have actually witnessed it, this procedure is usually performed with a sharp implement; a hypodermic needle or sharpened bicycle spoke were most often cited as the tools of the extractor.[3] After the teeth are removed, the dentist provides evidence that the teeth are diseased, according to witnesses, by showing the child's parent how the extracted tooth "plays" (*kyazina*), moving back and forth in a rocking motion. This movement (caused by the enervation of the tooth bud itself, according to biomedical accounts) is said to be a worm (*kijoka*) in the tooth. In this way, the plastic tooth might be said to have a life of its own, which threatens the life of the child.

In addition to the fact that there was widespread knowledge about the symptoms and treatment of plastic teeth, what was always pointedly made known to me was the cost of the therapy. People would always include in their characterization of the dentist's techniques the fact that he charged 200 Tsh (approximately $1) per tooth, a significant cost in a region where the median annual income from the sale of coffee totaled approximately $30 in 1988–89.[4] Moreover, the dentist was reported to have amassed a significant amount of money because of his practice, and this certainly seemed to enhance his reputation. This special concern with the specific costs of therapy, as well as the enigmatic appearance of plastic in the human body indicates the degree to which this entire phenomena and experience of affliction is permeated by the force of commodities and commoditized images.

Teething, Timing, and Naming

Plastic teeth may have arrived only recently, but the Haya have long been concerned with their children's teeth. There are legends about Kanyamaishwa ("The Beast"), a hunter who helped to found the kingdom of Kiziba. As a child he had been left to die in the forest because he cut an upper tooth before any of his lower teeth (Cory 1949, 69). Even today, the Haya are careful to make certain (sometimes by medicinal means) that their children cut a lower tooth first.[5] Failure to do so is said to be particularly dangerous for the child's mother's brother. Such dangerous teething is called *amahano*[6] ("strange, or odious action, or condition"; cf. Beattie 1960), a term that is also used for incestuous relations. For a child to be born with visible teeth is equally dangerous. The verb for teething in both Swahili and Haya is best translated as "to sprout" (in

Haya, *okumela;* in Swahili, *kuota).* I would suggest that this process of "sprout-ing" for both human and vegetable growth entails more than the appearance of what lies hidden beneath the surface. For the Haya, there is a sense in which this growth is both transformative and creative; that is, that teeth (to use this example) do not simply emerge out of the gum, but that they are *produced* by this emergence. This point is relevant to the Haya understanding of plastic teeth, as well. The mere fact that infants who have not yet begun to teethe actually have teeth that can be removed from their gums is evidence of ill health. As one friend who had seen his newborn cousin's plastic teeth extracted remarked, "What kind of a person is born with teeth? Maybe a lion, or a calf—but a human being??"

The particular forms of disorder manifest in the ill-timed growth of teeth are suggestive of the qualities that all teeth, and the teething process, signify for the Haya. The beastly name of the early exile and the explicit association of im-properly developed infant teeth with animals reveal the wild and fundamentally inhuman character of this inversion. Further, this brute, animal-like capacity is related to the subversion of reproductive and sexual relations. Not only is it categorized as *amahano,* just as is incest, but it is seen to be an active threat to affinity in the danger it poses to the mother's brother. Further, Beattie (1960, 146) points out that the Nyoro, like the Haya, do not permit married men to eat in the presence of their mothers-in-law. Such an act (which the Haya, as we have seen, explicitly associate with illicit sexuality between these in-laws) would be described as a form of *amahano.* Beattie also notes that the Nyoro consider it *amahano* for a mother to have sexual intercourse (or its symbolic equivalent) with "a man other than her husband before her child's teeth have appeared. If she allows this, the child's upper teeth are likely to appear before the lower, which is itself *mahano*" (1960, 146). Again, the suggestion is that proper affinal sexuality is directly linked to the condition of the child, a propriety that is signified by the child's teeth.

All these practices that Haya would categorize as *amahano* turn on associa-tions that suggest that the success of affinal corporal attachments (either sexual, commensal, or both) are realized, in the most direct manner, through the bodily development of these attachments' most significant product, namely the body of the child. Teething, then, can be seen to model the relational forms and orientations of sexuality that are characteristic of affinity, insofar as the proper development of each entails carefully regulating the direct manifestation and visible presence of potentially dangerous forces that are nonetheless recognized as integral to the construction of social, cultural, and biological activity.[7]

The concrete social ordering of productive and reproductive practices suggested by these connections to sexuality, and demonstrated in the category of *amahano,* is further indicated by certain associations of teeth and teething with the sequential unfolding and symbolic qualities of other Haya processes. For example, the verb "to bite" (*okunena*) is related to the verb "to cut" (*okushala*) in Haya usage. Thus, to say "I am in pain," one can either say "*Nanenwa*" (literally "I am bitten") or "*Nashasha*" (which uses the causative, *okushasha,* of the verb *okushala*). Both of these usages suggest that pain is characterized by the force of sharp, incisive penetration. Further, the verb *okutema* ("to slash"), typically used to describe the action of cutting through the banana stem when the stalk is harvested, can be used to describe eating with great gusto and pleasure. The significance of this link between biting and cutting can be seen in the cultural formulation of Haya cultivation techniques. Haya men are solely responsible for the preparation of the plantain and banana plants (*engemu*), which provide the staple food crop. And, as we saw in the discussion of bitter and "sharp" tastes at Haya meals, the principal men's activity in this cultivation is *okushalila* (the benefactive form of *okushala*) *engemu,* "to prune the plantain plant." This consists of cutting the desiccated leaves and outer husk of the plant and stem, which are then laid at the base of the plant as mulch. Women do contribute to the growth of plantain and bananas, not by cutting or altering the actual plants themselves,[8] but by preparing the ground of the farm through weeding and mulching. An important contrast in these forms of work is noted by the Haya themselves, who point out that "men work above, and women work below."

By elaborating on these practices I do not simply mean to imply that there is an array of symbolic associations or metaphorical connections between teething and cultivating. Rather, I am asserting that there is a systematic patterning to the sequential form of Haya (re)productive processes, and that the meaning embedded in these processes is realized in teething as well as other activities. Control of the sequential development of productive practices is managed by movement in space and time from women to men's agency. Thus, teeth, which "sprout" like plants, should properly go from below to above; and more insistently, *lower* teeth must come in before *upper.* This shift from (the initial) below to (the final) above embodies a passage from a female to a male position. Further, harvesting the banana stalk (*okutema*) "finishes" the life of the growing plant, just as devouring food (*okutema*) "finishes" the "life" of the cooked bananas.[9] In both cases, markedly female activity (weeding and mulching the farm and cooking the harvested plantain) creates the potential that *subsequent* male activity transforms and appropriates. Thus, it is the male position as the *completion* to the developmental process that is undermined by appearing *before* female potential can be properly generated. From this perspective, then, we can better understand why the child's mother's brother, *maento* (literally "male mother" and thus the masculine dimension of female productivity), is particularly threatened by the *amahano* posed by the premature growth of an upper tooth.

The measure of control realized in these processes of productivity and development, and focused on teething, is further demonstrated in Haya associations of teeth and names. Most Haya today will not give a child a "clan name" (*eibala ly'oluganda*)[10] until the child has cut its first tooth. Prior to "sprouting" a tooth, a child can be called *ekibumba* (from *okubumba*, "to be clogged"), because, say the Haya, "he can't pronounce any word until he has sprouted a tooth." Thus speech, or the culturally marked capacity for it, is the requisite to being named.

Children are given clan names by a senior agnate, preferably their father's father. Naming, then, firmly grounds the identity of the infant in the generational order of clan relations. Moreover, this transformation in identity is constructed in terms of a contrast between agnates and affines. Children are named and recognized with gifts and parties among their coresidential agnates. These gifts include, most importantly, money, as well as certain amulets, which are tied to the child's body. Subsequently, children, are taken to their mother's father's home for a second round of gift giving. In this way naming (which is facilitated by the presence of teeth) establishes social identity, *not* as an essential property of the person but as a relational dimension of the social being.

The importance of this relational quality is also revealed in the meanings of particular names, as clan names are supposed to refer to the social situation of children and their agnates. Although the rich significance of clan names is far too varied and subtle to discuss here, a few brief examples can demonstrate some of the ways in which clan names can signify agnatic position with respect to affines and others.[11] *Mutalemwa* is a fairly common male name, which means "Don't get tired" (or "Don't be discouraged"). As it was explained to me, this is a name that is given to a son whose father's previous wife or wives did not give birth to any children. The name *Mutalemwa*, therefore, is an agnatic response to the shifting reproductive fortunes of the child's father, which links fertility to a history of affinal relations. This name simultaneously makes an ironic commentary on the likely suspicions of the father's neighbors, who would undoubtedly have expressed doubts about his reproductive capacity.

This connection between names and particular clan and affinal histories further suggests the place of names in constructing *temporal* processes. The name *Tibaijuka* is a male name meaning "They don't remember" that makes these temporal implications even more explicit. As it was explained to me, a man whose wife leaves him (or "runs off" as Haya men often put it) will, if he is fortunate enough to marry again and have a son, name this child *Tibaijuka* as a means of acknowledging and admonishing his former wife's actions. One friend even suggested that if the woman with whom he was currently making marital arrangements were to break off their plans and marry another, he would name his future son *Tibaijuka* to show his disdain. A name like *Tibaijuka*, then, "remembers" a specific history and invokes that history by problematizing "memory" itself. The act of naming, as these examples illustrate, can be a means of creating and recognizing the temporal transformations of marital processes.

Giving a name after a child has cut its first tooth enables the child to be known as a distinct person. And, as the particular meanings of these clan names indicates, this knowledge and distinction are concretely situated in a specified spatial and temporal context and realized as a practical relation between patrilineal clan members and their affines as well as a wider social world. Like the activities of cutting and harvesting, as well as the process of teething as discussed above, Haya names also suggest that there is a determinate temporal order to affinal relations. Names, which define the children created through such relations, can be iconic of this order, creating temporal patterns by remembering past events and situations or acknowledging the passage of time.

Teeth, Speech, and Agency

The sociocultural transformations produced by naming are also embodied in important ways. Children who have not yet cut teeth are said to be totally dependent on their mothers. A mother could leave her child or be "kicked out" by her husband only once the child has its first tooth. It is as though this first tooth, and the naming process it indexes, severs the immediate intimacy of the bodily attachment of mother and child. One of the gifts that is given to a named child is often an amulet, usually in the form of a bored coin (*ekyapa*) tied through a string around the infant's waist, which ensures that the child will not have any trouble suckling. Moreover, the string that is used to tie the amulet also serves as a means of measuring the growth of the child. The expanding or shrinking belly of the child can be demonstrated by the relative tautness of this string, and this assures parents that their children are getting fat. This gift, then, suggests that the immediate intimacy characteristic of mother-child relations becomes problematic after teeth "sprout" and names are given.

It is also interesting to note that, in a sense, the toothless child is thought to be so thoroughly dependent on its mother as to lack an independent existence.

Children without teeth are thought to be immune from attack by snakes. For the Haya, snakes are animals that epitomize the surreptitious threat of penetration by dangerous, natural forces. Yet when a snake discovers that a child has no teeth, it will simply play with the child, as such a child poses no threat to this dangerous creature. In effect, the lack of teeth demonstrates not only an inability to act for oneself but, reciprocally, the inability of other agents to act on the child. What I am suggesting is that the child without teeth is in a condition of dependence that has a dual or reflexively structured orientation to the wider world. On the one hand, this dependence is characterized by intimate associations between the body of the mother and child; on the other hand, the child is thoroughly disengaged from action in the world. The child can truly be said to be "clogged," as it lacks the capacity either to act, or to be acted upon.

These forms of embodiment, then, indicate that the processes of teething and naming effect a passage from the bodily identification of the child and mother to the socially achieved personhood of a clan name. This transition from undifferentiated corporal existence to socially inscribed body and person is simultaneously a transition from mother to father, from the immediate intimacy of birth to the generational hierarchies of clanship. What is objectified in the child's teeth, and realized through these social transitions, is a situation of reciprocal engagement in the world. By opening the body, the tooth requires that the child (in practical terms) grasp the world, "take up" its "basic significance" (Merleau-Ponty 1962, 102) as an entity external to his or her self (for example, the child suckles from a mother now marked as a distinct person); at the same time, by grasping the world, the child becomes, in effect, grasped by that world and its inscribed orientations and potentials. Thus, in suckling, the child becomes bound by the string that measures weight gain—but which also measures the child's orientation to the sociocultural world that evaluates weight gain as an index of well-being. Through their "rootedness" in the processes in which this dialectical form of engagement is generated, teeth are produced as icons of agency. Their appearance signifies and exemplifies a capacity to act and be acted upon in sociocultural processes.

Speech, itself made possible by the appearance of teeth, epitomizes this engaged situation. To begin with, distinct forms of speech and conversation are identified with distinctions between men and women. Men's conversation and verbal exchanges, for example, facilitate a range of activities and experiences, from courtroom disputes to funerary mourning. Language learning, associated with the process of teething, has a gendered dimension; the Haya claim that every child's first word is *Tata* ("Father"), never *Mawe* ("Mother"). As Dauer notes, men's speech (by their own evaluation) should properly express the capacity for self-control in interpersonal relations. Men's relatively greater ability to be restrained yet forthright (*okwekomya,* literally "to make one's self bound") is contrasted with women's speech styles, which are more subtle and deferential. Women "pass behind" (*okulabya enyuma*), using euphemism, and even slips of the tongue, in order to avoid confrontation (Dauer 1984, 276–85). The point of this contrast is not that men control speech more fully than women, but that the form of men's speech is more openly assertive, while women's speech is typically effective through indirection. The distinction between these modes of agency is critical to the significance of teeth, for teething marks a point of differentiation that allows for the assertion (and ascription) of an individuated identity. The infant who teethes might therefore be said to pass from a condition of being "clogged" to an incipient capacity for "restraint."

For the Haya, speech is fundamental to the constitution and transformation of these differentiated forms of personhood. This capacity, and the meaning of these differentiated identities, can be demonstrated in the particular speech styles of mature men, and in the situation of certain types of speech over the course of the life cycle. As part of a marriage ceremony, the newly married son will address his senior agnates. He carries a spear and adopts a threatening stance towards his elders, while at the same time his speech extols the virtues of their clan and of his position in it as a worthy heir to its fame. This form of "boasting" (*okwebuga,* literally "to move or push one's self"), then, serves both to establish the mature, independence of a married man (as the threatening boasts and gestures make plain), while simultaneously expressing the necessary subordination of a man to the structure of clan authority with which he identifies. In the same way, naming signifies the independence of the child from its mother, by means of its dependence upon and identification with agnatic authority. At these critical moments of production and reproduction, speech coordinates the dialectical process of identity construction, in which separate, differentiated personhood is asserted as an aspect of collective identification.

Beyond the parallel gender markings of teething, naming, and speech acquisition, the significance of speech lies in its articulation of these three processes. The capacity for speech is the requisite for being named. By being named, the person submits to the authority and subjectivity of the namer. In the Haya case, this structure of authority is embedded in the collective forms of clanship and generation. At the same time, however, the child must possess the capacity for speech in order to receive a name. Thus, the power of the subjective authority to which the child submits as object is realized in the constitution of the child's subjectivity. The objective submission of the child implies the potential for subjective action.[12] The coordination of these potentials demonstrates that the child's self/world, subject/object orientation is reflexively constructed, and infused with the relations and meanings of power that produce it.

Haya teething considered as an embodied developmental process reveals a concern with the control of well-being that is not restricted to the infant. In preventing the penetration of animal forces suggested by upper teeth and by effecting the passage from mothers to fathers, from mere bodily being to clan identity, from disengaged closure to opened agency, the Haya achieve a measure of control over the body while simultaneously creating the productive capacities and orientations of that body. However, these empowering transformations are clearly more than mere transitions between these binary and rather generic positions. What is critical to the efficacy of these transformations is the fact that the body is both oriented to the world (including other bodies and subjects as well as a meaningful order of space and time) and realizes these orientations in actions that (re)construct that world. That is, bodily action and these actions on the body (such as teething, naming, speaking) go on in such a lived world and in so doing *produce* the world in which they "go on" (cf. Munn 1983; 1986). I have characterized this situation at the conjuncture of the subject/object relationship as the engagement of the body and the world, and suggest that the body is produced as an objectification of meaning, power, and the like, through its various forms of engagement.

Cut Off from Food

Given the significance of teething as a developmental process and of teeth as icons of the forms of agency it produces, we can address some of the specific ways in which plastic teeth are held to afflict children. As we have seen, plastic teeth are associated primarily with symptoms relating to food consumption; an afflicted child is both unable to retain food and refuses to eat. The body is reduced to a position of absolute isolation and inaction with respect to food. Such children can neither process food inside their bodies, nor can they appropriate food from others. In terms of the symbolic configuration of this condition, the child afflicted by plastic teeth presents a rather horrific negative projection of what should be the newborn infant's idyllic situation. As I have shown, the child who has yet to cut a tooth is in a condition of undifferentiated bodily being; disengaged from the world yet intimately connected to his or her mother's body. In contrast, the newborn afflicted with plastic teeth is disengaged from both the world and the bodily connections and capacities necessary to sustain this total dependence. A child should move from a position of total dependence to one of increasingly active separation. But plastic teeth produce a severance so total that the afflicted child is reduced to a state of absolute dependence on an inactive body. It is appropriate, then, that teeth, which condense the meanings of this complex transformation, should be pathologically linked to these gastrological inversions.

We have seen repeatedly that, for the Haya, food is a total social fact. Through all their food-related activities—consumption, production, and exchange; preparation, presentation, and anticipation—the Haya imbue their food with the moral order of their lives. Of course, the proper control over food and its manifold potentials is never unproblematic. For example, one's relation to these food processes often indexes, or provides a privileged and condensed expression of the experience of illness. The proverb "The parent gets sick, but doesn't vomit"—that is, "No matter how much trouble your children are, you can never totally divest yourself of them" (Seitel 1977, 199)—is indicative of the complex ways in which the experience of food is deployed in social commentary. Far from simply proverbial knowledge, vomiting is a condition that expresses one's own alienation from, and is explicitly contrasted to, the well-being embedded in proper food consumption. As my neighbor told me, upset with his daughter for failing to return from her grandfather's village, "There she stays and enjoys herself (*yalya obushemera*, literally 'eating happiness'), and we at home, we're puking!"

The problematic nature of people's relation to food lies not simply in the complications of illness or the threat of food shortage, but, as the example of vomiting suggests, in the range of often contradictory forces and meanings that food-related practices entail. In some African idioms, eating and being eaten are the quintessential acts of domination and appropriation, associated especially with political hierarchy and competition as well as sorcery and affliction (cf. Comaroff 1985b, 48). For the Haya, as discussed earlier, the ability to feed others is a critical form of asserting authority (Seitel 1977, 202), and those who eat are thereby subordinated. I have discussed the paradoxes of growing fat and wasting away, and demonstrated that, for many Haya, those who live well and without "worries" reveal their command over the productive dimensions of consumption through their control over themselves. Those who are well-off grow fat, yet do not eat a lot. In contrast, the troubled person experiences and demonstrates an absolute inability to separate the self from eating. No amount of food satisfies them, yet they continue to waste away. In this condition, subjectivity is so reduced to the immediate demands of the body that it becomes the object of that body. As the Haya say to anyone who is hungry, "Don't fool with your stomach!"—that is, the physical body or a particular feature of it can become the agent acting upon the human "subject" in this abject condition.

Plastic teeth replicate the bodily situation of this troubled condition, but in an even more extreme form. The person who is plagued by "worries" grows thinner, yet continues to eat and be hungry. Still, their subjective bodily experience continues to orient the person toward an appropriation of the object world, through which that subjectivity seeks to effect control over that world and itself. That is, the hungry person tries to eat well in order to get fat. What is particularly devastating about children with plastic teeth is that they lack both the ability to effectively appropriate food (as diarrhea, vomiting, and wasting suggest) as well as the subjective experience to orient them to food—to recognize, that is, the value of food. The child's refusal to eat or suckle signifies a condition of total detachment from food-related activities. Yet participation in these activities is the very means through which the subjective capacity that is at risk is able to demonstrate its viability. Plastic teeth are more than mere "worries"; they sever the person from their world, from themselves, and from the collective actions through which human beings process the world and so become human. They are, indeed, a fatal disease.

Sexuality and Social Diseases

There is certainly nothing novel in suggesting that food-related practices and experiences are redolent of sexual associations. Seitel has noted that Haya tales are replete with "metaphorical descriptions of sex that employ the vehicle of . . . food" (Seitel 1977, 203). Moreover, eating well is seen to be inextricably linked to sexual capacity and experience. To return to the example of bridal seclusion, Haya told me that a bride is supposed to be both fattened and, ideally, become pregnant during this period of time. This seclusion and fattening gives a husband sexual access to his wife and gives a wife the "heat" and "strength" for sexual activity.

In addition to these alimentary dimensions to the control of sexuality, there are also direct connections between the processes of teething and marriage. At one time, when a young woman was married for the first time, she had strings of beads (*enkwansi*), provided by her groom, tied around her wrists and ankles. Today, many women have lengthy strings of such beads wrapped around their waist at marriage, and may wear them underneath their clothing during the day. These beads are noteworthy in several respects. To begin with, infants also have these beads tied around their wrists once they have cut a tooth. Here, then, is an explicit connection between teeth and sexuality, as new teeth and nascent sexuality are similarly recognized. Indeed, each is carefully controlled and literally bound by the objects provided by husbands and fathers. This binding further marks a transition from natal homes (and maternal connections) to marital homes (and agnatic relations). The beads wrapped around the bride's waist also recalls the coin wrapped around the infant's stomach. Both signify the intimate dimensions of a new identity whose viability will be tangibly demonstrated by bodily growth and expansion. The beads that bind the bride and infant serve both to control and *display* their effective productive abilities. Teething and sexuality are each signified in the bodily forms of consumption and expansion under the careful control of fathers and husbands.

The symbolism of the spear (*ekyumi*) that is given to a man upon marriage is also significant in relation to teeth. As I have suggested, cutting is associated with teeth in idiomatic expressions that equate eating and agriculture. Spearing (*okuchumita*), in particular, is not only a crucial male agricultural activity but also a euphemism for sexual intercourse. Thus, just as the transitional process of teething, with its potential threats to sexuality, is mediated by collective clan actions that surround naming a child, so too is mature male sexuality ratified and controlled by its expression before the clan in the ceremonial presentation of a spear to the newly married son.

The perceptual qualities of eating and sexuality are also closely connected in Haya configurations of experience. As I demonstrated in my discussion of flavors, cooking, and eating, men's practices associated with cultivation are clearly encoded in certain alimentary qualities of food, the hot bitterness of peppers being especially significant for men. Moreover, these associations of men's gustatory perception with men's agricultural techniques are also laden with experiences of sexuality, as the "sharpness" of intense, bitter, "hot" spices suggests the implosive, sudden qualities of Haya masculine sexual experience.

Moreover, the physiology of reproduction and alimentation are also directly linked. The Haya point out that children develop in their mother's womb because they are fed with the food from their father's farm. The repeated acts of intercourse throughout pregnancy that Haya describe as necessary to a child's development are also said to "feed" (*okulisa*) and "grow" (*okukuza*) the fetus. Further, nonuterine siblings are called "stomach of the father" (*eibunda lya tata*)—or, collectively, "the stomach of one father"—as the stomach is the site of origin for both men's and women's sexual secretions (*amanyare*). In Haya forms of embodiment, the significance of the stomach (*eibunda* or *enda*) extends well beyond these gastrological, reproductive, or other physiological dimensions. The *enda* is a common term for "lineage" (or family)[13] in parts of Kagera (Reining 1967), as well as in Nyoro-speaking regions of Uganda (Beattie 1958b, 15). *Enda* can also mean placenta, and "to become pregnant" in the vernacular is *okutwala enda*, literally "to take a stomach/placenta." These Haya connotations of the stomach not only confirm it as a site of reproductive origins, they also identify the stomach with the products of that reproductive capacity.

The notions of "the stomach of one father" and the idea of lineal relations forming a single stomach/placenta indicate that feeding a child's or wife's stomach not only establishes the substantial connections of fathers to their offspring, it serves to create his *own* stomach, the *enda*/family as well. In this respect, it is important to note the connection of the stomach/*enda* to another term for an agnatic group of common origin discussed earlier, the hearth/ *amaiga*. The hearth, you will recall, can be used to denote the uterine offspring of a single household. A "hearth," then, is an integral component of a "stomach"—that is, a man may father several sets of uterine siblings (hearth/*amaiga*) with different women, and collectively these are all his offspring (stomach/ *enda*). A hearth might be said to "feed" a stomach (although this is my *own* and not a Haya metaphor) in this agnatic as well as alimentary fashion. But a stomach also "feeds," or serves to constitute, a hearth insofar as the stomach is the bodily point of origin that serves to create a father's children. In this reciprocal pattern of constituting bodies and relations, households and practices, the hearth and the stomach each instantiate and stand in relation to each other as both points of origin as well as final products. Each focus heightens or condenses the process of origin and completion that I have identified as integral to the spatiotemporal form of Haya productivity.

As a way of confirming this sense of condensation and further revealing how critical the stomach is to Haya bodily being, I must point out that the very word "stomach," *enda*, is intrinsic to the Haya sense of "inside." The word *omunda*, "inside" (see chapter 2), is composed of *omu-* (the prefix for interiority) and -*enda* ("the stomach"); thus, "inside" is literally "in the stomach."[14] The stomach might therefore be thought of as the quintessence of interiority and enclosure, spatial forms that are crucial to Haya configurations of viable, productive, intimate, and enduring sociocultural relations and activities. The stomach is a Haya embodiment of the processes of focalization that are essential to their orientation to their world and themselves, and it is these vital processes, control of the stomach itself, that are directly threatened by plastic teeth.

These associations between teething, feeding, fattening, and reproduction are not exclusively sexual in nature. They clearly link up with the more general Haya concerns with the form and organization of productive processes, as has been discussed in relation to questions of growth, cultivation, and developing social identity. They suggest that the fattening achieved through feeding a bride is entailed in the productivity of social relations and the success of affinal attachments. Sexuality is one aspect of the affinal experience that is signified through bodily growth, just as the growth of the child signifies another related dimension of affinity. The productivity and value of sexuality, childbirth, and successful affinal relations are literally embodied by alimentary processes and experiences. Yet, these are the very processes that are threatened by the appearance of plastic teeth.

I point to these interconnections between affinity, sexuality, and alimentary experience in order to further suggest (somewhat tentatively) certain relations between plastic teeth and AIDS. To begin with, there are some formal similarities in Haya characterizations of both diseases. Like plastic teeth, AIDS is said to have originated in Uganda and come to Kagera through the sexual contacts of rich Haya businessmen. More significantly, both plastic teeth and AIDS are seen to have their most deleterious effects in the physical wasting of the body. Victims of "Slim," as the nickname suggests, are always recognized by their weight loss (and gossip abounds as neighbors remark on, or anticipate, their fellows' fluctuations in size). This concern with weight loss, as my assessment would suggest, is clearly motivated by more than the simple observation of AIDS symptoms. Those who suffer from AIDS, like those with plastic teeth, are clearly isolated from the processes through which personal well-being is achieved, and it is this diminishment that is signified by such drastic slimming.

Affinity and sexuality, for the Haya, have become increasingly fractious and uncertain aspects of their lives. This fracture, moreover, has a long and varied history. Indeed, recurring epidemics of venereal disease, and a continuous increase in the number of women from Kagera who practice prostitution in urban East Africa have proved the abiding interests of social science, medicine, and missionization (Culwick 1939; Richards and Reining 1954; Reining 1967; Sundkler 1980; Swantz 1985). This shifting history of disease has also seen the emergence of local medical personnel like *watu wa sindano* (Swahili for "people of the needle"), whose injections of chloroquine and penicillin are sought to cure malaria and to prevent the infertility of syphilis (Reining 1967, 87–88).[15] There is, then, an historical connection between sexuality, reproduction, and the practices that address their complications, practices that articulate biomedical categories of disease (the word "malaria," for example, has entered the Haya vernacular) in the Haya context of bodiliness and (re)production.

The fact that "rich businessmen" are said to have brought AIDS with them from Uganda may also be relevant to the appearance of plastic teeth. The spread of AIDS in the late 1980s,[16] which has made sexuality so intractable, is often linked explicitly to the use of money, not simply in the profession of prostitution, but in the everyday acts of people (especially, but not exclusively, women) whose desire for money is said to be insatiable. In this respect, it is important to note the connection to Rwandan migrants that many of my neighbors cited in their etiology of plastic teeth. Rwandans who have come to Kagera in recent years are thought of as a kind of "homeless" population, who live largely as unpaid tenants in the farms of absentee Haya landowners. It seems possible that these migrants' dependence on the productivity of land that they do not and cannot control is a powerful image of the intransigence of the local economy in relation to the wider world. The "product" that is generated by this kind of tenuous situation—that is, the milk from Rwandan cattle—thus, carries with it the instability of the conditions under which it is created.[17] Given this experience of an unregulated and unstable movement of money, persons, and objects in a complex economy, it does not seem accidental that a highly visible commodity form, plastic (the significance of which I will return to), has infected children, just as the pervasive flow of commodities has undermined adult sexuality.

It was once suggested to me, by a man whose own son had had several plastic teeth removed, that "Plastic teeth are a kind of children's 'Slim'; but fortunately there are doctors to take care of children. We adults don't have any medicines. We just die." This claim[18] clearly reveals a far from subtle and certainly widespread resentment of the medical alternatives for a community whose abject suffering is ever increasing. However, by pointing to the contrast between the therapeutic courses for these diseases, it seems to suggest that the Haya are seeking to redress the ruptures in their world. While AIDS may spread unabated, plastic teeth can be removed. The fact that plastic teeth is a disease of very young children requires that parents demonstrate concrete control over them in pursuing treatment. The child/parent relationship provides an occasion for the real exercise of power that is otherwise unobtainable. Moreover, the symbolic configuration of these diseases indicates that plastic teeth may be a product of an AIDS-infected world, for the children who are born with plastic teeth suffer from the inability to engage with the objects and processes of the *world* through which agency and identity are realized and signified. And they are the offspring of parents who face the same inability to engage in the stable and enduring attachments with *each other* that enable them to constitute themselves.[19] Is it too far-fetched to suggest that parents in a world of sexual instability and fracture give birth to children who cannot sustain their own bodily integrity?

While the concerns of parents are undoubtedly experienced in the condition of their children, and this experience might provide some measure of amelioration—an opportunity, perhaps, to take action against unendurable yet enduring suffering—I do not mean to diminish the trauma that plastic teeth extraction imposes on Haya fathers and mothers and their infant children. If plastic teeth are an apt image of tragic contemporary conditions, this only makes the very drastic actions that parents feel compelled to perform on their own children an integral part of that tragedy. When I first met Sebastian in November of 1988, his infant son was just a few months old. This child's mother, Hilalia, was in poor and degenerating health. She had developed a cough that could not be treated and was so weak that she found it increasingly difficult to leave her home during the day. Hilalia was Sebastian's third successive wife, in a string of unsuccessful marriages. According to Sebastian, one wife, the mother of his eldest daughter, had "become lost" and left him for a life of prostitution (*kupiga malaya*).[20] Hilalia had become Sebastian's wife three or four years earlier; her parents continued to object to their marriage, and by his own admission Sebastian was still at the point of "planning" to make bridewealth payments at some unspecified point in the future.

As Hilalia's health declined, so did that of her young son. Over the months that I knew him he was consistently underweight and never developed any of the motor skills that might be expected of a developing infant. At a year of age he was barely able to sit up on his own, and unable to feed himself or crawl. Even before I met him, according to Sebastian, this boy had had four plastic teeth extracted.

Eventually, Hilalia was put on the TB ward at the local hospital and underwent a brief course of anti-tuberculosis treatment. While her HIV status was never actually tested, in this local hospital a clinical diagnosis of AIDS was often associated with TB. This period of hospitalization precipitated the collapse of her marriage to Sebastian. When she left the hospital, she accused Sebastian of refusing to provide for her during her treatment and promptly returned to her parents' village. Less than a month later she was dead.

Sebastian made a half-hearted effort to meet his affinal mortuary obligations to his wife, an effort that was met with more than mild disdain by Hilalia's kin. In the meantime, he had to attend to his son's health. In September of 1989 Sebastian took his son to the local hospital after several days of the child's refusing to eat. While at the hospital, Sebastian was instructed by some older women attending to their own relations that his son was clearly suffering from plastic teeth. The news was devastating to Sebastian. This was certainly a life-threatening condition. And where, he wondered, was he going to find the money necessary to pay for this costly procedure? I asked him how it was possible for his child to have plastic teeth when he had already had them removed. Couldn't Sebastian at least wait to see if he recovered? "Those old women," he told me, "they know about these things. They've seen this disease a lot. They can't be wrong. These teeth will have to come out."

A week or so later I found Sebastian at home in an obviously somber mood. "Life is hard. To hear your child crying and crying when he takes out those teeth. You have to be sad! A woman, she couldn't watch. Even for his father, it's really hard."

Sebastian's son's suffering is not a "typical case" of plastic teeth, but it is by no means unusual. The circumstances surrounding his parents' well-being, the state of their marriage and the states of their health, are not the common condition of children with plastic teeth, but neither is there anything extraordinary about these conditions. Not all parents of children with plastic teeth have AIDS, but many do. The specific set of relationships and events surrounding Sebastian's child are, of course, unique. But, the kinds of concerns that are linked together in this particular affliction are widespread in this context. For Haya men and women, marriages are often fragile, economic resources are generally scarce, and infectious disease is pervasive. Sebastian's son's malady is not the predictable outcome of these mere facts, but in fact it comprehends the insidious connections between these sociocultural realities.

Plastic

Thus far I have focused on the significance of teeth and plastic teeth as expressive icons of Haya developmental processes, and as symptomatic of a disintegration of personal, bodily capacity in the related fields of alimentation and sexuality. I want to turn now to the question of why these teeth are said to be plastic.

Haya can use the term *plasta*, from the English "plastic," much as speakers of English do, to describe a substance. However, in everyday usage, a *plasta* refers to a plastic bucket with a twenty-liter capacity. So, for example, a person might tell you to "use two plastics of water" when making beer. Other objects with which the Haya are very familiar—bowls, plates, containers, and the like—are also made of plastic. My point is not that there is something about a twenty-liter bucket that makes it a privileged vehicle for expressing the "idea" of plastic. What I do mean to suggest is that the general substance, plastic, is *practically* understood by the Haya in terms of commodity forms and media that enter into their lived experience.

These commodity forms are, as I have said, very much enmeshed in everyday life. Haya villagers commonly note that plastic objects are very useful because they are more durable than other products. Moreover, food, and especially beer, is thought to keep longer when stored in plastic. These claims, I suggest, are not simply utilitarian observations. Rather, given the importance of the concrete, sequential ordering of productive processes (especially processes relating to the consumption of such "valuables" as food and beer) these statements reveal a concern with plastic's capacity to transform and arrest the temporal processes of cooking, preserving, and decaying.

Plastic's ability to alter the temporal ordering of these processes is specifically linked, in Haya commentaries, to the thermal properties of plastic objects. The durability of plastic containers, as well as the durability they impart to the foods they contain is seen to derive from the fact that, from the Haya perspective, plastic keeps things cold. Thus, for example, buckets and jerry cans can be used to store beer for several days. But the beer cannot be *produced* in plastic containers. Proper banana beer (*olubisi*) is always made in large dugout canoes. The production process entails extracting banana juices and then storing the juice in the covered canoe, which must rest on a bed of the residue of desiccated bananas (*enkamelo*, "that which has been squeezed"). This residue is essential to the fermentation process, as it was described to me, because it transmits the necessary heat to the beer. Similarly, drinking gourds—which, particularly for men, are strongly identified with their owners—develop a reddish patina over time which many of my informants attributed to the heat that is generated by continuously holding and touching the gourd.

These examples indicate that heat is essential to local notions of ongoing transformation and development; and they further explicitly locate the source of this heat in the bodily connections that people establish with particular objects (the heat of the *enkamelo* is generated by the men who squeeze it, and the warmth that transforms a gourd's appearance comes from being held). In both of these respects, this example recalls the significance of heat that is derived from feeding, fattening, and sexual contact. The coldness of plastic, therefore, would suggest the introduction of a kind of restriction or limitation on these warm, ongoing processes, one that stands in an uneasy relation to the forms of bodily connection that are the source of this heat. Other commodity forms are also experienced as particularly cold. Houses with zinc roofs and cement floors, for example, are said to be colder than the thatched beehive huts (*omushonge*) that are rapidly disappearing. Fernandez (1982, 112ff) also notes that Fang experience new residential structures as "cold houses" that lack the warmth of both the cooking fires and the convivial sociality present in former styles of housing. For many Haya these concrete symbolic properties— durability and preservation, as well as coldness—are expressions of the ways in which plastic is experienced within a cultural order: as a powerful substance that possesses the capacity to transform as well as threaten those carefully constructed processes of growth, production, and consumption of which it has become an intimate part.

We have seen that thermal regulation is critical to Haya productive practice in a wide variety of processes. From the heat of sexuality that is implicated in the heat of bitter foods to the focality of the hearth as a centrifugal point for orienting heat within the household, control for the Haya is often assured by securing and enclosing the generative capacity of heat. Plastic containers, cement floors, and zinc roofs, on the other hand, are all objects that either repel heat or allow it to dissipate. This dissipation or dislocation of heat makes these objects problematic, and enigmatic. On the one hand, they are widely desired as consumer goods, objects that are not only "useful" for their durability but highly prestigious for the kind of lifestyle they suggest. At the same time, the control of these very same "desirable" features poses problems when—unlike the regulation of heat that is carefully monitored at all levels at the hearth—the *source* of such durability cannot be known; and the "prestige" of such objects *discloses* a family's resources for others to evaluate, the very process that domestic production consistently attempts to *enclose*. The dissipation of heat produced and concretized in these object forms clearly demonstrates the potential dissolution of Haya attempts to control productivity in a wider sense.

In addition to these perceptual and symbolic qualities, plastic goods are also clearly recognized as commodities. This means not only that they can be marked as foreign objects, but that they embody an order of circulating media, especially money, that stands in uneasy relation to productive processes such as eating and sexual activity. The tensions of this relation are well illustrated by the gifts and amulets provided when a Haya child is teething. As we have seen, gifts of money are given to the child at this time; indeed, a coin is tied to the child's waist. Here, the first tooth of the child indexes the development of the child and demonstrates the child's capacity to engage in social interaction as a defined, named person. The gift of money demonstrates the child's new identity, but the meaning of money is mediated by the form and timing of the gift, which carefully controls its circulation. Plastic, and especially plastic teeth, are inversions of this relation between persons and objects. While the child who has cut a tooth demonstrates the capacity to be independent and thus to control and participate in the circulation of objects, plastic teeth possess a life of their own that subverts this very form of independent agency and personhood and thus control the child they afflict.

What seems especially important about plastic goods is the way in which the substantial and material form of plastic objects—that is, their very plasticity—is closely linked to their form of social circulation, that is, the commodity form. There is clearly a "ready-made" quality to available plastic items in Kagera. The fact that bowls and sandals, buckets and combs are all seen to be made of the same substance, yet assume such thoroughly distinct forms further suggests the dynamic interconvertibility of plastic itself. Plastic goods are therefore presented to Haya consumers as *fully realized* objects whose distinctive commodity form (for example, as sandals, buckets, and other objects) bears no recognizable relation to the common *content* of plastic, nor to the production process through which such mutability is achieved. In this respect, plastic is an inversion of teeth (and other bodily forms). Clearly, teeth should not be present in a child's mouth as "ready-made" products, as fully realized objects that bear no relation to the process that creates them. Indeed, the fact that plastic teeth *do* present themselves in this way is taken as irrefutable evidence of their pathological character. When proper teeth ultimately present themselves, they do so as bodily forms that have been scrupulously observed, sequentially organized, and rigorously grounded in a broad nexus of interpersonal relations. Their particular qualities and symbolic configuration are built up over the course of everyday practice, as well as ritual actions, so that their specific properties are linked to their unique, concrete form. Plastic is meaningful in such a context because it intrinsically conflates or obscures its production process and reveals itself in nonunique forms. Plastic commodities, then, are evidence of the dynamic ability of the contemporary political economy to assume all manner of transposable forms.[21]

Epidemic Commodities

I am not suggesting that commoditization exists or can be assessed as a process unto itself. Commoditization is a totalizing process that transforms all productive practice, just as it transforms the potential of all the objects of this practice. For the Haya, commoditization, with its easy convertibility of objects, especially alters the spatiotemporal connectivities between persons and things that are generated through work, cultivation, inheritance, affinity, and other generative activities. To cite perhaps the most important instantiation of this process (one explored in detail in the following chapter), land alienation results in a severance of the attachments between clansmen and their clan farms, attachments that can be realized only through the transmission of the land from clansmen to fellow clansmen. As we have already seen, those who sell their clan lands "just eat" their money, but they "can never get full," an act that equates "eating" with "finishing" in a complete way. The symbolic/material potential of this kind of commoditization is often represented in consciousness in the concrete forms of the media through which it operates. Plastic is just such a form and, I would argue, has the same disruptive potential. Used in the daily course of domestic affairs, plastic is a part of every person's intimate experience. At the same time, plastic carries the symbolic weight of commoditized practices, which render transient and dislocate the forms of well-being that should characterize this experience. Thus, far from being the predictable scourge of meaning in social relations, material forces and commodity forms like plastic often *engender* such dense symbolic representations and practices. Commoditization provides tangible evidence of the plenitude of possibilities that is characteristic of modernity, a situation in which the total procedures of production and circulation are largely unknown, and to that degree uncontrollable. And yet, precisely because of this seemingly inexhaustible potential for creating meaning, such commoditized objects are highly prestigious and intensely desirable. This commoditization process is always simultaneously destructive and creative, both alienating and intimate. Plastic teeth, then, are a vivid image of the degree to which Haya experience and the social body have been imbued, indeed infected, with the power of this historical transformation.

I have discussed the significance of an affliction by situating its signifying process in a concrete order of cultural practices and historical transformations. Plastic teeth have emerged under specific conditions, and are caught up in a nexus of relations with other diseases, forces, and objects. The imagery of these wider powers are tangibly objectified in the body, but their effects can be traced through every aspect of the condition in which the Haya find themselves today. In a time of increasing land fragmentation, a collapsing coffee market, incomprehensible currency devaluations, and growing rates of HIV seropositivity, the Haya experience their increasingly eclipsed capacity to control the forces that give their lives meaning. Perhaps we should not be surprised to find that through engaging in such a fragmented and fragmenting world the Haya have produced themselves in its image.

If plastic teeth are a form of affliction whose symbolic qualities evoke the terror of corporal and affinal disintegration as embodied in the Haya community's children, AIDS is a syndrome of epidemic proportions throughout this society. The spread of AIDS and HIV disease is a phenomenon equally infused with images of displacement and disruption, with palpable bodily and interpersonal consequences. In the next chapter I discuss some of the problems surrounding AIDS that emerge in the continuous everyday discourse that addresses its appearance and unabated transmission. This discourse, as we shall see, addresses not only relations between affines, but relations between men and women and the gendered nature of Haya society as a whole. Moreover, we also find that the issues surrounding the process of commoditization, which are so central to the image of plastic teeth, are also prevalent in Haya discourse on AIDS. In particular, this discourse explores not only a variety of commodity forms, but the place of *money* in the contemporary world.

7 "BUYING HER GRAVE":
MONEY, MOVEMENT, AND AIDS

This World and Its Troubles

I begin with a bit of conversation: Three of us were talking, having just received the devastating news that a close friend of ours had died of AIDS. "This world!" began the senior member of the group, "All of this trouble is because of money." "Absolutely!" my younger friend replied. "Take a young girl. If she sees those beautiful cloths and dresses do you think she can give them up? She can't! She'll say 'If I'm going to die, let me die!' She doesn't care." "A woman," continued the elder, "she thinks she's getting rich. Goodness! She's buying her grave."

It will come as no surprise that these were three males talking about the death of another man (although I often heard women discuss "trouble" in very similar terms). But what may be surprising about these exceedingly common-place remarks is the very explicit and matter-of-fact way in which they link together such apparently disparate phenomena. How are sexuality and the rapid spread of a fatal disease connected to economic ambitions and fortunes? Women are held responsible for the spread of AIDS in many African societies (Bledsoe 1990, 208ff), but why should women's relation to money assume the symbolic and moral load of this culpability? This chapter attempts to address some of these questions by focusing on the cultural dimensions of certain transformations in the Haya political economy. Of particular interest are the forms and operations through which values are generated and transacted in the course of rapid sociocultural transformation. Haya understandings and prac-tices relating to money will be considered as exemplary of these transforma-tions, and representative of their distinct potential for the creation, destruction, circulation, and subversion of value in the Haya world. Money is essential to this order of values, both as an object whose formal properties introduce distinctive (if not *new*) possibilities in the local political economy and as a feature of the circulation, extraction, and introduction of value—processes of control that are fundamental to the articulation of this local economy with a wider world.

As I indicated previously, rates of HIV seropositivity increased dramatically in the Kagera Region of Northwest Tanzania during the late 1980s. Moreover, there has been a recurring incidence of venereal disease epidemics in the region, as well as a history of Haya women from Kagera marketing sexual and domestic services in urban East Africa since the early parts of this century. These experiences and practices alone, however, are not sufficient to account for the distinctive character of Haya understandings of the relationship between a desire for commodities and the uncontrolled transmission of disease. Haya accounts of this relationship suggest, instead, that questions about the nature of disease and the practices of prostitution must be subsumed within the wider problem of the cultural and historical formulation of value as a gendered process.

Focusing on such questions of value further allows us to explore this articulation as part of a wider context of Haya meanings and potentialities, for the expansion and deployment of values is always concretely embedded in a lived world of action and experience. This lived world incorporates a range of orientations and qualities, including forms of mobility and directionality, speed and pace, fixity and dispersal. Such a dynamic order of space and time is (re)generated in the flow of objects, and—as the conversation above suggests—in the variety of pursuits that people undertake to obtain them. Thus, I argue that our analyses must consider the processes that produce persons and empower objects as well as the concrete forms and qualities that persons, objects, and the relations between them can assume. In so doing we can better assess the ways in which sexual transactions and economic seductions are culturally constructed and represented in Haya experience and action.

Except where indicated otherwise, my comments here attempt to address specifically a Haya *male* perspective on the practices I will describe and the particular configuration of the rhetorical claims made by Haya men. I have tried to be forthright and explicit about the masculine perspective of those that elaborate the particular connections between women and land, sexuality and money, while making clear, whenever possible, that many women also participated in this rhetoric—a participation that ranged from very specific criticisms of daughters, nieces, and neighbors to broad generalizations about the unreliability of their "fellow" women *tout court*. The acknowledged biases of these perspectives, I feel, reflect not only the sources for my data on such frequently sensitive questions but also the fact that such transformations in culture and economy are always gendered processes. In the Haya case, the discourse and practices of the men I knew were especially concerned with the ways in which changes in the world were "about" gender relations. Why and how this is so is a central question in this analysis.

Cash, Cars, and Class

In January 1989 an event of no small importance to the Tanzanian economy took place—the first 500 Tsh note, the highest denomination in the nation's history, was issued. The significance of this new tender was not lost on my neighbors in Kagera: "Prices will go up! It's just like when they brought the 200 Tsh note, instead of the 100 Tsh. You go to the market, and everything goes up twice as much." While the 500 Tsh notes were first issued that January, I did not notice them in circulation in the far reaches of the Muleba District, Kagera Region until October. Even then, the utility of these notes was rather limited, given the fact that it remained difficult to get change for a 100 Tsh note at the weekly markets where most household goods were purchased. The newly minted 500 Tsh notes stood in sharp contrast to the withered and frayed twenty and fifty shilling notes and the smoothed surfaces of the five shilling pieces that passed through numerous hands on market days. I mention these conditions, which are obvious to anyone who has spent any time at all in any rural area of Africa (and, perhaps, other regions), in order to convey a sense of the substantive qualities of money itself, which are certainly a part of the everyday experience of its use and possession. Money as an object is never simply a unit of measurement or transparent medium of exchange. As the practical requirements of such a mundane affair as making change suggest, the very form that money takes, its graded denominations and its transactability in notes and coins, provides a clear means for those who engage in sales and purchases to demonstrate their own capacity to command that system of exchange. I am stating more than the obvious fact that those who have more money have more control over its circulation. What is more important in terms of these substantive aspects of currency, are the *ways* in which different people have different kinds of money. The multiplicity of ties and transactions that accrue to small denominations and the inaccessibility of larger ones are tangibly realized by everyone in the very material condition of the currency itself. Furthermore, the empowering dimensions of this differential relation to differentiated media are experienced both as an aspect of people's abilities to control money but also as an aspect of money's ability to control people. As the casual logic of my neighbor suggests, it is the very form that money takes, the ever-rising 100 Tsh, 200 Tsh, and 500 Tsh notes, that determines what people will charge in the market.

The logic of this system (which strikes me as fairly generic, and might well be applied to any system that uses hierarchically graded exchange currency) is also given more concrete expression in some intriguing representations of money in popular consciousness. The 500 Tsh note, freshly minted and striking in its complex and colorful design, was widely known as "Pajero." Pajero is the latest model overland four-wheel-drive vehicle; made by Mitsubishi, it is now seen on the often impassable roads along with its predecessors, the Toyota Land Cruiser and the ever-popular Land Rover. The automobile as a privileged vehicle for the expression of wealth and status is well known in Africa and elsewhere.[1] The fact that this newest note is known as Pajero suggests that it is a prestige object definitively beyond local origins as well as local control. Again, the inaccessibility of the Pajero (both the car and the currency), and the fact that even the knowledge of how such an object works is commanded by only a select few are highlighted by this nickname.

Automobiles (*magari* in Swahili, *emotokaa* [from "motorcar"] in Haya) and the roads they travel are not only highly charged representations of class differences in Kagera, they are also central icons of the very process of class formation. While the kingdoms (*engoma*) of Buhaya were highly stratified hierarchical systems, present-day class differences, and the process of production and commoditization that enable them, have emerged principally in relation to the intensive growth and marketing of coffee since the turn of the century. Raising coffee as a cash crop was first made compulsory in 1911, although coffee had long been planted for other purposes prior to colonial administration (Curtis 1989, 89). Haya coffee marketeers contributed to the expansion of commoditization, while reaping tremendous profits from the early boom in coffee prices (Curtis 1989, 72). The extent to which coffee remains central to the structure of class relations is illustrated by the fact that an overwhelming percentage of the coffee grown in Kagera today is marketed by an extremely small percentage of the total number of "farmers" (*wakulima,* the Swahili term used by coffee cooperatives for its members) who sell coffee to the cooperatives.[2]

My purpose in focusing on the significance of coffee and coffee trading to class formation is to point out the concrete connections between coffee as a commodity form and the system of roads and automotive transport that link this commodity to a wider political economy. At all levels of the local political economy, among both wealthy coffee entrepreneurs and poor cultivators, the transport system is inextricably linked to coffee as a commodity form because, in everyday parlance, cars and lorries are what might be called a "standard measure" of coffee volume. That is, when speaking of an amount of coffee produced or sold, the Haya with whom I spoke would always refer to, for example, "one lorry" or "three cars" of coffee as a measure of total volume. The use of cars and lorries as standard measures indicates that the very logic and means of commoditization are embedded in the concrete forms (i.e., these automotive means) through which this historical process is effected and understood. We saw the same constructions of consciousness with regard to plastic as both the widespread content of many commodities as well as the specific buckets known simply as "plastics." The poetics of cars further suggests that transport vehicles are recognized as powerful and prestigious forms of travel, which simultaneously embody the commoditization process they facilitate. The ways in which commoditization is embedded in automotive transport in the case of lorry and car loads, moreover, return us to the poetics of the Pajero. In the example of the 500 Tsh note, it is money that is characterized as a motor vehicle; while, in the coffee trade, motor vehicles are concrete measures of cash crop. Cars, for the Haya, operate as complex poetic devices. They are both indices of class position as well as icons of the process of commoditization, which in the history of this particular local economy has given rise to class relations.

Money and Mobility

"He was drawn to markets and straight roads . . . And not any dusty, old footpath beginning in this village and ending in that stream, but broad, black, mysterious highways without beginning or end." (Achebe 1972, 3)

I would further suggest that the symbolism of the automobile cannot be reduced to its prestigious and intractable "economic" origin and circulation. Nor can it be fully accounted for in terms of the process of class formation, which so clearly demonstrates discrepancies over the control of wealth. Indeed, even the relatively available five shilling coin, introduced in the early 1980s to replace the five shilling note, is known as "Scania," the Swedish company best known in Tanzania for its passenger buses. Scania lorries are also found throughout Tanzania. The term "Scania" was at one time used to describe large women, which again suggests certain popular connections between women and mobility as well as sexuality, given Haya aesthetic preferences and their associations of gaining weight with well cared for newly married brides.[3] This terminology (found in many parts of Tanzania, not only among the Haya) suggests that there is something about money and its potential that is akin to automotive travel. The critical aspects of this similarity, I would argue, lie in the command over space and time exercised by cars and buses, that is, their speed and mobility. Schivelbusch, for example, writing about the development of railways in Europe and America notes that

physical speed and the commodity character of objects . . . were intimately
connected in that the physical speed achieved by means of a vehicle of
transportation was merely the base for the economic circulation of the
commodities: that circulation increased the commodity character of the
goods with a rapidity that is in direct proportion to the physical rapidity of
the vehicles. (1986, 193)

Here, I want to suggest that speed and rapidity are not "merely" means of
moving commodities, but that the character of mobility in a concrete sociocultural order of experience may actually determine particular meanings
and values of commodity forms.

Cars not only move quickly but they move over large main roads (*barabara*,
highways), which lie between villages and connect groups of villages to regional
towns, in contrast to the narrower paths (plural, *emyanda*) on which neighbors
travel within their residential villages. The system of transport in Kagera is
complex and gives rise to a variety of experiences of travel on the roads. Buses
run irregularly between villages and the regional capitol, Bukoba. Travel to
town often requires people to wait for buses along the road at early hours of the
morning, often uncertain of whether a bus will be making the trip that day.
Smaller cars often make the trip and pick up passengers who "*omba lifti*" ("ask
a lift"). But such car trips depend entirely on car owners, who follow no routine
schedule. The fares for car travel are also two to three times higher than those
for buses. In either case, vehicles are always overflowing with passengers and
cargo. As is true in so many contexts throughout Africa, if not the world, the
unreliable schedules and maintenance of vehicles, the ever present possibility of
breakdowns or accidents, as well as the markedly poor condition of the roads
combine to give most travelers in Kagera a sense of transport as unregulated
and irregular movement. Thus, although automotive travel is markedly fast, it
is also circumscribed and fraught with tension, unreliability, and danger.

To understand the concrete symbolism of the Pajero, we should also consider
the significance of speed. As we have seen throughout the discussion of food
production, the pace of any movement, its speed or slowness as a general
quality and cultural category, is very important to Haya notions of well-being
and moral control. The term for a "nice," friendly, and well-behaved person is
omupole or *mtaratibu*, literally, a "slow person." Speed, however, is characteristic of important bodily conditions in which it is associated with "heat" and,
thus, disease. For example, drinking too quickly, especially "hot" *enkonyagi*
whiskey, will cause one's blood to "run quickly" and "boil," which leads to
fever.[4] The point is that excessive speed can lead to a degeneration of the proper
balance and control, which are necessary to easy-going sociality and bodily

well-being. If speed is indeed characteristic of cars, and money is represented by the images of particular car models, then the potential danger suggested by this capacity for great speed should be seen as an aspect of the power of money and monetized exchanges.

The varying potential for movements of different kinds within this lived world and the significance of money as a part of this world can also be seen in the contrasting practices and orientations relating to paths and roads. The contrast between paths (*emyanda*) and roads (*barabara*) lies not simply in the kind of vehicles that can and cannot travel on them, but in the forms of activity they permit and the concrete orientations they establish. Paths and roads are not simply empty regions in which external action takes place. Nor are they mere representations of the different agents or authorities—state and regional, entrepreneurial trader and household farmer—that produce them. Rather, the very configuration and situation of paths and roads in a lived order of space and time serve to orient and thereby constitute the meanings of movement as it is undertaken.

Thus, for example, when I traveled with friends and neighbors from our home to a neighboring village, most of them would insist on returning home by a different route than the one we had gone out on. They expressed concern, in such situations, that "others" might have noticed their route of departure and planned to do them harm (usually through theft or sorcery) by meeting them on the way back. In general, the Haya do not like to have their travel plans known to others, and the flexibility of alternate pathways allows them to control this kind of knowledge. On the other hand, inflexibility and fixity are in many ways inscribed in the landscape in the form of highways. I often heard complaints that a local town that was a convenient center of marketing and other exchange relations for people throughout the district would have been a better choice for the district capital (*wilayani*), but the actual district capital had been selected because it was located on the highway from Bukoba to Biharamulo. In this way, the location of the highway serves to establish an inflexible contrast between centers and peripheries. As Achebe's distinction suggests (albeit with reference to a different African context), paths can run from "this village" to "that stream," but "straight roads" run "without beginning or end." The flexibility of Haya pathways allows persons to construct multiple relations between themselves and the specified locales they inhabit, while villages and towns become mere sites, whose uneven and in many cases unnegotiable relation to the fixed highway either marginalizes or enhances their interests.

The flexibility of pathways is also made use of in an interesting form of spatial orientation, an orientation that engages money and commodities as well. We have already seen in our discussion of "binding" rites that crossroads are important sites of transformation and conjunction. They are used as points of protection, for example, when hatched eggshells are left in a crossroads in order to preserve the life of the chicks they harbored. More often, crossroads are sites of removal and transformation. In such acts of "binding" or encompassment, signs of mourning or disease are left in crossroads in order to "drive off" (*okubinga*) these afflictions. One particular form of therapy that uses crossroads to "bind" and cure illness involves coating a single coin with the incised blood or secretions from a diseased person, and then placing this coin in a crossroads. My informants suggested that money, as well as newly purchased clothing, could be used in this way to effect a cure because the disease would surely be passed from the afflicted to any person who came across the item at the crossroads and then took it with them. Crossroads, as many Haya say, are effective sites of transformation because "you know for certain that someone will pass through a crossroads." They are concrete points of interconnection in the land that facilitate personal relatedness (see MacGaffey 1986; Jacobson-Widding 1989). The use of money and commodities in this way also suggests that currency is recognized as having a capacity for fixing, indeed, for "binding" aspects of personal identity and value in their very form and substance. The placement of commodities on the path conjoins the power of crossroads to encompass multiplicity in social interaction with the power of money to condense transposable values. Money, through its many associations with roads and paths, can operate on both the multiplicity of personal relations—through the assurance that others will intersect at the same site—as well as the ability to fix and encompass the flow of these personal relations.

I have tried to suggest that there is a tension in the Haya understanding of the form of money as an object. These tensions are illuminated by an understanding of the lived world in which money and commodities circulate, a world that is constructed through the movement and transformation of value across the landscape. The potential for fixity or dissolution that movement makes possible is well illustrated by the Pajero, a 500 Tsh note that is a high-powered vehicle in the hands of well-ensconced elites. For the very potential that the Pajero represents also poses the dangerous threat of speed and uncontrolled movement. Toward the end of 1989, the popular nickname had inspired a cautionary pun: *Pajero, pa jura!*, "Pajero, the fool's place!"

Sexual Transactions and Economic Seductions

Thus far I have attempted to account for the Haya association of monetary exchange with women and sexuality, but seem to have slid further into the symbolic abyss of money and its concrete qualities of mobility and speed. Let me return to some issues relating to sexuality and AIDS, which may become clearer in light of these symbolic qualities. The opening conversation and other comments similar to it make clear that it is women's relation to money and consumer goods that is perceived by men, and many Haya women as well, to be especially problematic. AIDS in Bukoba was originally (in 1984–85) thought to be a disease of wealthy businessmen, who contracted it on their trips to the urban centers of Kampala and Nairobi. Yet I rarely heard accusations made against these men's desire to acquire money as a "cause" of AIDS. It might seem to us, nevertheless, that men are implicated in the dangerous transactions that the Haya so often denounce. After all, according to the local understanding, men are the ones who provide these "young girls" with access to the goods they desire; moreover, the woman who "doesn't care" whether she lives or dies is *still* acquiring AIDS from a man, even if it is as a result of her reckless behavior. But, despite the fact that men are engaged in the same actions as women, men are simply *susceptible* to the potential of these actions, while women are *responsible* for their consequences. I would suggest that the focus of moral judgment, and the source of moral worth for both men and women, is the production and control of desire. What is particularly reprehensible about women's behavior, in the folk accounts, is their inability to curb their desire for money and wealth. Given the prospects of material gain, a young girl is unable to "give them up," *kuviacha*. Moreover, her desire is doubly dangerous, as it is both insatiable and incomprehensible. Money seems to promote a deluded subjective sense of value, such that the outcome of its acquisition seems completely irrelevant to its immediate demands—"If I'm going to die, let me die!" Further, money does not even allow one to consider the consequences of one's own action. It is so deceptive that its potential cannot be determined from its possession. Thus, a woman "thinks she's getting rich" while in reality "she's buying her grave." Desire of this sort is not simply selfish greed. It poses a more active threat that knows no bounds and can induce one into unrestrained and unrestrainable kinds of action.

The dangerous desires that money encourages, in these views, are an important subjective dimension of the overall economy and its representations. But the economy and money itself are seen and felt to have an intractable quality, as well. In a situation of hyperinflation, recurrent currency devaluation, and the worst collapse in the world market for coffee in fifteen years, it is not surprising to hear the Haya say that Tanzania has "money like paper!" What seems paramount in the Haya understanding of this condition is the unpredictability of money and its contexts. The runaway effects of inflation are always under discussion; the value of 100 Tsh, its purchasing power today in comparison to only a few years ago, is a source of constant incomprehension. What seems especially pernicious about this incomprehensibility, at least in Haya accounts, are the unforeseen and unforeseeable demands of expenditures, and the transience of any amount of money in the face of these demands. A person may seem to have money, but a sudden rise in prices or, especially, sudden illness, might rapidly deplete this apparent wealth. Similarly, the black market in coffee is most effective in taking advantage of the sudden need for cash. Those who have access to cash are able to purchase the prospective coffee harvests of their clients who cannot wait for the state's payments. In this way, control of the annual processes of coffee cultivation are cut short in favor of the immediate requirements of money. In sum, just as the physical form of money is characterized as fast and mobile—indeed, as *automotive*—so are the processes by which it operates seen by the Haya to be sudden and immediate. Money seems to confuse and distort temporal processing itself, a capacity that is well expressed in a phrase the Haya commonly use to describe the evanescence of their economy: *Ebyo mbwenu ti bya nyenkya, n'ekibi kya mpya*—"The things of today are not those of tomorrow, that's the evil of money."[5]

From the perspective of the Haya men with whom I spoke, both young and old, desire is seen to delude women in ways that have become critical to men's susceptibility. This is not simply because men's sexual desire can lead to their own demise (an issue that is far less often the focus of moral judgment). In Haya men's account of their own sexual experience, their sexuality is constituted in large part by the creation of a sexual experience that entails control over a woman and that woman's desires. It is certainly not accidental that my friend, a young man preparing to find a wife and thus especially sensitive to the reputations and "behavior" (*omuze*) of young women, should refer to a "young girl" (*omwisiki* in Haya; *msichana* in Swahili), a term that often denotes a virgin in both vernacular Swahili in Kagera and Haya,[6] as a particularly threatening and deceptive figure. Haya men's—and, as we shall see, in important respects, women's—notions of proper and satisfying sexuality are premised on the careful control of female sexual potential. These premises are realized explicitly in the passive grammatical construction of female sexual/marital activity—a woman is married/is slept with (*okushwelwa*), while a man marries/sleeps with a woman (*okushwela*)—and implicitly in such practices as bridal seclusion in order to "teach" and "calm down" a new wife. To return once again to this practice, I have argued that the control of a new bride through the activities surrounding seclusion is essential to her husband's capacity to establish himself as a household head. Moreover, the control of incipient female sexuality is equally the concern of the bride's female relatives. As Reining notes, Haya senior women told her that prior to marriage a bride

is harangued by her mother and female relatives . . . The facts of intercourse are explained to her and her role of compliance is also made very
explicit. It is assumed that she is a virgin, or at least her virginity is the
issue of the questioning and formal examination which takes place during
this period . . . Girls find this traumatic, both because the information is
designed to be frightening and because the attitude of the older female
relatives is harsh. (Reining 1973, 2:210)

In the contemporary situation, both men and women told me that if a bride
does not display the modesty and restraint (*obugole*) that are appropriate for a
new bride, her mother and her father's sister will be held accountable for
raising their daughter poorly. This confirms the fact that "virginal" sexuality is
of interest to both husbands and the senior women who seek to control young
married women.

The capacity for this kind of control is further suggested by a practice that
conjoins sexual and economic transactions. The Haya currently engage in a
form of exchange (*okulongola*) in which the giver makes a small offering, usually of food; the recipient of this token (*akamwani*, literally "a bit of coffee," the
ubiquitous offering in everyday visits and encounters) is then expected to
present a large gift in return (*longolo*), usually a sum of money or commodity
much greater than the "price" of the token gift. To understand the meaning of
this disproportionate return, we need to understand the relationship between
those who offer the opening gift and those who make the return. This kind of
exchange can, in one instance, form a part of marriage payments. The groom's
family will place a substantial monetary payment in the bride's mother's basket,
which has been used to bring food to the married couple. Further, *okulongola*
exchanges often precede a marriage as part of courtship. In such cases, a young
woman will offer a small gift to a young man who interests her. The receiver of
such a gift is then expected to display his interest in this woman by the value (in
some accounts, by the very monetary price) of his return. As such returns will
characteristically consist of a dress or a pair of shoes in return for a bowl of
sweet potatoes, some Haya men jokingly describe *okulongola* as "women's business" (*biashara*, the Swahili term used, means women's *commerce*, not just
women's matters). Lastly, it should be pointed out that first fruits (*omwaka
gw'okulosa*) gifts, especially the delectable grasshoppers (*ensenene*) that arrive
in December and the prized Bambara nuts (*ensholo*) that are offered today as
part of these transactions, were once offered to royals in anticipation of a
longolo of land or cattle.

Let me explore the significance of this kind of exchange in order to draw out
the forms of control it entails and to contrast it to the deadly connection of

money and sexuality made by so many Haya. To begin with, the directionality of the *okulongola* exchanges is always gendered. A young woman may offer a young man an initial gift in anticipation of his generous return, but a young man will *never* make an initial offering. Men may give *akamwani* to other men, but never to women. This gendered dimension of *okulongola* is further played out in its importance to affinal relations. The groom's family always return the *longolo* to the bride's, just as premarital *longolo* returns, which may lead to marriage, are given by men to women. Moreover, the gifts of *akamwani* offered by women to men have important sexual and affinal implications. The grass-hoppers that are most prized as initiating gifts are said to give men sexual strength. The fat in this seasonal food gives heat to the body, which, as we have seen in a number of contexts, has sexual potential. Grasshoppers were also once forbidden to married women, for if a married woman were to eat one, her husband would die. Many Haya food taboos take the form of such gendered distinctions. Women in the past, and some women to this day, avoid goat, chicken, and eggs (all of which the Haya men I spoke with considered to be the most desirable of foods) with the understanding that if they were to violate these prohibitions, they would inflict damage, not on themselves, but on their husbands. Given the pervasive associations between sexuality and consuming food, which have been discussed extensively, we might say these taboos suggest that a woman's ability to control her own "appetites," to constrain herself in her alimentary and sexual activities, is critical to men's well-being.

The Bambara nut, a highly desired women's crop that is commonly offered in these exchanges, is also a euphemistic term for clitoris (*gw'ensholo*, literally "of/from the Bambara nut"). Thus, sexuality itself is represented in these foods, as well as its affinal potential through the eating taboos and exchange relations they constitute. In effect, a woman offers up her corporal sexuality for con-sumption. And by properly consuming these gifts (i.e., by eating these foods *and* by making returns for them) a man may direct and transform this sexual potential into affinal ties. These relations, in turn, are signified by a restriction *for women* (i.e., the taboo) on the very symbols that they themselves use to gen-erate affinity. A young woman offers a gift which, if successful, will be alienated from her completely. These sumptuary practices simultaneously create, trans-form, and restrict sexuality by delimiting its proper orientation and expression.

This kind of offer and return present a very different model of sexuality and transaction than is implied in the disparaging remarks about women's in-satiability. In these practices it is clear that women can and must initiate the exchange; and it is only proper for them to expect a significant return for their offering. While it is crucial to acknowledge this potential that these offerings entail, in many important respects women are also subordinated by these exchanges. Just as commoners once offered royals gifts in the hopes of a magnanimous *longolo,* so too can women anticipate returns from men. More importantly, it is clear that the concrete form of these exchanges ensures men a measure of control over the values that are engaged in them. To begin with, it is not unimportant that the food gifts offered by women, and the first fruits once offered to kings, are highly seasonal products. This restricts the timing of women's initial gifts. Under these conditions, women's demonstrations of their desires and intentions will be limited to predictable and known seasons. This link to seasonality assures men a measure of control over the expression of these sexual and economic potentials—most significantly, in a way that directly contrasts with the demands of money, which, as we have seen, "knows no season." But above all, the specific value of the *okulongola* exchanges, and what differentiates them from simple payment for goods or services rendered, is the clear inequivalence of the exchange, the vastly disproportionate return that men make to women. The women's offerings are intentionally meager, for this allows her to display her modesty, which is the proper disposition of a new bride. And this modesty also affords a man the opportunity to demonstrate his ability. This includes the ability both to control (literally to consume) the sexuality of the woman, as we have seen, but also to demonstrate his ability to control *money.* Unlike the insatiable desire for money—which undermines male sexuality and makes both men and women susceptible to the vagaries of monetary speed, mobility, and intractability—the *okulongola* exchanges actually allow women to initiate their own relations with possible affines, indeed, to offer men the promise of reproduction and ascendancy, which the particular qualities of the food gifts embody. In this way, women may acquire the returns this initial effort may yield while simultaneously allowing men to feel they control their own sexuality and display their command of money.

I suggested above that Haya women's desire for money and the goods it buys appears both insatiable and incomprehensible to Haya men. The consuming desire for money can render some women completely enigmatic and clearly demonstrates to men their own inability to control the interests and intentions of women. However, as the example of *okulongola* suggests, it is not simply the intrinsic desires of women, either economic or sexual, that are necessarily problematic. A woman motivated by the monetary processes of buying and selling, the demands of which are limitless and unpredictable, will often be understood by both men and women to be controlled only by her desire. Men's experience of their own sexuality, in this instance, is susceptible because the sociocultural forces through which women's sexuality is effectively contained and fulfilled are at risk. This is not the case in *okulongola* exchanges, which clearly mediate and restrict the exchange of money by constituting the relative positions of the transactors, thereby *expressing* and *controlling* their sexual and economic relations. Men, then, feel themselves to be increasingly susceptible to women's desires, precisely because the form of control that men hope to realize most tangibly over women and themselves is their ability to delimit and transform women's desires.

"Buying Her Grave"

Money, I am suggesting, operates in a world that is dynamic and fluid but potentially transient and intractable. The mobility and speed of cars and buses embody forms of both power and inaccessibility. The same is true for the unpredictable quality of monetary desire, a desire so consuming and immediate that men feel it undermines their ability both to satisfy women and to create and control the very capacity for satisfaction. But how does money come to take on these specific qualities? Surely there is nothing intrinsic to the substantive form of money that could strictly determine these Haya characterizations. Moreover, these specific symbolic qualities of speed and such dangerous insatiability were certainly not *introduced* with the arrival of money. The problem, then, is to assess these qualities from the broader perspective of the Haya lived world. The processes of this culturally constituted, lived world have certain potentials for productivity and creativity, and the apparently threatening and subversive potential of money must be understood in terms of these constitutive processes. To understand the ambiguous processes and potentials that money and monetized transactions objectify, it might be useful to examine certain objectifications and transactions that have for the Haya more positive and constructive potential. Fortunately for this analysis (and perhaps not accidentally, given the Haya rhetoric), one of the most salient condensations of such constructive potential is offered in the conversation quoted above; that is the grave.

The Haya bury their dead on their family farms. These farms, as we have seen, are not merely agricultural lands but are the sites of continuous residential occupation. Patrilocal households are formed as residential land is bequeathed across generations. Moreover, access to and continuous occupation of land that is acquired in this way is intimately connected to the burial of one's agnates. Reining, drawing from field research from the early 1950s, noted that "the continuity of the land, and the appointment of an heir is also bound up with a man's fate after death . . . For the living, the most convincing statement a man can make in justifying the validity of his ownership is to say that his father is buried in his *kibanja*" (1967, 234–35). When discussing residency and migration, I often heard Haya men speak of the importance of "staying by the grave of your father." The royal *nyarubanja* system of land tenure (referred to in the introduction)[7] was perhaps the most debated issue throughout the colonial and early postcolonial periods. Today, my Haya neighbors insist that the greatest injustice of this system was its disregard of the significance of burial. As one friend put it, "Your father worked his whole life on his farm, and you bury him there, and then somebody comes along and kicks you off of the land he's left you! It isn't right!" The little cemetery set up by the Catholic parish in Rubya is seen as an especially pitiful place to be buried. Only the totally indigent who die in the hospital are unfortunate enough to be buried there. Many of my neighbors were convinced that the graves are unmarked, despite the presence of a number of wooden crosses. Many others told me that even if these graves are marked, these memorials are totally meaningless because, as a neighbor once told me, "they only dig a shallow grave in the cemetery, and all of the bones get dug up and mixed up" with all of the others as each new corpse is buried. Other people who are dispossessed, either because they are migrants with uncertain attachments to particular localities or thieves who threaten communal viability, are said to be "tossed out" into holes in the uninhabited woods, and thus denied the propriety of a burial on residential farms in a recognizable grave. As these various burial styles suggest, having a grave, both to be buried in and to remember, confers stability to the land as well as to the identity of those who inhabit it.

Over the course of successive transmissions, residential lands become sites of what I will call focalization. Sons are always entitled to have access to their father's land. Those who are required to leave their natal farms, (because, for example, of employment or when land partition has provided a parcel of land too small to sustain agricultural production) are expected to maintain possession of some land given to them by senior agnates. Both sons and daughters today are expected to be given parcels of land, often no larger than a few square feet, at the death of their fathers. Indeed, specific trees, usually coffee trees, can be designated for the use of certain relatives at any time by the household head of an *ekibanja*. These practices reveal the ways in which a household's land is more than simply an object owned by a corporate group or its current representative. Rather, a residential farm objectifies a meaningfully oriented order of space and time. Relations between persons and the land are constituted in this spatiotemporal order so as to link persons back to specific locales—that is, to create a focus—and, in this way, reciprocally to assure the social endurance of those very sites.

This reciprocal ordering of persons and objects in space and time is, in fact, what makes a Haya farm a form of "wealth" (*eitunga*). As I suggested earlier, this kind of wealth and the acts of "endowing" through which it is generated are commonly used to describe the passage of land from seniors to juniors. It also applies to the presentation and provision of a wife for a husband, and this connection of affinity to land devolution, as well as the relation between receiving and endowing, suggests that wealth and wealth production are generative dimensions of social relations. Moreover, it is essential that the most emphatic demonstrations of the wealth production as it is realized in the focalizing potential of the *ekibanja* are made at death. Inheritance, as I have suggested, provides the occasion for asserting the relatedness of persons back to their natal farms. Further, the Haya are especially concerned to make certain that one is buried on the appropriate farm. No matter how far one might travel from one's household, a Muhaya will always return to be buried on his or her farm, and corpses are often returned from great distances for burial at home (see White [1990b, 241] for an interesting account of this Haya concern with home burial). If someone is inadvertently buried on the what is later determined to be the wrong farm, some of the earth from the proper farm is taken to their grave site in order to establish the connection between the right farm and the deceased. Thus, death provides an occasion for re-centering persons and objects, as the dead are returned to the land and these central lands are reidentified with those who inherit from the deceased. The way in which death conjoins these two processes of creating a spatial focus suggests that possession of a farm provides a form of temporal focality as well and that death is the moment at which this time-binding quality is achieved. Death, in temporal terms, serves to determine future activity by creating obligations for succeeding generations (e.g., obligations to "remain by the father's grave," to retain access to natal farms, etc.— thereby fulfilling the demands of generational authority). At the same time, the deceased fully realize their own authority over their descendants, thereby achieving the promise that the gift of the *ekibanja* made in the past. Death and burial on the farm establish a position from which to orient future activities as an aspect of activities in the past out of they are created.[8] The near and the distant, the past and the future are thus continuously cycled through the focal site of the *ekibanja*. The grave, then, is an objectification of these processes of continuity and identification. It is a site that encompasses the horizon of the past that has created it and the future that will ensure it.

This spatiotemporal process of focalization embodied in residential farms and the relations and exchanges in which they are engaged are, and have long been, difficult to realize. Fractious relations between brothers, a royal system of land tenure that made residence on certain lands a rather tenuous proposition, and the occasional war and famine made holding a viable *ekibanja* over successive generations a critical problematic in everyday Haya politics. In the contemporary context, however, nothing is more central to Haya concerns about the disintegration of this form of spatiotemporal integrity than money. To keep to the example of landholding, residential farm land *can* be sold. The current land holder is supposed to offer agnatic kin the right to match any offer to purchase any land acquired through inheritance; and the courts also recognize the rights of agnates to redeem a farm if the redeemer can return the purchase price to the new landholder. Land that has been inherited is, therefore, a semi-alienable property. It can be purchased and sold, but *not* as a freehold. However, land that has been acquired through purchase can be disposed of in whatever way the purchaser likes. Thus, despite the limitations on alienability, every farm has been infused with the potential for commoditization. Money, therefore, has the capacity to dislocate the landholder and thus to disrupt the power of the land itself to focus the sociocultural processes of continuity and identity. In contemporary popular consciousness, those who sell their estates fail to remember their parents and can only destroy the lives of their children as they wander through perpetually unproductive and alien lands.

The Legacy of Tomas

Let me illustrate some of the dilemmas posed by the values that attend to Haya lands by exploring a family history. This history can begin, as those who offer this history as their own begin it, with a founding figure, a patriarch named Tomas. According to his sons and heirs, Tomas was a renowned and highly respected local figure. One of his sons held that he was an *omukungu,* a regional officer during the kingdom's colonial administration. Tomas' son William told me Tomas was appointed to this position because "he was a very well-mannered person [an *omupole,* in the sense described above]. Every person like him a lot."

Tomas moved his family from a neighboring village to the one in which his sons now resided and, perhaps because of his administrative position, was able to acquire a rather large *ekibanja*. At his death, he left four sons: Oswald, Samuel, William, and Ezekiel. The eldest son, Oswald, was recognized as Tomas's *omusika,* his principal heir. Beyond this formal recognition, Oswald also retained the admiration of his neighbors, as his father had. Almost universally, the village residents I spoke with remembered Oswald as a wealthy but generous man. Ezekiel, his youngest brother, also remembered him as a very powerful brother, one who was able to assert the authority (*obutwala*) of a principal heir and, especially, to preserve the continuous legacy of their family.

These contemporary memories of Oswald as a generous and powerful man are important because of their implications for subsequent events. While Oswald's character was widely attested to, the men and women I spoke with were even more familiar with the unusual circumstances surrounding his death. If Oswald was known to be a wealthy man, this fact was most often recalled as a motive for his wife Elizabeth and their son Vedasto to murder him. Many of his neighbors told me that Oswald had undoubtedly been poisoned by his wife and son. Elizabeth, according to many of the most detailed reports, had convinced her son that he could live very well on Oswald's wealth, could marry whenever he wanted without waiting for his father to provide him with bridewealth, and that she, in particular, would not have to worry about being cut off from Oswald's affections and (therefore) fortunes if they could have it all now. By most accounts, then, Vedasto was by no means the unwitting accomplice to his mother's treachery. Yet it was clear that the motivation for pursuing Oswald's wealth by any means necessary was generally attributed to Elizabeth.

Oswald, I was told, was poisoned by Elizabeth at an evening meal. Vedasto and Oswald ate together, but Elizabeth had carefully set aside her son's portion of the meal from his father's, so that only Oswald ate the deadly food. The detail in which some people described the actual events that took place that evening is quite unusual, especially given Haya concerns with intimacy and seclusion surrounding a household meal. Ezekiel told me, "when we neighbors saw Oswald that night, he had turned completely black, and his whole body was swollen. We knew this was poison." At Oswald's funeral, Vedasto began to exhibit signs of possession and, according to Ezekiel, was about to speak and tell of his plotting, but he was attended to by "those old women" whose medicines counteract the intervention of the deceased.

I was never able to confirm these accounts of Oswald's demise, nor did I find anyone who disputed them. In 1988, however, Vedasto was living in his father's house with a wife and two small children. Elizabeth, however, was no longer living in her marital village. Many neighbors suggested that Vedasto had "kicked her out" not long after Oswald's death, either repentant for their nefarious deeds or perhaps unwilling to share the bounty they had acquired.

While these events are striking, they gave rise to circumstances that most Haya men and women would recognize as all too commonplace. Vedasto's culpability in Oswald's death was the topic of occasional speculation, but an increasingly widespread issue for discussion amongst his neighbors was the way in which he had begun to sell off the farm land in which his household was established. William also saw the death of his brother Oswald as an opportunity to sell off some of the farmland with which he had been endowed upon Tomas's death. Ezekiel took this sudden interest in selling land as the work especially of William's first wife, who would never have been able to persuade William to sell had Oswald been alive. These transactions, especially Vedasto's most recent ones, often prompted local invocations of the dubious consequences of selling land that I have described above. In particular, Vedasto was widely scorned for selling land to provide cash that went toward the purchase of frivolous pursuits: a radio, a bicycle (again suggesting the dangers of mobility), and, above all, lots of *enkonyagi.*

Oswald had a sizable tract of land, and Vedasto was able to make at least three separate land sales of that I am aware of and still provide for his household on the remaining land.[9] At one point, however, his own wife became concerned about the amount of land Vedasto had sold, and came to Ezekiel for help. As Ezekiel was both a member of Vedasto's clan and the local cell leader (*balozi*), she hoped that Ezekiel would be able to prevent Vedasto from selling off what remained of their farm. Ezekiel was also quite worried about the loss of what was ultimately his own father's legacy, and he asked me to help him compose a letter to the district judge in order to prevent any transactions that Vedasto might be planning. Ezekiel drafted the letter claiming to speak on behalf of the members of his clan. He indicated that in the past Vedasto had sold land without reporting to his clansmen and that without this prior notification they had been unable to prevent these transactions. Now, however, his wife had informed the members of his clan of Vedasto's plans, and they were asking the judge to prevent these plans from being realized. At one point while transcribing this letter, I read back a sentence to Ezekiel in which I had written "We have received a report that Vedasto wants to sell his farm" (in Swahili, *anataka kuuza shamba lake*). "You can't say that!" insisted Ezekiel. "That farm is not *his* farm. Not at all! That farm is his *children's* farm!" (*shamba la watoto wake*). Of course, Vedasto's children were all of two years and six months of age. Yet Ezekiel's objections to my haphazard wording were an exact and elegant statement about the temporal qualities of Haya landholding and the implications those qualities have for the ways in which it can be transacted. Endowing land from a father to his son (even under such suspicious circumstances as those surrounding Oswald's death) entails a commitment to securing its continuous endowment. Such a relationship to "clan" lands is distinctly oriented toward the future (as Ezekiel said, this farm is Vedasto's *children's* farm) precisely because it has been endowed *in the past* to its current occupants. My mistaken missive, in Ezekiel's understanding, revealed the crux of Vedasto's mistaken transactions; each of us had disregarded the temporal connections embodied in the land and considered only what were actually contingent "present" circumstances.

The Gender of Landholding

In view of the consequences of money for land acquisition and the ways in which these consequences form part of a gendered discourse, it must be pointed out that women from Kagera have been engaged in prostitution throughout urban East Africa for several decades. White notes that the "wazi-wazi" form of prostitution (an appellation derived from the Waziba of Kiziba, the Haya kingdom nearest to Uganda) began in Nairobi in the early 1930s (White 1990b, 103ff); and in urban centers throughout East Africa, neighborhoods known for prostitution have names associated with Buhaya and the Haya (Parkin 1969; White 1990b, 110). In rural Kagera,[10] women who return from their urban labors are resented by men, because they use their funds to acquire land for themselves and their family. It is even more important, however, to point out that the complaints made by Haya men such as those expressed in this everyday context of conversation are not addressed strictly, or even primarily, to prostitutes. Nor is the disconcerting desire for money seen to be an attack on prostitution. The point of these complaints and critiques is that they are part of a discourse about gender in which men use prostitution as simply one kind of activity to demonstrate essential differences between men and women. All women, in this view, pose the threat of dislocation, and prostitution is merely one aspect of this threat.

At the same time, all women are engaged in the system of clan-based landholding from a position that makes their access to farmland more closely bound up with purchase and sale. As daughters, women are entitled to receive parcels of farm land from their fathers, and occasionally they will be given land or specific trees by senior agnates. The position of women as legitimate heirs to clan farmlands, or as landholders of any kind, is a rather recent phenomenon in Kagera. Until the early 1950s, Haya women were not recognized, by either administrative courts or clan authorities, as legitimate heirs to clan-held lands, and a man who had only daughters would have a difficult time assuring his clan's possession of such land (Reining 1967).[11] On the other hand, sons receive access to farmland from their seniors upon marriage, as they are expected to farm clan land in order to provide for their families. Daughters, however, are expected to have access to resources from the farm of their husbands, and so are more likely to be given access to their own clan's lands at the time of inheritance. The fact that sons remain to reside on their clan's land and establish their access to the land through their continuous occupation and cultivation of their own farms even during the life of their fathers, while daughters occupy and work their husbands' farms and generally receive access to clan land only at the death of senior agnates, means that sons are in a much better position to maintain control over the devolution of farm land than are daughters. The potential conflict between brothers and sisters intrinsic to this situation is exacerbated when women divorce or simply leave their husbands and expect to reside on the clan lands worked by their brothers. Moreover, these brothers can pass their *inherited* farm land on to their own children, while sisters cannot pass on their inheritance to their own children, who are members of their *father's* clan. Thus, in order for women to control farm land as clan land, and therefore as wealth (*eitunga*), they must bequeathe their farmland to the children of their clan members, not to their own children. If, however, a woman wants to provide for her own children, she can make land available to them only by *purchasing* land, which she is then free to give to anyone she pleases. To acquire land through purchase is an expensive proposition, and it is likely that a woman will have to *sell* her clan-inherited land in order to buy land for her own children.

These structural features of agnatic clan-focused processes of property de-volution mean that women are more dependent on both *purchasing* non-clan land and *selling* their own clan land as means of acquiring control over land. As daughters, women acquire farmland much later and in a much more delimited way than do sons. As sisters, women's control over land is restricted by assum-ing patrilocal residence upon marriage (a restriction that is severely compli-cated when marriages end). As mothers, women cannot simultaneously main-tain farmland as *clan* land and endow their children with that land. These different positions (daughter, sister, mother) are not meant to be an exhaustive characterization of the life of any woman and certainly not of Haya women in general. But it is meant to suggest that over the ongoing, contentious, and fractious process of clan and family formation, women's capacity to control farm land is severely restricted and that, as a consequence of these restrictions, women's practical attempts to control farmland disposes them to both buying and selling.

Migration and Dislocation

Of course, the sociocultural significance of buying and selling land is not exhausted by these structural limits. The concrete Haya experience and conse-quences of land selling, for example, confirm the earlier characterization of money's dislocating potential. The refrain of a popular rural tune is "*Yaguz'eki-banja, yater'ekigendo!*" ("He sells his farm and makes tracks!"). This is a less than subtle critique of the young men, like Vedasto, who have sold family lands to acquire radios, clothing, beer, and, especially, bicycles. The "tracks" of this tune are literally the tire tracks of the speedy new bike. Again, the force of mobility is both a sign of luxury and a transformation of the farm's "stable" values. By many Haya, and throughout Africa, the dangers of mobility of this kind are also directly linked to sexual susceptibility, AIDS in particular. *New Vision* in Uganda (quoted in Bledsoe 1989, 204) reports: "Big men, traders, drivers to name but a few used to go to nearby schools to steal [seduce] girls and spoil them . . . Special hire men were in business by transporting men and women to nearby lodges," confirming an explicit connection between the vertiginous movements of transport and illicit sexuality.

The experience of those who must move their residence is seen (especially by those who do *not* move) as equally unsettling. As I mentioned in my discussion of food preparation techniques, most Haya prefer to live on the high, cool escarpments (*omugongo*, literally "on the back") that overlook Lake Victoria (see also Beattie [1957, 317] on similar preferences in Bunyoro). Those who move, in contrast, are seen as forced to move down to the valleys (*oluhita*). The life there is characterized as desperate. The people are unprotected from the hot sun, which brings disease and makes the land too dry to grow the bananas necessary for any proper Haya meal. The urban areas to which Haya might migrate in Tanzania in search of a living—especially the cities of Mwanza and, above all, the nation's capital, Dar es Salaam—are always described as "too hot!" An often repeated account suggests that Dar es Salaam is "so hot that you can't even cover yourself with a sheet when you lie down to sleep." Mobility, speed, and excessive heat are, then, bound up in the Haya understanding of land sales and their consequences, just as money is a condensation of these critical qualities.

Women have a less "fixed" relation to residential lands than do men because of the meanings of social practice, as well as its structural configuration, described above. In a patrilocal culture, the mobility of women is essential to social reproduction. Marriage is constituted by women's movement between the focal sites of agnatically held households. Moreover, this mobility is not simply women being moved by men; nor is it exclusively the movement of an individual woman from the house of her father to the house of her husband. Rather, there is a coordinated control of the complementary relation between women's mobility and men's fixity. Female kin, both matrilateral and agnatic, move together, accompanying new brides to their marital homes; provide prized crops that have often been cultivated by groups of women at *okuzilima* events; or work collectively to mourn and cook for other mourners in intervillage work parties. Movement is thus critical to the potential and productivity of women, but it is also a focus of restriction and control by men as well as other women. To return to the example of bridal seclusion, both men and women say that this practice is necessary in order to "calm down" a new wife and to ensure that she does not "run off." Moreover, any new groom is expected to have fevers in the first few days of marriage because of his intimate exposure to the extreme heat that is produced by a woman's body. At the same time, a bride in seclusion is expected to become fat and hot. In effect, the threatening heat of a newly married woman must be transformed into the generative heat of fertility and growth (*okugomoka* meaning both "to fatten" and "to get healthy") by this seclusion within her husband's house. These explicit concerns suggest both that women have a naturalized capacity and tendency for mobility and heat and that this tendency makes women less bound to the households and localities they occupy. Women's mobility and heat are clearly essential to household formation; marriage and reproduction are impossible without them. But they are dialectically opposed to men's focality, which always mediates women's attachments to a household. This dialectical relation, when well managed by both men and women, transforms ambiguous mobility and heat into generative households.

Given the spatiotemporal contrasts in these practical dimensions of gender identity, it is not surprising to find that a woman's capacity for movement is easily assimilated by men to the threat of dislocation and discontinuity. Women, like money, move in mysterious ways, often coming and going in the course of activities that seem incomprehensible to men.

The rhetorical reference to "buying her grave," then, presents a highly condensed statement about the position of women, and of gender relations more generally, at the crux of dynamic processes of sociocultural continuity. The grave, which is the essential site of focalization, the binding and returning of diffuse spatial and temporal phenomena to concrete localities, is undone by sales and purchases, the quintessential acts of disruption, dislocation, and uncontrolled mobility. The fact that it is women, in men's view, who are the agents of this disintegration is testament to men's own inability to comprehend this capacity for perpetual motion, which women seem to embody *and* command. To "buy a grave" when you think you are "getting rich" is not merely an ironic commentary on the terrible consequences of death for those who seek only their own gain. Rather, it is a statement about the ways in which sweeping transformations in economic and bodily conditions render impossible the very forms of death that allow for the living to realize and perpetuate their own well-being.

8 ELECTRIC VAMPIRES: FROM EMBODIED COMMODITIES TO COMMODITIZED BODIES

Rumors and Circulation

During my field research I occasionally heard reports of "greedy" people who had made their fortunes by stealing and selling other peoples' blood. As my neighbors talked with me about such diverse matters as the number of well-stocked stores in a particular town or the dangers of life in urban areas, they often brought up rumors of blood stealing. In their accounts, the victims of blood extraction and blood selling were not of much interest. I never heard anyone claim that someone they knew, or even knew of, had been murdered by blood sellers. What was of interest was the fact that vast sums of money could be made by such blood sellers, who acquired their victims by a variety of means. As one young Haya man described this phenomena to me:

> You can see a person who has a brick house, a store, cars. And you think a year ago he was the same as me, but he hasn't done any work. How did he get these things? You know he has been selling people's blood.

Wealth in itself, in such accounts, is not a sign of wrongdoing, but the perception of a sudden and inexplicable shift in fortunes can invite suspicion.

As the previous chapter illustrates, Haya discourses surrounding AIDS reveal many of the fissures in their contemporary sociocultural order. These ruptures relate not merely to affinal relations but to gender relations more generally, as well as to sites of contestation in clan and agnatic relations. And central to Haya concerns in their grappling with this epidemic and its attendant social implications is the sense of displacement it engenders. This same set of concerns can also be assessed in a somewhat different domain, in narrative forms of popular consciousness that describe such threatening and deceptive business transactions in human blood. The images these accounts elaborate reveal further Haya understandings of the importance of locality in relation to the control of wealth. They also re-pose important problems of embodiment—and disembodiment—in relation to the world of circulating commodities.

Cars, both icons and means of such circulation, were frequently cited in Haya rumors as objects typically acquired through such nefarious actions. While most rumors spoke of the practices of blood stealing in general terms and without reference to particular cases, the one named individual I knew of who was identified as being a blood seller was reported to have purchased his Land Rover with money made from his victims' blood. Moreover, this person was said to be using his car in order to further his bloody business. Owning a car enabled him to lure unsuspecting travelers looking for a lift into his car, and then to transport his victims' blood for sale outside the borders of Tanzania. Cars, in these accounts of blood stealing, are both the quintessential objects purchased through blood selling and a principal means of engaging in the blood trade.

The centrality of transport and travel is another important feature of blood stealing rumors. The most elaborated reports of blood stealing concern travel to urban areas, to Bukoba the capital of the Region, and especially to the town of Mwanza, a ferry's voyage across Lake Victoria. Several Haya told of *Matende* ("Evil Doers") at work in Mwanza employing a dangerous technological apparatus to procure their victims' blood. According to one typical report,

> There are houses in Mwanza where they steal people's blood. They use electricity, and your body, it dries up. They steal your blood and just toss your corpse into a big hole in the back. I have been in these houses! The front door is made of wood, and they have written "Danger, Electricity" (*Hatari: Umeme*) on it. But if you just touch it, straight away that electricity catches you and your blood is sucked out (*imevutiwa*).

In such cases I was told that blood stolen in this way could be sold to hospitals in Mwanza, Dar es Salaam, and Nairobi, to "specialists" (*wataalamu*) who knew what to do with human blood.

The final "type" of rumor circulating in Kagera while I was there has to do with youth (*vijana* in Swahili; usually synonymous with *abasigazi*, "unmarried *men*" in Haya) who are, as Haya villagers say, "lost in the city" (*babula omumji*). Young men who leave their rural homes in search of work in Bukoba, Mwanza, or beyond, are often said to be "lost," but in certain stories some young men become the victims of blood stealers. In these accounts, newly urban youth are kept alive by blood sellers who feed them very well so as to fatten them up in order to extract their blood every month (see White [1990a, 430] for a description of "pits" where men were kept "just like dairy cattle"). Urban areas in such reports as well as in the rumors of blood stealing by electrocution are places of extreme vulnerability and insidious activity, where even the apparent benefits of "eating well" and being "well-fed" can become a means of destruction.

These rumors of blood stealing seem to speak to the uneasy tensions that local cultural orders experience in the face of global political-economic processes. In these accounts the effects of commodities as forms of objectifying and displaying value or the ongoing project of urbanization and migration are represented as very immediate aspects of personal experience. And yet, even in the face of such powerful forces as these, the precise *nature* of that experience is not as predictable as one might expect. What is particularly arresting about reports such as these are the ways in which they clearly *conjoin* discourses of economics and physiology; they articulate the circulation of commodity forms and bodily fluids, and characterize certain qualities of monetary transaction and accumulation in the terms of physical destruction. The variety of these commonplace, popular experiences may be less well documented than the activities of international banking institutions or biomedical epidemiological projects, entities that are typically looked to as the *agents* of rapid social transformation. However, popular Haya experiences such as these are equally integral to the unfolding historical processes in which *both* local and global actors are engaged. In this chapter I explore the implications of blood stealing rumors as a particular Haya form of consciousness and in so doing attempt to assess what they reveal about the ways in which contemporary Haya imagine and construct their *own* place in making the history of which they are a part.

Looking for Work and Leaving Home

Stories of blood stealing clearly suggest that the pursuit of wealth is highly problematic in the East African context. Not only can the accumulation and display of particular forms of property be looked on with suspicion, but the very project of simply seeking to make a living, either by selling labor or engaging in trader, poses imminent dangers. To begin to comprehend these rumors and the iconic forms of evil they deploy, we have to examine the ways in which the people who tell and listen to them attempt to make a living; in turn, this requires that we understand a certain history of how the Haya are situated with respect to the *places* in which such material gains are sought. The Haya who shared these stories with me all lived in agrarian communities and were engaged to some degree with maintaining farms and fields. Although the rumors they exchanged were about urban areas and forms of work that are not centered on agricultural activities, it is critical to point out that these accounts of blood stealing are *not* merely exoticizing reports about the alien character of strange and remote locales told to the stable residents of familiar home regions. The people telling these stories were reporting on their own experiences in places they may have routinely traveled to, and those who listened were often equally well acquainted with these places. Even those who had never been as far as Bukoba were very much aware of the property that might be acquired through travel, as well as the means of transport that made this travel possible. Blood stealing rumors, then, despite their images of the unfamiliar, are less about the contrast between the country and the city and more about their *mutual* constitution (see Williams 1973). Indeed, the central themes of Haya rumors suggest that between country and city there are interconnections of the most intimate sort.

As a consequence of explicit colonial divisions imposed at the Berlin Conference of 1884–85—which split up East Africa into British and German "spheres of influence" just north of the precolonial Haya kingdom of Kiziba (Coulson 1982, 34)—Kagera is separated from Uganda by a national border. The Haya living in this region find themselves on the margins of the Tanzanian state with respect to Dar es Salaam, rather than integrated into the flow of traffic and trade surrounding Kampala, as Haya kingdoms were throughout the nineteenth century. Due to political ebbs and flows in the East African community in the postindependence period, culminating in the invasion of Uganda by Tanzanian forces in 1979, the border with Uganda has been little traveled in the 1980s.

The Kagera Region remains rather peripheral to the national transport system. It is possible to travel from Bukoba to Mwanza by ferry, and from Mwanza the railroad can be taken south and east to the capital, Dar es Salaam. This is a two-day trip, and the third-class compartments (a colonial "survival" in spite of Tanzania's African Socialism), which is what most Haya travelers could afford, are notoriously dangerous. The roads that connect Kagera to the rest of the nation are largely impassable, and there is no regular bus service that travels from Bukoba to Mwanza.

In spite of these obstacles, Haya do travel extensively throughout East Africa. The relation between Haya peoples and urban East Africa is long-standing and extensively documented. Many older men I spoke with recalled their military service in Tanga, Kampala, and Nairobi during World War II. White has evidence of Haya women arriving in Nairobi as early as the mid-1930's (White 1990b, 103). In contemporary Tanzania, many Haya routinely travel to Mwanza, where goods like clothing, soap, and housewares can be acquired for resale in Haya markets. Factory work is also occasionally available in Mwanza; those who come to either Mwanza or Bukoba with less certain prospects often make a temporary living selling goods, especially prepared foods and similar snacks, in roadside kiosks. In all of these cases, the stay in town, while it may last for a few years, is transitory. Traders return to market their wares, factory work is rarely long term, and those who rely on less dependable employment return home even more quickly.[1] In fact, White observes that a high rate of mobility with no attempt made to establish permanent residence in urban areas was the defining characteristic of Haya women's forms of prostitution in colonial Nairobi of the 1930s and 1940s, a residence pattern that is widely recognized as markedly distinct from other East African women who work as prostitutes (White 1990b, 103ff). Haya women were and continue to be motivated to migrate to urban areas in order to acquire resources that secure and enhance their standing in rural Haya communities. Again, this pattern of mobility indicates that an array of urban experiences insert themselves profoundly into rural ways of life through the continuous actions of coming and going.

Haya efforts to seek financial gain or employment have given many of them direct experiences of the world beyond their natal villages; but the form of this experience is largely itinerant and is characterized even in cases of long-term residence by rather tenuous attachments to urban locales. White's essential research on blood stealing in East and Central Africa has concentrated largely on the significance of blood stealing as a means of articulating this tenuous position and on disclosing disjunctures in the control of property relations and labor under colonial regimes through an *idiom* that rather strikingly objectifies notions of descent, inheritance, and productivity (White 1990a; 1993). The history of Haya engagement with East African urban life tells us that Haya experiences of work and property are similarly fraught with the tensions of uncertain control, and it is not surprising to find that the ways in which they describe the places where they seek such work and property are charged with the same graphic accounts of horrific physical destruction.

While I think the connection between rumors of blood stealing and the transforming colonial and neocolonial constructions of property relations is absolutely essential, I also think that the specific qualities of both the images of violence and bodily attack as well as the concrete, experiential dimensions of property, wealth, and value can be examined more closely. The characteristic semantic values of these material forces are not simply *represented* by such discursive forms; the meanings of the contemporary Haya political economy are in fact constituted by the *mutual* construction of personal experience *and* property relations. Blood, that is, is more than an idiom, it is an iconic form, a concretely experienced substance—in effect, a qualisign, as I argue below—

whose meanings actively inform the values of a transforming political economy. Property, money and commodities, I am suggesting, are significant features of Haya and other Africans' lives not only because of the transformations they bring about or because of what they do, but because the very meanings of property, commodities, and the like are created in the course of this unfolding historical process. Stories of blood stealing and blood selling, for example, tell us that aspects of the body can literally become commodities—indeed, commodities that can be reduced to the price of their constituent parts. But at the same time, these rumors indicate that for many Haya, the very processes of social transformation—from the technological forms of electrical wiring and automotive transport to the institutions of biomedicine, innovations that are, of course, dependent on the kinds of property relations characteristic of the colonial and neocolonial encounter—are concretely realized and made meaningful through their bodily effects. Put succinctly, components of Haya bodies not only become commodities, but the process of commoditization becomes embodied.

Circulations of Blood in the Body

The potential of blood described in these stories, as an *alienable* substance to be exchanged and evaluated according to a monetary measure, certainly seems to suggest a capacity for circulation that is inimical to Haya notions of blood. Yet blood is a tremendously generative fluid in Haya models of both physiology and sociality. According to Haya understandings of circulation, blood operates in ways which are dynamic and enabling. I want to address these understandings of circulation and transaction in order to asses their relevance to the conception elaborated in these rumors of blood as a *commodity* form; this in turn may allow us to appreciate precisely what kind of exchange *commodity* exchange is in the Haya world.

Within the body, according to the physiological theories offered to me by numerous neighbors and informants, blood is not simply a constant volume that is altered only by traumatic intervention.[2] Rather, the quality, consistency, and volume of blood is in constant flux in an active body. For example, Haya men and women often refer to the ability of certain foods to "increase the blood" (in Haya, *okukiza obwamba;* in Swahili, *kuongeza damu*) or to "decrease the blood" (in Haya, *okuiyao;* in Swahili, *kupunguza*). According to informants, meat (especially organ meats), leafy vegetables, and fish are held to increase blood, while bitter foods like black coffee and citrus fruits will decrease blood.

Moreover, the ability of blood volume to increase and decrease is not simply a matter of quantitative measure but of qualitative potential. Thus, blood content fluctuates according to the thermal properties of the body's situation. Blood itself is considered to give heat and energy to the body (one friend actually compared the function of blood in the body to petrol in a car), and increases or decreases in blood volume can be gauged by how hot or cold a person feels. For example, eating foods or engaging in activities that are considered particularly hot—foods such as chili peppers or certain bitter greens, and activities like working in direct sun or, in the case of newly married couples, excessive sexual activity—are frequently sighted as causes of illness such as feverish chills, which are characterized by a lack of blood. In the practical logic of Haya physiology, excessive heat causes the blood to "race" (in Haya, *okuiruka;* in Swahili, *kukimbia*) and "boil" (*okutagata*), which in turn diminishes blood volume. Women's bodies, by both women's and men's accounts, are held to have more heat than men's bodies,[3] and this heat leads directly to blood loss in the form of menstrual flow, which is held to be the hottest of all blood.

The thermal qualities of blood, and the management of blood volume are also of concern in relation to drinking, especially, as we have seen, to drinking distilled banana gin. Drinking gin to excess is typically conceived of as a sure way to cause the blood to race too quickly, heat up, and eventually diminish. A Haya hangover is typically described as feverish. In order to counteract the effects of banana gin, many Haya drink sweet, unfermented banana juice (*omulamba*) or eat fatty, deep-fried fish (always a popular seller at gin-drinks). Both sugar and fat are blood-building and *hot* substances that replenish the heat lost from drinking by restoring blood volume. Similarly, neighbors of mine often sat out in an area of direct sunlight after a day of excess in order to reheat their blood-reduced bodies.

These understandings of physiology add an important dimension to Haya concerns with the control of heat in sociocultural processes, which I have discussed at length, for they reveal a specific interest in the dynamic and thermodynamic qualities and potential of blood. Blood circulates within the body at variable rates. It can race ahead quickly or move slowly under certain conditions. The circulation of blood within the body is also intrinsically linked to a quantitative blood volume, as fast or slow blood tends to increase or decrease blood. These characteristics are further interconnected with the thermal qualities of blood, as relative heat influences both speed and volume. All of these dynamic, fluctuating properties suggest that blood is a substance whose shifting form can be taken as an acutely sensitive index of well-being. However, what is especially critical to point out is that the condition of well-being represented by blood is not merely an individuated condition of the physical body. Rather, the qualitative condition of the body is generated through the interrelation of *active* persons with the material world in which they are situated. Personal well-being is a *product* of particular ways of interacting with other subjects and with other objects; it is *realized* through practices like work and sexuality or eating and drinking. And the qualitative and quantitative state of blood concretely and directly signifies this interactive and practical process. Blood, in these Haya physiological conceptions, is iconic, perhaps even symptomatic, of the engaged character of persons and objects. This description of blood clearly follows my analysis of "growing fat" and "wasting away," each of which is iconic of the subject's well-being as signified by a capacity to control food (see also Munn's [1986, 17] analysis of such qualisigns). Blood, I would argue, is a more general medium, whose precise semantic qualities are more nuanced (hot, slow, increasing, etc.) and more sensitive to changes than are growing fat or thin. In this way the condition of blood can serve as an index of a general sense of "feeling" good or bad on a day-to-day or hour-to-hour basis. Blood signifies changing conditions of the body as an internalized aspect of a subject's relation to the wider world in which he or she acts.

The fact that blood can be dynamically and continuously transformed within the body in ways that signify shifting relations between the body and its encompassing situation is, I would argue, integral to Haya suspicions that blood could be converted to a commoditized object. These physiological understandings tell us that rumors of blood stealing do much more than simply make metaphoric connections between profit-making and murder. These rumors in fact suggest that certain aspects of commoditization can eclipse the capacity of the body to act effectively, that is, to produce itself through engaging in productive collective activity. Moreover, given the concern with enclosure and interiority that is so crucial to Haya control of productive activity, it is significant that blood is not only removed from the body but literally whisked away in cars. These local understandings of extraordinary exposure, extraction, and mobility speak to an ominous challenge that undermines the kind of secured containment integral to viable social practice. Even those who seem to enjoy the benefits of being well fed, so strongly embedded in these sociospatial qualities, are ultimately doomed. In effect, these victims embody the kind of "worries" that Haya generally recognize can cause a person to eat abundantly without generating and demonstrating the productive values of food, without ever "growing fat." It is this capacity for effective and productive action, what amounts to a Haya bodily dimension of agency, that is indexed and experienced through blood, and therefore extracted and appropriated through blood stealing.

Power Embodied and Extracted

The qualitative dimensions of blood as both a substance that can be transformed by food and heat and a resource that must provide heat and energy in the body point to its enabling aspects as well. Blood conditions clearly *signify* the potential of the body in the ways I have described. But these Haya accounts also indicate that blood *is* the potential of the body. This dual form of signification—the fact that blood both provides a concrete *index* of a general bodily capacity and also intrinsically *embodies* that capacity—provides a critical connection to the commodity forms that circulate in these stories and in Haya experiences.

To begin with, it hardly seems accidental that blood should be compared with gasoline and that blood stealing should be so strongly associated with owning cars. While the suggestion was never made to me that blood could be used in place of petrol, the very point of these accusations, it seems to me, is that blood can be *converted* into gasoline when it is sold. This convertibility is essential to the activities of blood sellers, and (to follow Marx) the seemingly infinite potential to interconvert objects created by monetary values is an essential feature of commodity exchanges. However, this dimension of commoditization is not sufficient by itself to account for the meanings associated with transformations in processes of exchange and conversion. The fact of convertibility tells us little about the *specific* objects or the various *forms* of conversion that stories such as these suggest are characteristic of contemporary Haya experience.

For example, the link between transport and commodities in Africa, as described in Haya accounts of paths and roads, has been much discussed in recent scholarship (Bastian 1990; Masquelier 1992; White 1993). These arguments focus on the connections between the space of colonial road systems, high degrees of mobility, and privatized control over the mechanisms of mobility; and the potential for commodities and capital to dislodge and transform the ways in which persons construct and control the spatial order of the worlds they inhabit. Here, I want to suggest that a further aspect of these connections can be seen in the substantive qualities of both blood and gasoline. I have argued that in Haya understandings, the power, or *potency,* of blood is achieved and utilized through the control and regulation of heat. The fact that blood and gasoline, as well as electricity (which I discuss later) are all hot substances is, as I have demonstrated, quite relevant to this commoditized nexus. In Haya experiences, buying and selling and the pursuit of money in general are hot procedures. These activities may involve travel to hot distant cities or require migration to arid farmland. If, as we have seen, it is blood in the body that is especially susceptible to depletion through exposure to excessive *heat*, it is not surprising to find that gasoline, cars, electricity, and money—all of which are integral to activities that are considered significantly hot—can be construed as central to the radical extraction of blood.

Beyond its substantive properties, the *form* of power and potential objectified by blood suggests further connections with these processes and experiences of commoditization. Haya statements suggest that blood is both a means of empowering the body as well as a *medium* that allows other sources of power (i.e., specific foods or other bodily conditions) to be converted into bodily power. This characteristic poses some intriguing similarities to electricity, another technological capacity notable for its associations with blood stealing. Electricity itself certainly suggests connections with the blood-depleting effects of extreme speed and heat, particularly at a moment when the Haya say that "*AIDS yairuka nk'obumeme*" ("AIDS is racing like electricity"). There is no electrical power provided to households throughout the region, but many individual buildings, especially hospitals and occasionally government offices, do generate their own electrical supply. Most Haya residing in rural areas are familiar with electrical power through their encounters with institutions such as these. This context in which electricity is experienced—the actual buildings, generators, and phone lines that for many Haya so tangibly *are* the State, in both its colonial and neocolonial incarnations—make electricity a form of power that is not only beyond the control of even elite rural people, but also a *threat* to the control of value they can exert, for such institutions concretely embody a structure of privileged appropriation that has forcefully reconfigured the rural moral landscape.

Batteries used to operate radios, cassettes, flashlights, and the like make electricity a somewhat more pervasive and available commodity. But the effective control of electricity, especially on the scale implied by electrified blood stealing, remains elusive. The weak life of the ineffective batteries available in Tanzania (a very common topic of Haya complaints) confirms this elusive character. As a form of property or commodity, then, electricity is very much like the automotive transport with which it is associated in popular consciousness. Both of these high-speed media are markedly privileged resources, something well beyond the means of most people, that are owned and operated only by those who can afford to procure them for themselves.

As a form of *power*, that is, as a specific potential or capacity for effective action, electricity is often spoken of, not only as a *source* that provides power to other mechanisms, but as a *substance* that is *identified* with the products of those mechanisms. For instance, in many Haya descriptions, the radiance of electric lighting is not simply said to be produced by electricity, it actually *is* electricity. The rumors of blood stealers in Mwanza would seem to be based on such a conception of electricity as well. Remember that in these accounts, the door to the blood stealers' house is made of wood, but when you touch it you are instantly "caught by electricity." Electricity, here, does not operate through some other mechanism; rather, it contains within itself the capacity to effect certain results. The victims, in these accounts, are not killed by electrified property, they are caught by electricity itself.

This view of electricity suggests that certain Haya understandings of substance and power are founded on notions of causality and efficacy that condense the product of a procedure into its source. I have indicated earlier that Haya experiences of plastic reflect a similar understanding of the ways in which process and product are embodied in commoditized objects. In this regard, electricity can be seen as a form of energy that can be both supplied to various mechanisms as well as directly experienced. Blood, as I have described it, seems to be a similar substance. It is both intrinsically a form of power and capacity, one that manifests a range of different qualities; but it is also experienced as the most immediate index of the body's power, a medium in terms of which other resources (the sun, gin, red meat, etc.) can be expressed in bodily terms. As they are represented in a range of Haya activities and discussions, electricity and blood can be seen to be similar configurations of potential. And these similarities do seem relevant to their conjunction in these stories of blood stealing. However, such similarities also point to the fact that blood stealing rumors are not about the easily reconciled compatibility of blood and electricity as forms of power. Indeed, they suggest that these meaningful compatibilities can provide a pathway for uneasy transformations.

Part of the significance of these transformations can be seen in the very different applications of these alternative forms of power. Electricity, for many Haya, is a form of energy that is simultaneously concrete and diffuse. It can be directly seen in electrical lighting, but it can also be encapsulated in batteries. It is a singular source of power, and yet it can serve a seemingly infinite array of mechanisms. Thus, electricity conflates singularity and multiplicity in a way which suggests the hypermutability of power, a capacity that is also discernible in the qualities and appearance of plastic. This sense of diffusion can be seen in the description of the blood sellers' building, where electricity seems to pervade the entire structure of the house. In effect, those who are "caught by electricity" are ensnared in its capacity for permeable transposition. Perhaps the ultimately deceptive warning "Danger: Electricity" is meant to indicate not that electrical power is contained within but that electricity is essentially uncontainable. Moreover, this form of uncontained permeable power identified with certain urban architectural forms is certainly at odds with Haya domestic productivity, which is predicated on carefully demarcated enclosure.

In elucidating these distinctive properties I do not mean to suggest that Haya conceptions of electricity are somehow inadequate or mystified. Many of my Haya friends devised elaborate adaptors and mechanisms to use oversized batteries in minuscule cassette players, which amply demonstrated that if anyone's knowledge of electricity was inadequate, it was my own. What I do mean to suggest is that the power of electricity has distinctive applications in Haya experiences, and these particularities help to shape its concrete meanings. Moreover, these distinctive possibilities indicate that although electricity and blood may be similar *forms* of power, the contexts in which they are deployed make electricity into what might be seen as an anti-blood. Where electricity is a diffused and highly mutable source, blood is necessarily localized and absolutely specific. While the same batteries can be and often are transferred from radios to cassettes to flashlights, human blood is *productive* only in the human body.

I emphasize productive because, of course, human blood can be powerful outside of the body. As I indicated in my discussion of the crossroads (a site where diseased blood can be passed on to unsuspecting passersby), exposure to discarded blood or, worse, the unmediated ingestion of another person's blood is a sure way to contract disease, and would almost certainly be attributed to sorcery. Haya did engage in blood brotherhood relationships, a practice that entails the exchange of blood (*okunywana*, literally "to drink each other"; see also Beattie 1958a). Through these practices, however, Haya always stressed to me that they were creating "one blood" out of two different men but also out of two different clans. The implication is that blood is not a generalizable substance that can empower different bodies, but rather that each body is categorically *different*. Any *similarities* between them must, therefore, be carefully constructed—that is, blood brothers must be *made* into men of "*one* blood" when they begin as two. Moreover, the physical connection that is created through blood brotherhood is one that does not *encourage* the interchange and circulation of bodily substance, but actually creates regulations that further restrict and delimit such circulations. That is, one of the principle effects of blood brotherhood is that it establishes exogamous prohibitions, not only for the "blood" relations of the two men who enter into blood brotherhood but for all members of their two clans. Marital exchanges extending to persons quite distant from the blood brothers themselves are thus cut off through this exchange of blood. In marked contrast to the hypertransposability and generalizable applications of electrical power, then, blood works only within the body and only within the *specific* body in which it originates or those who have been *made into* members of that "one" body. Indeed, according to both members of the staff at Rubya Hospital and my lay informants, Haya considered blood transfusion a threatening procedure even prior to widespread local concerns about AIDS. Thus, while the contexts of convertibility for electricity seem limitless, blood's capacity to be converted is much more narrowly defined. Attempts to *distribute* the potency of blood outside of its strictly regulated position in the body, therefore results in a radical subversion of its proper effects.

Of Cannibals and Vampires

Thus far I have described various Haya accounts and experiences as they relate to distinctive constructions of power, in the specific sense of a potential or capacity for action. The forms of power embodied in blood, gasoline, and electricity, and the range of qualities that are interrelated through these forms reveal certain correspondences between these different substances, correspondences that suggest the appropriateness of their being brought into direct relation in blood stealing rumors. Similarities in the ways in which these substances are experienced, especially in terms of their thermodynamic potentials, are recognizable. Important inversions in the experience of these dynamic substances are also evident, particularly in the ways in which their distinct potentials are applied and distributed. But the semantic configuration and interpenetration of all of these forms—as when blood races like electricity or fuels the body like petrol in a car—demonstrate the fact that they are mutually defined and redefined in the processes of ongoing social changes.

The semantic features of these accounts, features that are simultaneously about power, are crucial to their contemporary expression in Haya consciousness. But these stories are not simply about the imaginative correspondence and free transposition of one symbolic substance for another. In fact, what motivates these correspondences, both establishing and organizing the specific relations between these substances, is not just blood stealing by means of cars and electricity but the fact that blood can be sold to create wealth.

The principal means that blood stealers have of making money, according to these stories, is to sell their victims' blood to hospitals, a claim that should tell us something about local perceptions of biomedicine. Practical attitudes toward medical treatment, according to the reports of regional hospitals themselves, are skeptical at best. One hospital estimated that only 12 percent of women in the area have their children delivered under any kind of biomedical supervision; they also estimate that the population of AIDS cases in the region is roughly six times higher than the population that ever seeks medical treatment.

The community I lived in has a lengthy familiarity with biomedical practice. A local hospital was established by Dutch Franciscan missionaries over thirty years ago. Originally administered by the regional diocese, it has recently been named a district designate hospital and is now subsidized by and run in conjunction with the state.[4] One of many results of this transition is that medical care and pharmaceuticals are provided free of charge to the resident population. This is a change that, in the main, has *not* been well received. Many Haya men and women made their feelings known to me on this subject. A typical complaint was: "If you go to the hospital and tell them you have malaria, what will they give you? *Vitamins!* That hospital is free, it's of no benefit at all!" Indeed, those with any means tend to seek attention at other regional hospitals that charge for their services.

Of course, the reception of biomedicine, and the ways in which its practices are articulated with or kept at a distance from indigenous systems of therapy and health management, is a complex issue, with an uneven history throughout Africa and the Third World more generally (Young 1978; Janzen 1982). The Haya experiences and claims I have described, from routine problems with local dispensaries to the services of plastic teeth extractors, indicate that local interactions with biomedical health care are ambivalent at best. But the special concern many Haya express with regard to the cost of health care in relation to its benefits reveals that over the course of their ongoing relations with local hospitals Haya have come to evaluate biomedical efficacy in monetary terms. In effect, the bodily experience of health acquires a price when it is mediated by the institutions of biomedicine, and this recognition certainly seems to make the understanding of blood as a valuable commodity more plausible.

However, the significance of bodily commoditization, especially as it is configured in the nefarious acts of stealing and selling blood, is not reducible to experiences of hospitals, transfusions, and medical fees. We also have to pay attention to the consequences of blood *selling,* not only for the biomedical enterprise that purportedly purchases blood but for those who *sell* it, to begin to understand the meanings of these kinds of transactions. Recall that the wealth accumulated by reputed blood sellers seems not only extravagant but especially mysterious. Indeed, the fact that such riches are suddenly and *inexplicably* possessed is taken as evidence of their illicit acquisition.[5] What is particularly unfathomable is the sudden *discrepancy* in wealth, the rapid accumulation of goods by those who one once knew and recognized as economic equals.

This concern with the relation of knowledge to the relative wealth of one's neighbors along with a recognition of inexplicable rises and declines in economic fortunes suggests important connections with another form of Haya popular consciousness, namely, a concern with sorcerers (*abarogi*). Reports about the activities of sorcerers, frequently neighbors and kin, are a pervasive theme in Haya conversation. Virtually every funeral that I attended was accompanied by suspicions that death was brought on by such malevolent actors. Haya friends told me that sorcerers act out of "obstinacy" (*oluango*, literally "refusal," from the verb *okuanga*, "to refuse"). "He doesn't like to see that you exceed him" (in Swahili, *Hataki kuona kwamba wewe unamzidi*) is a standard description of a sorcerer, as I indicate in the discussion of meals and refuse. "Jealousy" is the way anthropologists have generally translated African terms for the sorcerer's motivations, and this word might be applied in the Haya case; but it must also be remembered that Haya sorcerers are clearly not driven by a desire to possess what others who "exceed" them possess but rather by an ambition to destroy those others completely. No sorcerer that I heard of ever accumulated a fortune by destroying his or her victims, and wealthy people were less likely to be suspected of being sorcerers than they were of being potential victims of sorcery.

These popular rumors of both blood stealing and sorcery present icons of evil that are intimately connected with perceived economic[6] differences within the Haya community. Yet, interestingly, blood selling, according to my Haya sources, is categorically *not* the same as sorcery.[7] To begin with, we can see that blood sellers and sorcerers represent differences within a community in opposing ways. Whereas blood sellers embody an idea of sudden, inexplicable (and implicitly illicit) advantage and inequality, sorcerers always act to radically invert these very sorts of inequality. Moreover, the wealth accumulated by blood sellers is conceived of as arising from unknown and impenetrable sources, while most Haya fear that neighbors who are constantly scrutinizing their households (those who "have the evil eye," *baina ekiisho*) are likely sorcerers.[8] Blood selling is made evident by tangible *displays* of wealth, while sorcerers are obtrusive *observers* of internal household resources.

Blood selling and sorcery not only embody alternative "visions" of economic inequalities, they are characterized by alternative actions on the human body. Blood sellers, as we have seen, sell their victims' blood in order to acquire houses, cars, and the like; but sorcerers, by most Haya accounts, kill their victims in order to dig up their corpses and eat them. These distinctive forms of consumption tell us something about the ways in which the significance of property relations and economic transaction are constituted and embodied in Haya experience.

Blood sellers make use of their victims by a decomposition of their constituent *parts*.[9] The victims' blood is always thoroughly extracted and alienated from the rest of their body. This is no mere trivial observation, for the rumors themselves focus on and elaborate this aspect of the blood stealers' actions. Once the bodies are drained of blood, the victims' corpses are merely piled up in open holes, an image of chaotic death and *burial* that Haya find as horrific as the idea of blood stealing itself. The lost young men, kept like cattle in the city, present another image of bodily detotalization. These young men's bodies are effectively converted into transactable units by this blood-sucking operation. Blood thereby becomes a resource, a *utility* that is thoroughly separable from the context in which it is produced.

By contrast, sorcerers in the Haya context are interested in much more than the fragments of their victims' lives; they seek to encompass them completely. Death and burial, as we have seen, establish a fixity and finality in personal identity; and it is the finalized identity established through mortuary that is the sorcerer's true object. As I have indicated, Haya descriptions of sorcerers always elaborate their techniques for exhuming newly buried bodies, and certain amulets are buried with a corpse in order to prevent this from happening. By eating their victims' corpses, sorcerers finish off, in effect, the completed and total person. This form of consumption is also in keeping with the sorcerers' excessive scrutiny of their potential victims while they are alive. Sorcery establishes a thoroughgoing identification between sorcerers and their victims, an identification that proceeds from intrusive observation through exhumation and consumption of the finalized corpse.

These characteristic actions of the sorcerer reveal important correspondences (albeit in the form of inversion) to many of the fundamental qualities of Haya productivity and viability discussed throughout part 1. The concern with the sorcerers' invasive scrutiny and observation of the household confirms the centrality of *enclosure* as an essential characteristic of domestic activities. It also demonstrates that this spatiotemporal pattern is not only a matter of concrete forms or practical techniques, but one that is intrinsic to what I described as Haya *sociality*, a basic orientation that Haya households and persons have toward each other. The understanding of neighbors as ever-present witnesses, carefully evaluating fluctuations in household fortunes, as a most insidious threat, demonstrates how crucial (and so, how fragile) are Haya attempts to establish their household as an acknowledged locus of independence, self-sufficiency, and separation from surrounding "others."

The fact that cannibalism, *eating* the dead is the ultimate expression of this threatening agency also reveals how central the practices surrounding (food) consumption are to this model of domestic security. The preparation and presentation of food within the home and literally behind closed doors ensures the kind of enclosure that is essential to the viability and endurance of the household. The dramatic disinterment of a household's recently deceased member enacts a violent dislocation on a number of levels. Such an activity not only suggests the graphic and shameless exposure of eating (which in itself should be kept from view) and its consequent threat to household productivity; it also clearly portends the disruption of underlying processes of generativity, which, as the admonishments about "buying a grave" also make clear, are so deeply embedded in Haya family farms. Cannibalism of this sort, then, signals a totalizing dislocation and disorientation of the household and the immediate landscape it inhabits. It is a form of undoing that is deeply rooted in (and hostile to) the practices, techniques, and spatiotemporal organization of domestic life as well as to the forms of property that sustain it.

On the other hand, blood stealers present a threat that is oriented toward a different form of property and transaction, an orientation that is concretized in their distinct use of their victims' bodies. The threat of blood stealers is not something that emerges in the context of landholding disputes, which is so often the case in sorcery accusations. Blood stealers are, instead, a model of "business" taken to its horrifically logical conclusion. Indeed, I would argue that it is even misleading to describe their actions as "vampirism"; for "true" vampires (at least in their Euro-American (re)incarnations)—with their sexual as well as alimentary interests in their victims and the fact that they sustain their own eternal lives, as opposed to lining their pockets, with the bodily substance of their victims—are bound up in the kinds of intimacy and destruction that are of little interest to blood stealers. Instead, blood stealers convert their victims into transactable resources, while it is sorcerers, through their totalizing consumption, who make the very practice of transaction with others an impossibility for their victims. Thus, while blood stealers present the tangible evidence of economic success, however tainted it may be, sorcery, say many Haya, is bad for business.

Diabolical Divisions and Articulations

Presenting the contrast between blood stealers and sorcerers in this way clearly demonstrates that the changing social worlds in which such actors are situated inextricably fuses political economic and semantic processes. This contrast suggests, for example, that a putatively economic category like "consumption" can be assessed only by breaking it down into specific historical modalities. The concrete forms of consumption, from appropriation to accumulation to purchase to ingestion, must then be related to the variety of practical contexts in which they are configured. These practical contexts reveal some of the ways in which the meanings of blood, heat, speed, and the like construct the values of commodities, while the forces of market transactions simultaneously appropriate bodily conditions and capacity.

At another level, blood stealing rumors demonstrate dialectical relations of a different sort. The contrast between blood stealing and sorcerers is not to be taken as indicative of a historical *transition* between discrete spheres of transaction or regimes of value. Blood stealers embody economic inequalities generated through skillful transactions, the very phenomena sorcerers attempt to subvert. But local understandings of sorcery have been penetrated by the same forces that pervade its iconic representation of blood stealing. Sorcery is not something that threatens some set of exchanges that are clearly demarcated from the market transactions exploited by blood sellers. Rather, both forms of consciousness indicate that all such activities have become inextricably conjoined in the contemporary world. The connection of sorcerers to money, landholding, and consumer goods is as firmly a part of these forms of Haya consciousness as are the links of certain businessmen to blood and corpses.

On the surface these stories may appear to be concerned with contrasts between former ways of life and the hazards of the modern world. However, they clearly address notions of power and capacity, and represent forms of efficacy and potential that underlie commodities, bodies, and the actions in which they engage. In short, rumors such as these describe a series of articulations, articulations that illustrate connections between bodies and commodities, semantic values and economic transactions, rural livelihoods and urban travels, as well as local "experience" and global "events."

9 CONCLUSIONS: THE ENCHANTMENT OF THE DISENCHANTED WORLD

This study of contemporary Haya culture and society has attempted to demonstrate the relevance of symbolic dimensions of quotidian activity and experience to an understanding of broad political economic processes. My analysis of these issues proceeds from a concern with the construction of a lived world, an order of spatial and temporal relations created by persons engaged in productive practice, that simultaneously orients and motivates those social agents. In the course of their actions, Haya men and women are making and unmaking this world of objects and places, a world that has become infused with powerful possibilities, both alluring and threatening.

The effects of such powerful processes as labor migration, cash crop production for a world market, and commoditization more generally have often been considered so encompassing as to overwhelm and undermine the efforts of peoples like the Haya to assert their own agency as they pursue their livelihood. It has become commonplace to assert that social transformations at the peripheries of the so-called "world system" entail the systematic marginalization of culturally determined orders of activity and experience, as meaning itself is rendered irrelevant to a calculus of rational interests. Such theories tend to argue, as my discussion of Taussig suggested, that modernity not only transforms the relation of subjects to objects and persons to each other, but that it decisively severs these relations, producing only "alienation" out of what was once "authentic" value.

This view of social transformation corresponds to what Bourdieu calls "the disenchantment of the world" (1979, 1–94), a moment at which the "economic function" of activity becomes recognized as distinguishable from its "social function" (26) by the social agents of that activity. Bourdieu's understanding of this process is noteworthy, and particularly relevant to the arguments and analyses that I have put forward, because of the terms in which he conceptualizes this transformation or what he describes as an "adaptation to the capitalist economy" (6). The analyses Bourdieu proposes proceed from his trenchant observation that "the functioning of any economic system is tied to the existence of a definite system of dispositions towards the world, and more precisely towards time" (6). My analyses of Haya sociocultural processes have been equally concerned with the nature of these "dispositions" and with their temporal (as well as spatial) character. However, the ways in which I have described Haya sociocultural activities are also clearly different from Bourdieu's account of Kabyle practice. I want to draw attention to these differences as a way of summarizing the ethnographic themes of these analyses and of suggesting some important theoretical conclusions to my argument.

The reciprocal aspect of Bourdieu's notion of disenchantment is his vision of the enchanted social world. Again, Bourdieu demonstrates this view of enchantment through his account of the temporal form of the "pre-capitalist economy." In such an economy, consciousness of the future (*le futur*) best reveals the character of social practices. For Bourdieu, pre-capitalist dispositions construct the future as a time of "forthcoming" (*à venir*), which is "implicit in the directly perceived present" (6). Perhaps Bourdieu's clearest example of the forthcoming character of the future is the Kabyle agrarian production cycle, in which agricultural products are immanent in agricultural practices (10). This understanding of the passage of time as a *possibility* embedded in immediate conditions at hand recalls Thompson's understanding of the "task-orientation" in noncapitalist contexts (1967, 60).

This notion of "forthcoming" is certainly an important insight of Bourdieu's more general theory of practice. The fact that future possibilities can be grasped in present contexts, or that certain activities are "pregnant" with their potential outcomes (Bourdieu 1979, 10) seems to suggest that temporality is constructed in the course of social action, an argument that I have made throughout my analyses. However, in Bourdieu's view, this quality of temporality is only characteristic of an "enchanted" social system. For Bourdieu, the embedding of a temporal order in social practices is linked to activities that have "no other goal than to ensure reproduction of the economic and social order" (26). In effect, pre-capitalist dispositions result in a consciousness of time that is strictly repetitive and static. Indeed, Bourdieu claims that "the practices of fore-sight [i.e., activities oriented toward the forthcoming future] stem from the desire to *conform to inherited models*" (9, emphases added). In his view, practices disposed to a forthcoming future "enchant the experience of time [*la durée*] by magico-religious stereotyping of the techniques or rituals which [tend] to make the unfolding of time 'the moving image of eternity'" (26). Such enchanted social worlds, it would seem, resemble those of the "fortunate" Nuer for whom "time is an illusion" (Evans-Pritchard 1940, 107). Thus, while the notion of "forthcoming" implies that temporality is created through practical activities, Bourdieu ultimately dispenses with actual time itself by grounding such pre-capitalist activities in a timeless social order.

I have tried to specify the implications of Bourdieu's views of temporality, and of "forthcoming" in particular, because they are quite relevant to my ethnographic account of Haya sociocultural practices and to the phenomeno-logical perspective developed in my description of these practices. I have as-sessed the forthcoming character of productive Haya activities across a number of fields. In Haya house entering activities, I noted the ways in which fires can establish points of origin that encapsulate within themselves the trajectory of a household's "life." This point of a household's origin becomes a terminus at the conclusion of the household head's life and upon the establishment of descen-dant generations. This pattern of periodicity in time is characteristic of Haya agricultural practice on the family farm, as banana plants embody a cycle that is more than merely repetitive or cyclical, but one which is oriented toward forthcoming generations of plants. This periodicity actually creates the tem-poral pattern of the agrarian cycle. In the culinary activities surrounding the hearth, forms of consumption as realized in certain bodily conditions (e.g., growing fat, going hungry, or eating well), the socialization process of infants and children, and the inheritance of family lands, I continually pointed to the ways in which the products of Haya processes are seen to be immanent in the nexus of temporal relations that give rise to them.

I would add that there are spatial interrelations that implicate, if not *antici-pate,* each other, as the notion of forthcoming suggests. Thus, Haya forms of "enclosure" typically entail forms of exclusion and inclusion. We saw this most clearly at the level of the physical house, where interior space implied the exclusion of exterior space, a dialectic that is realized through a whole host of domestic activities. This dialectical character in spatiality could also be seen in the form of gifts that worked both to define *interior* space (through wrapping, tying, etc.) as well as to establish *distance* between households (as in the visible display of gifts and the significance of vision to sociality and hierarchy). These co-implied spatial relations are also apparent in Haya constructions of the body, where, as the case of the infant's relation to food suggests, proper en-closure and differentiation *from* the world also demonstrates adequate integra-tion *into* the world. Haya constructive processes (from socialization through planting techniques) seem especially concerned with constructing these dimen-sions of space as integral aspects of Haya agency and engagement in the world. This kind of simultaneous multidirectional orientation, a form of embeddedness in place that allows an encompassing spatial orientation to be grasped as a whole, might be thought of as a spatial complement to temporal dispositions toward a forthcoming future.

Although these temporal (and spatial) relations might indicate Haya dispositions toward the forthcoming products of actions, I have also tried to demonstrate that even the routinized or "stereotypic" activities of everyday life are in no way static or guided by a strict conformity to past models of action. Practices as varied as burying a clansmen and preparing cassava have potential consequences for changing the world, which may make their outcomes uncertain. Haya men and women often challenge the categories of everyday activities (Was your food purchased, or farm-raised? Do you brew beer for flavor or for money? Is a woman's "business" going to secure access to land for her children, or simply buy her a grave?) in ways that open the significance of these activities to explicit, often quite public, debate. Further, unequal access to the control of such activities—as in the systematic attempts to exclude women from *ekibanja* farmland or, more directly, the ability of royals to alienate land from commoners in the early colonial period—is typical of Haya social relations. This means that even the most standardized practices in which potential future outcomes seem to be immediately grasped in the present can be threatened, undermined, or transformed by forces that can interrupt this temporal unfolding. The Haya processes I have described indicate that dispositions toward the future as a forthcoming possibility do not prevent sociocultural practices from being *politicized*. The temporal form of these practices does not doom them to mindless repetition, for Haya temporality embodies the power to produce and control action.

If "forthcoming" is a form of temporal consciousness characteristic of precapitalist contexts, a disposition toward the future that guides action in the "enchanted" world, then "disenchantment" occurs when the future can no longer be grasped as "forthcoming" but must instead be "forecast" (Bourdieu 1979, 8). According to Bourdieu, capitalist economic activity demands a view of the future that is abstract, and this abstraction severs the "organic unity which united the present of labor with its 'forthcoming' [future]" (8). This abstraction of time is most strongly associated with "the spirit of calculation" (17), as it is rational calculation of potential outcomes that allows one to *forecast* the future, whereas previously the forthcoming products of an act could be immediately grasped in the present. As Bourdieu puts it, "rational calculation [has] to make up for the absence of an intuitive grasp of the process as a whole" (10), as though pre-capitalist labor were both mystically "enchanted" and naturally intuitive.

I have already discussed throughout this work my differences with theorists such as Bourdieu who posit such clear-cut oppositions between pre-capitalism and capitalism, gifts and commodities, meaningful relations and rational trans-actions. While Bourdieu's interest in temporality and temporal consciousness does seem a useful methodological focus for analyses of social transformation, his shift from the embodied, concrete, immanent forms of experience to a world of abstraction and alienation makes it difficult to account for the fact that temporality is grasped and concretized even in capitalist economies. My analy-ses of Haya practices, on the other hand, has paid particular attention to the ways in which the experience of commodities is grounded not only in the body (as in the cases of plastic teeth, AIDS, and blood stealing) but in the symbolic qualities of productive processes—in the ways, for example, that money is related to heat and speed and that the control of commodities like banana gin, fried fish, and bicycles is bound up with the spatial constructions of enclosure and movement. Yet, Bourdieu's analysis makes it seem as though the bodily anchorage of temporal consciousness and the condition of being *as* time ceases to exist under capitalism (see also Battaglia 1992 for a similar critique of the contrast between embodiment and inscription).

There is one final dimension of Bourdieu's argument that is critical to my own analyses and suggests an important theoretical conclusion for this eth-nography. According to Bourdieu, pre-capitalist dispositions not only avoid rational calculation, they seek to negate convertibility in exchange relations. The difficulty of money in pre-capitalist contexts is both that it requires a "fore-casting" of the future, a calculation of potential products whose outcome can be grasped in the indeterminate form of money; but also that it converts temporal values via an economic calculus into financial values (Bourdieu 1979, 13). This convertibility is an anathema in the "enchanted" world where "the rule of the game is that objective convertibility and calculability must never appear as such" (21).

These problems of calculability and conversion are at the very heart of the matter in my analyses. I have indicated that, indeed, Haya practices do seek to enclave important objects from monetary transactions. Food grown at home or family farmland—to say nothing of bodily fluids like blood—are not willingly or readily converted into cash. However, convertibility also proved to be a recurring theme in my description of Haya lived world, and especially in the dynamic process of production at numerous levels.[1] At one level, conversion can be thought of in terms of transformations in substance. For example, certain qualities of heat can be produced that are conversions of particular kinds of food (fat and spicy, or moist and soft). In other contexts, Haya men and women also think of these qualitative conditions as conversions of the form of an activity (i.e., its speed, direction, degree of mobility). At another level, the idea of conversion is integral to the problem of mutability, that is, to the ways in which the production and development of objects or persons can be traced through a series of stages. Thus, the generative potential of a household can be converted into the fertility of a banana crop; or the consumption of food by a child can be converted into health and independent agency; or the value of beer can be regulated by manipulating the conversion of beer bananas into beer. Each of these processes are explicitly characterized as a series of conversions, and their relative success is evaluated in terms of how well these conversions are carried out.

Embedded in all of these processes is the idea of conversion as a concrete means of reckoning differential values through commensurate forms. For example, my analyses began by looking at food as a condensation of particular values. Through these analyses we saw that food is an object into which all sorts of other objects and practices can be converted. The reasons for a host of actions, from marriage to raising children to migrating to a different village are all routinely evaluated or accounted for by many Haya in terms of their consequences for providing food. In addition, relative shifts in personal well-being— both in the bodily terms of weight gain and fortitude as well as in (re)productive terms of the number of children one has or the kinds of agricultural activities one can engage in—are all experienced and signified through food as a condensed medium of conversion. The bodily dimensions of these processes also emerge in relation to blood as a medium of conversion. Blood is the primary medium by which efficacy can be evaluated in bodily terms. For example, the effects of particular foods, or of particular kinds of activities are converted into relative decreases or increases in blood level and thereby evaluated. Values can be made commensurate through their relation to blood, just as states of being and health are analyzable in relation to their consequences for blood. Blood is, therefore, a critical medium of conversion for Haya productive processes.

Convertibility also provides a means of comparing different kinds of productive processes in the Haya sociocultural order and therefore can lend insight into the transformation of that order. We have seen, for example, how different *rates* of conversion are indicative of the kinds of value that can be embodied in the products of a production process. This is essential to the value of different kinds of food (hot vs. ripe, soft vs. hard, moist vs. dry) as well as beer (slow vs. fast, cool vs. hot, gustatory pleasure vs. financial gain). In addition to the speed or rapidity of conversion, the extension and variability of conversion is crucial to the significance of productive processes. In bodily terms, I described the extensions of blood as a medium that converts the values of a wide range of substances and activities into bodily qualities. The same is true of food, which condenses a breadth of social values into a tangible medium. This dimension of variability, or what I have also called mutability, is especially crucial for evaluating the meanings that Haya attribute to commodity forms and to money itself. Haya images of commoditization—both in bodily conditions like AIDS, plastic teeth, or even fever, as well as in the qualities of specific commodity forms like automobiles and electrical lighting—consistently instantiate a concern with the mutability of form and the seemingly infinite potential for conversion that commodities present. It is also interesting to note that, unlike Bourdieu, who closely associates the convertibility of cash transactions with rational calculation, Haya forms of popular consciousness suggest that the convertibility of money makes calculation virtually impossible. The hypermutability of commoditized goods, as I have described it, seems completely beyond the control of the Haya who seek to possess them. When, as the proverb states, "the things of today are not those of tomorrow," it is not the rational calculus of money that "forecasts" the future, for the convertible potential of the money form makes that future intractable.

Much has been made in theories that address modernity (and postmodernity) about the consequences of convertibility for systems of signification and production. The capacity of signs to interconvert semantic values has been taken by many analysts of discourse, texts, and discursive texts to mean that social life is constituted by a free play of signifiers in which everything can signify everything—or nothing at all. What I have attempted to show through this account of a specific sociocultural context is that it is possible to discern principled and systematic relations of space, time, and agency in productive activities; but also that this systematicity is intrinsically dynamic and fluid. The dynamic character of these systematic relations is apparent in the *processes* of Haya social life, processes through which meanings, values, and orientations are generated, embodied, and concretized—but also debated, subverted, and dislocated. I have argued here that this ongoing challenge—the continuous movement between making and unmaking, which is characteristic of collective experience throughout the world—is illuminated by careful attention to the specific qualities and concerns that motivate the men and women engaged in their lives' activities.

NOTES

1 Introduction

1   I discuss the relation between "outside" and "inside" in some detail throughout this work. Chapter 1 deals directly with the interpenetration of these locations, as suggested in this example.

2   The Kagera Region in Northwest Tanzania is the political division in which rural Haya communities reside. I lived in the Muleba District within this region in the course of my research.

3   My characterization of this kind of "visual objectification" and its "point of view" derives from Bourdieu's renowned critique of objectivism in the social sciences (Bourdieu 1977, 96ff).

4   See Certeau's critique of Bourdieu and Foucault on this point (1971, 45ff).

5   It is this feature of sociocultural practice that is invoked in Sahlins's account of a "naive phenomenology of symbolic action" and its significance to cultural transformation (Sahlins 1985, 143ff).

6   See also Hanks (1990, 81–83) on the relation of *schème corporel* to *habitus*.

7   I recognize that for Mauss this activity amounts to fulfilling the demands of "reciprocity," a position (extensively criticized in current debates on exchange, esp. Weiner 1978, 1980; and Strathern 1988) that makes these "actions" less than dynamic or productive. Nonetheless, I do feel that Mauss recognizes the degree to which objects become points of orientation in concrete interpersonal relations.

8   In his discussion of the strategic exchange of valuables, Appadurai adopts the notion of diversion from Munn's discussion of *kula* (Munn 1983).

9   From 1917 to 1931, Kagera was called the Bukoba Province, Bukoba being the regional capital. In 1931 it was administered as part of the Lake Region, with its capital in Mwanza on the southeast of Lake Victoria. In 1959 the area regained its regional status under the name West Lake. The current name, Kagera, from the Kagera River that circumscribes the area, was given in 1981.

10 The term "Haya," originally used only by fishing peoples along the lake, was applied to the inhabitants of this entire region by German administrators (Cory

1949, 13). Today, "Haya" is routinely used by the people of Kagera as a term of ethnic identity, and is typically used in the noun form *oluhaya* (literally "the Haya way(s)") to describe language and cultural practices.

11   The racist dimensions of this conjecture are rather transparent, given the assumption of many observers that the invading Hamites were "pastoral 'Europeans'" (Seligman 1966, 100; see also Curtis 1989, 45) or of ancient Abyssinian and early Christian origins (Speke 1863), and therefore easily overwhelmed the indigenous African population.

12   From 234 tons in 1905, to 681 tons in 1912, to over 12,000 tons in 1939 (Dauer 1984, 72).

13   See Mutahaba 1969 for an extensive discussion of the *nyarubanja* system and its reform.

14   See Newbury 1991 for an extended discussion of the flexibility of clan identities throughout Interlacustrine Africa.

15   See also Buchanan 1978 regarding migration in precolonial interlacustrine cultures.

16   Based on data gathered in the mid-1950s, Reining (1962) reported an average size of from one to three acres. Anecdotal evidence suggests that farm sizes have declined significantly since then.

17   Although the *possibility* of such conversions is, in fact, a premise of the very distinction between clan-held land and open grassland. The implications of this possibility are discussed at greater length in chapter 7.

18   I discuss prostitution in the context of transformations in gender and sexuality at greater length in chapter 7. Smith and Stevens also report that only 37 percent of male-headed households and 7 percent of female-headed households in the Muleba District had any income from employment outside of their farms (1988, 554).

19   In this study the words I have cited in translation are from Oluhaya, except in those cases where I have indicated that the word is Kiswahili or where I have given the terms in both Oluhaya and Kiswahili (hereafter usually referred to as "Haya" and "Swahili," respectively). The speech reported in English only is generally from conversations with me in Swahili, except for those cases where I have noted and translated specific Haya terms.

20   See Weiss (forthcoming [a]) for an extended discussion of Haya clothing practices.

21   Based on figures compiled from local coffee cooperatives.

2   Creating and Securing Domesticity

1   I must admit that I never witnessed the rites that I am going to describe, nor have I found any account of them elsewhere in the literature on Buhaya. However, I did find a rather high degree of consensus in the accounts that my friends and neighbors offered to me. In any event, I am less concerned with presenting a detailed analysis of these rites in themselves than I am in sketching out a more general

model of form and action. My assessment of rites such as these is intended only to provide evidence of this broader issue.

2   This was also a common architectural form in most of Interlacustrine Africa (see Roscoe 1911, 369).

3   This term is derived from the Swahili abstract noun *utamaduni,* meaning "culture," and is used in the Haya vernacular to refer to "tradition" or "traditional ways."

4   The specific qualities of this storage area, a space constructed in the highest region of the house, and therefore especially well protected, are discussed in greater detail in chapter 3.

5   Bantu nouns typically are derived from verbs, and this kind of linguistic evidence is not enough on which to rest a cultural exegesis. In any case, what interests me is not the fact that these medicines' names derive from verbs and therefore relate to action, but rather the *kinds* of actions they describe that are relevant to this analysis.

6   The significance of relating endpoints to origins is discussed at greater length in subsequent chapters.

7   See also my discussion of *okulola* ("living") and its relation to "seeing" in chapter 4.

8   Devisch describes a similar dual orientation in Yaka understandings of the body as a sociocultural focus of both "bounding off and interrelating"(Devisch 1993, 132–33).

9   In Swahili, the root *-zinga* can also mean to coil or circle around.

10   See De Boeck (1994) on "tying" in aLuund communities as a similarly powerful act.

11   See Weiss (forthcoming [b]) for a more extensive discussion of coffee in Haya social life.

12   See chapter 7 for further discussion of crossroads in relation to highways as well as human mobility more generally.

13   The significance of these values is discussed at greater length in chapter 4. Here, I am pointing only to the similarities in orientations that underlie both household and bodily space.

14   It is worth pointing out that bananas are also parthenogenetic, and put up shoots that surround the senior plant. But bananas are cultivated, and only a single shoot should properly replace the senior plant. However, my friends report that in certain cases a banana plant associated with the birth of an infant will be left to put up as many shoots over as many generations as is possible. In such instances, the resulting flora resembles the growth pattern of bamboo.

15   The generativity of smoke and other by-products of domestic food processing are explored in greater detail in chapter 4.

3   Hearthplaces and Households

1   This also suggests the ways in which centers and focal points may be both original and *final* spaces—that is, they are the places from which things originate and to which they return, as indicated in my discussion of binding invocations. See chapters 4 and 7 for different aspects of this argument about focality.

2   Yaka coresidents are also referred to as "those who share one hearth" (Devisch 1993, 93).

3   I am grateful to Debra Spitulnik for suggesting the applicability of the notion of a "set."

4   Different uses of the terms *amaiga* and *ekisibo* may reflect regional differences. Indigenes of the southern areas of the Kagera Region, where I lived for most of my field work, used *ekisibo*, while those who used *amaiga* as the term for "place of origin" tended to come from northern Kagera.

5   The Haya are historically linked to the Nyoro, their neighbors to the North who speak a mutually intelligible language.

6   See chapter 8 for a more extensive discussion of the thermodynamics of the body, viz. drinking, fat, and blood.

7   As I discuss at length in chapter 4, in many ways, fried fish becomes an icon of the commoditization process. Fried fish is always a commoditized product, cooked to be sold and consumed only when it has been purchased.

8   See Comaroff and Comaroff (1990, 210) for a discussion of the Tswana category "cattle without legs," which has a similar effect on the pace and rhythm of money's circulation.

9   In Bemba, *ukutala* means "to start," and *ubutala* is a "granary" (D. Spitulnik, personal communication). The sense of this lexical root, *-tala*, as "foundation" seems consistent across these contexts.

10   See chapter 5, especially the section titled "Counting Food and Spending Money."

11   In urban areas an individual-meal portion of bananas can be purchased. This feature of urban life, the necessity of purchasing even a single meal, is discussed as a particularly distasteful situation in most agrarian Haya communities.

12   Bananas might also be steamed by placing the curled up vein of a banana leaf (*omugogo gw'olubabi*) in the bottom of the pot and resting the *ebitoke* on top of it. However, according to my informants, this method is used to prevent the food from scorching, not to steam the bananas, which do actually sit in the water as well. All these methods of cooking (*okuchumba*) *ebitoke* are called *okutagata*, "to boil."

13   There are a number of other reasons (viz. markets, commoditization, and colonialism, which I discuss in chapter 5) for the Haya lack of enthusiasm for *ugali*. Taste and texture, however, are the most common objections.

14   Haya do cool down their bananas at a meal, but only enough to allow the food to be picked up and eaten without burning their fingers or mouth. The point is that intense heat needs to be applied to bananas in order to fully and successfully cook them.

15   I have given a banana-centric account of cuisine thus far, and this does unfairly exclude women's foods. I return to these when I discuss food provision and cooking in greater detail in chapters 4 and 5.

16   See chapter 4 for more discussion of the aesthetics of taste, viz. sweet and bitter.

4 Mealtime

1   Such weddings (*okukaitwa* in Haya, *Kufunga ndoa* in Swahili) are not common-place. Only a small percentage of Haya marriages (perhaps less than a third) are ever "officially" sanctioned in this way.

2   For more information on the agricultural dimensions of cassava cultivation, as well as Haya interpretations of this food, see chapter 5.

3   Prohibitions on using salt are widespread in African rites of passage (Turner 1967; Comaroff 1985a); see also Lan (1985, 79–80) on the association of salt prohibitions and ancestors in Shona practice.

4   In the area I knew best, two cattle were butchered daily for sale.

5   According to the Inter-Territorial Language Committee's Swahili-English diction-ary, *uto* means "semsem" (sesame); I found that what was sold as *mafuta ya uto* in the market could be anything from cottonseed to corn oil.

6   See Weiss (forthcoming [a]) for a discussion of the use of emollients as an impor-tant feature of Haya clothing practices.

7   This area is discussed at greater length in chapter 7.

8   On my few trips to these regions I was struck by the arid climate and the poorer vegetation on the farms there; but these are merely my anecdotal impressions, and I confess to being thoroughly prejudiced by the unfavorable impressions of my Haya friends and neighbors.

9   We can contrast this property with Lévi-Strauss's understanding of boiling as a process in which water is strictly a *medium* of cooking and not part of the cooked cuisine itself (Lévi-Strauss 1966, 588).

10   Considering the paucity of cattle in the region, this is a minor sanction that would be effective only against the well-off who, in practical terms, are unlikely to be "avoided" in this way.

11   This kind of avoidance actually continues to this day. The only example with which I have firsthand experience involves a man who, by virtue of his clan affiliations, claims to be able to control the rains. He was "avoided" (*"Bamuzila!"* "They are avoiding him!" as I was told) when the summer dry season of 1989 lasted far too long.

12   A very few households do have water collection tanks, which, given the high monthly rainfall of approximately sixty millimeters a month, are sufficient to provide water for all of a household's requirements year-round.

13   Such views of gestation and its relation to intercourse are widespread in East and Central Africa (Taylor 1992, 68).

14   The same is true for the Swahili *tamu*, which is both an adjective and adverb.

15   *Okushalila* has its equivalent in Swahili as well: *chungu*, again used as either an ad-jective or adverb, with a semantic range similar to that described for the Haya term.

16   See chapter 7 for a more extended discussion of the significance of Haya sexual practices and sexual secretions.

17   The significance of cutting and gender is also discussed in chapter 6.

18   Rald and Rald (1975) note that these large plants are usually called *Engemu za-nyineka*, "Bananas of the Household Head."

19   Agricultural policy has discouraged intercropping of coffee with bananas. Haya farmers are encouraged to plant new coffee trees by themselves, on a separate plot of land within the *ekibanja* (Rald and Rald 1975). This technique is now known as *kilimo cha kisasa* ("modern farming" in Swahili), but it has not been widely adopted in most Haya villages.

20   I discuss the relative values of different edible agricultural products and their variable status as food more extensively in chapter 5. Here I am pointing out that this evaluation has a distinctive spatial implication.

21   Meal bananas and their relation to markets and money are discussed more extensively in chapter 5.

22   I return to this very important point in the sections on hunger in chapter 5.

23   With respect to these qualities, recall the contrast of beer and gin and monetary increments described in chapter 3. Also see the discussion of money, food, and *ugali* in chapter 5.

24   It is also quite possible that my experience of being a "guest" at certain households for meals was entirely idiosyncratic, a function both of the kind of guest *I* was and the kind of hosts I frequented. Rather than base any important argument on this evidence, I am only suggesting the possibility of alternative practices to the ones I focus on.

25   See chapter 6 for a discussion of masculine verbal performance.

26   See chapter 7 for an extended discussion of the focality of the grave.

27   See chapter 5 for extensive discussion of hunger or food troubles of any kind that can actually be brought about by the undue attention of a larger community.

28   Many Haya suggested to me that the "binding rites" at a house opening would protect a household from sorcery.

29   I also heard many reports of poisoning that involved a household's meal, but such actions were considered categorically different from sorcery. Poison (in Swahili, *sumu*) is not the same as "medicine" (*omubazi*), and murderers are driven by motives different from sorcerers'.

30   See my discussion of origins and completions in chapter 3; this pattern is also relevant to my discussion of human death and burial in chapter 7.

31   In effect, the banana stem forms the bridge between agricultural and comestible cycles, since it becomes garbage when the last of its fruit are eaten.

32   Kagera is just south of the equator, and it is dark year-round by 7:00 p.m., well before most Haya eat dinner.

5   A Moral Gastronomy

1   Indeed, in contemporary rural Tanzania, wage labor is only a marginal source of income and certainly not disparaged in the eyes of the villagers I knew. Smith and

Stevens (1988: 554) found that only 37 percent of male-headed households and 7 percent of female-headed households in Kagera derived *any* income from nonfarm employment; this suggests that a far smaller percentage of total income comes from such employment.

2   This cassava (*makopa*) is usually already soaked and dried and rarely pre-pounded into flour.

3   This is not to say that bananas *never* have to be purchased. I am instead referring to the fact that there are a number of ways in which bananas can be acquired without purchasing them.

4   See chapter 7 for additional discussion of the significance of speed, as well as its relation to heat.

6   Plastic Teeth Extraction

1   I never participated in the diagnosis or treatment of a child afflicted with plastic teeth. What follows is a description of the symptoms and treatment of plastic teeth which is compiled from the accounts of others, in some cases those whose own children and siblings had been treated for the disease.

2   *The New Vision* reports that diagnosis by the "quack dentists" can also be made when "the canine prominence turns red or white when little pressure is applied" or "by the presence of an itchy whitish or reddish or yellowish-green prominence at the unerupted incidious [*sic*] canine region" (False Teeth 1987, 4).

3   The use of these implements and the entire phenomenon of teeth extraction is of tremendous concern to the biomedical community in Muleba, particularly because of its relation to the spread of AIDS through infection. The Public Health Campaign/AIDS Programme in Nshamba Division, begun by staff at the Rubya District Designated Hospital in early 1989, has focused on plastic teeth as one of its principal concerns. I am grateful to many of the staff at Rubya Hospital for their discussions of *ebiino* with me.

4   Based on figures from local coffee cooperative societies, discussed more extensively in chapter 7.

5   The temporal order of teething seems to be significant in other parts of East and Central Africa as well (cf. Thornton 1980; Hutchinson 1988).

6   The plural, *amahano,* is used by the Haya speakers I know in the Muleba District. The singular, *eihano,* may be used in other parts of the region.

7   In these arguments I have tried to carefully distinguish these developmental processes from what might be inadequately described as "socialization." The Haya understanding of "sprouting" teeth as a constitutive activity, for example, makes it clear that human development is not conceived of as a process of "domesticating/taming" otherwise natural/wild children, but rather that properly realized social identity is *intrinsic* to the well-formed (i.e., carefully *constructed*) human body (see Strathern 1980).

8   In practice, women do occasionally attend to these plants; but in the accounts of both men and women, this is described as properly the activity of men. Moreover, I often saw women ask men from other households to harvest banana stalks, suggesting that this was men's work in both theory and practice.

9   Recall also the connection of "eating" to "finishing" with respect to "eating money," as an activity that completely "finishes" what should be perpetuating forms of value.

10 Clans (*oluganda,* singular; *enganda,* plural) are categories (rather than "corporate groups") that organize generations of agnatic descent. The term "clan name" has arisen in opposition to baptismal names.

11 See also Sundkler's discussion of Haya names (1980, 83ff).

12 Cf. Devisch's analysis of "interiorizing listening" among the Yaka, in which he argues that dynamic subjectivity is developed as one is passively acted upon (or named) as "'passive' listening implies the possibility of 'active' speaking" (1985, 607).

13 Haya clans are not divided into distinctive segmentary lineages in the "classic" Africanist sense. The term *enda,* if it is used at all, would refer to all agnates of a single clan who *recognize* a common ancestor. The key term is *recognize,* for, given the fragmentary nature of Haya clanship relations, uterine brothers might well recognize no common line if they opt to "forget" their common descent. In other words, the term "lineage"—which is rarely used—typically refers to a cluster of relations.

14 Similarly, in Swahili the word for "inside" is *ndani,* composed of *nda-* (which, while it is a cognate of the Haya *enda,* is a Swahili term for "heart") and *-ni,* the locative suffix for "inside" or "on top of"; *ndani* is, literally, "in/on the heart." Both terms, therefore, locate the concept of interiority with respect to bodily orientations.

15 I am grateful to Peter Seitel for suggesting this important connection to me.

16 While exact rates of HIV seropositivity are difficult to assess, there is reliable evidence that reports 33 percent seropositivity in the town of Bukoba; one rurally located hospital reported 13 percent seropositivity in its blood donors for the year of 1989 and estimated an overall rate of 15 to 25 percent seropositivity for the entire population of the Muleba District.

17 In Uganda, according to *The New Vision,* plastic teeth are said to have originated among Luo populations in northern Uganda and it is reported that "the majority of [the] quack dentists are Luo" (False Teeth 1987, 4). I might speculate that the structural position of Luo with respect to the stable landholders along Lake Victoria could be similar to that of Rwandan migrants in Kagera, but this is a hypothesis that would surely require greater evidence to substantiate.

18 While I never heard anyone else make the explicit connection between AIDS and plastic teeth, those who heard this conversation did not seem to find the suggestion untenable.

19   In epidemiological terms, my data do not clearly support a claim that adults who have AIDS or who are HIV-positive produce children with a higher rate of plastic teeth extraction. In any case, most Haya I spoke to indicated that *all* children are born with or may develop plastic teeth. I am merely suggesting here that there is an interesting concurrence between plastic teeth and AIDS in the configuration of their symptoms and the wider sociocultural processes in which they are embedded.

20   The implications of being "lost" in the city are discussed in further detail in chapter 8.

21   Barthes makes a similar point, in a very different context. He writes that "more than a substance, plastic is the very idea of its infinite transformation; as its everyday name indicates, it is ubiquity made visible" (1972, 97).

7   *Money, Movement, and AIDS*

1   See Masquelier (1992, 59ff) for a discussion of the pervasive symbolism of automobiles in much of African popular culture.

2   My data, admittedly for a small number of cooperatives, suggest that less than one-quarter of the overall number of "farmers" sell more than three-quarters of the total volume of coffee marketed in Kagera. In my sample, of 122,342 kgs of coffee marketed by cooperatives with a total of 481 members, the 97 members marketing the highest volumes of coffee (20.1 percent of membership) sold 91,823 kgs, or 75.1 percent of the total volume. This figure, moreover, is skewed by the fact that those who market the greater volumes of coffee are much more likely to be registered as members of several cooperatives. Therefore, the 97 memberships cited above represent many fewer *individuals,* each of whom has multiple memberships. This, in turn, means that an even smaller percentage of *individuals* controls this share of coffee volume.

3   I am grateful to an *Africa* reviewer for these suggestions.

4   See my discussion of further bodily dimensions of speed and heat, especially in relation to blood, in chapter 8.

5   I am grateful for Fred Kaijage of the University of Dar es Salaam for pointing out the *second* half of this proverb, which makes the link of time conflation to money most explicit.

6   While *bikira* and *mwali* are standard Kiswahili words for "virgin," the term *msichana* as used by speakers of Kiswahili *in Kagera* is taken to mean "virgin." Moreover, Haya commonly use the abstract noun *usichana* to mean "virginity."

7   See Mutahaba 1969 for a detailed discussion of the history of the *nyarubanja* tenure system.

8   See Munn (1970) for a discussion of this use of objects to establish such connections between the past and future.

9   Haya farms are often quite small, on average just over an acre in size; Vedasto re-

ceived a farm of just under four acres, allowing him to sell off substantial amounts of land.

10   My data, drawn from a rather small sample, suggest that approximately one quarter of Haya women have at some point in their lives spent time in urban areas in activities associated with prostitution.

11   Survey research by Smith and Stevens (1988) indicates that to this day women in Kagera have much less secure tenure on farmland of any kind and that female-headed households have smaller farmland as well.

8   Electric Vampires

1   This characterization of Haya patterns of work-related traveling does not include those of an important educated elite, many of whom live and work for many years in places like Dar es Salaam, London, and Chicago. Yet even in these cases (perhaps especially in these cases, because of their economic capacity to do so) most Haya make concerted efforts to maintain attachments to their agrarian homes, not only by regular financial support to family members but by actually owning and maintaining homes and farms of their own in a village.

2   Haya medical practice does call for bloodletting in some instances, usually in response to the thermal conditions described below.

3   This heat comes from the greater amount of fat that Haya usually says women have. Heft, as earlier chapters indicate, is also an aesthetically desirable condition, especially for women, and this preference certainly inclines Haya to think of women's bodies as fatter than men's.

4   The physicians who work at this hospital are still all European, but the staff of medical assistants, nurses, and administrators are currently all Tanzanian.

5   Cars, especially, are seen as outwardly visible forms of wealth of ultimately unknown and unknowable acquisition and operation (see White 1993). Haya often comment that one can never be sure exactly who owns a car; it can be driven by different people, so its *control* seems open to multiple agents.

6   Here I take "economy" in a broad sense to include forms of value that are not equivalent to commodities or even to possessions. Children and fertility, for example, are attributes of a family that will characteristically incite the *oluango* of sorcerers. The economy here concerns the control of all forms of value, which the iconic forms of sorcery—and blood selling—implicitly recognize are bound up in social relations.

7   Luise White confirms this distinction. Her informants insisted that blood selling was not something carried out by sorcerers, since sorcerers "couldn't get a market for blood" (personal communication).

8   This concern with scrutiny and observation is another instance of Haya understandings of vision and visibility as sensory dimensions of hierarchical control (see chapter 4).

9   Misty Bastian (n.d.) also discusses the significance of commoditization as a process
     of detotalization in her analyses of *juju,* or money magic, in Nigeria.

9   *Conclusions*

1   Nancy Munn first suggested the importance of convertibility as an analytic focus
     for my analyses. I am grateful to her and to Bill Hanks for helping me to develop
     my ideas about this crucial process.

REFERENCES

Achebe, Chinua. 1972. The Madman. In *Girls at War and Other Stories.* New York: Fawcett Premier.

Appadurai, Arjun. 1981. Gastro-politics in Hindu South Asia. *American Ethnologist* 8:494–511.

———. 1986. Introduction: Commodities and the Politics of Value. In *The Social Life of Things: Commodities in Cultural Perspective,* ed. A. Appadurai, 3–63. Cambridge: Cambridge University Press.

Austen, Ralph. 1968. *Northwest Tanzania Under German and British Rule: Colonial Policy and Tribal Politics, 1889–1939.* New Haven: Yale University Press.

Barthes, Roland. 1972. Plastic. In *Mythologies,* trans. A. Lavers, 96–98. New York: Hill and Wang.

Bastian, Misty. 1990. Blood and Petrol. The Dangerous Eroticism of Roads and Transport in South-East Nigeria. Paper presented at the annual meeting of the African Studies Association, Baltimore, Md., November.

———. n.d. "My Head Was Too Strong!" Body Parts and Money Magic in Nigerian Popular Discourse. Unpublished manuscript, Franklin and Marshall College.

Battaglia, Debora. 1990. *On the Bones of the Serpent: Person, Memory, and Mortality in Sabarl Island Society.* Chicago: University of Chicago Press.

———. 1992. The Body in the Gift: Memory and Forgetting in Sabarl Mortuary Exchange. *American Ethnologist* 19:3–18.

Baudrillard, Jean. 1981. *For a Critique of the Political Economy of the Sign.* St. Louis, Mo.: Telos Press.

Beattie, John. 1957. Nyoro Kinship. *Africa* 27:317–39.

———. 1958a. The Blood Pact in Bunyoro. *African Studies* 17:198–203.

———. 1958b. Nyoro Marriage and Affinity. *Africa* 28:1–22.

———. 1960. On the Nyoro Concept of *Mahano. African Studies* 19:145–50.

———. 1963. Sorcery in Bunyoro. In *Witchcraft and Sorcery in East Africa,* ed. J. Middleton and E. H. Winter, 27–55. London: Routledge and Kegan Paul.

———. 1970. *The Nyoro State.* Oxford: Oxford University Press.

Bledsoe, Caroline. 1990. The Politics of AIDS, Condoms, and Heterosexual Relations in Africa: Recent Evidence from the Local Print Media. In *Births and Power: Social Change and the Politics of Reproduction,* ed. W. P. Handwerker, 199–221. Boulder, Colo.: Westview Press.

Boddy, Jannice. 1989. *Wombs and Alien Spirits: Women, Men, and the Zar Cult in Northern Sudan.* Madison: University of Wisconsin Press.

Bourdieu, Pierre. 1977. *Outline of a Theory of Practice.* Cambridge: Cambridge University Press.

———. 1979. The Disenchantment of the World. In *Algeria 1960.* Cambridge: Cambridge University Press.

———. 1984. *Distinction: A Social Critique of the Judgement of Taste.* Trans. R. Nice. Cambridge, Mass.: Harvard University Press.

Buchanan, Carol. 1978. Perceptions of Ethnic Interaction in the East African Interior: The Kitara Complex. *International Journal of African Historical Studies* 11:410–28.

Carlson, Robert. 1989. Haya Worldview and Ethos: An Ethnography of Alcohol Production and Consumption in Bukoba, Tanzania. Ph.D. diss., Anthropology Department, University of Illinois.

Carrier, James G. 1992. Occidentalism: The World Turned Upside-Down. *American Ethnologist* 19:195–212.

Carsten, Janet. 1989. Cooking Money: Gender and the Symbolic Transformation of Means of Exchange in a Malay Fishing Community. In *Money and the Morality of Exchange,* ed. J. Parry and M. Bloch, 117–41. Cambridge: Cambridge University Press.

Casey, Edward. 1987. *Remembering: A Phenomenological Study.* Bloomington: Indiana University Press.

Certeau, Michael de. 1984. *The Practice of Everyday Life.* Berkeley: University of California Press.

Cesard, Edmund. 1937. Le Muhaya (L'Afrique Orientale). *Anthropos* 32 (1–2):15–60.

Comaroff, Jean. 1985a. Bodily Reform as Historical Practice: The Semantics of Resistance in Modern South Africa. *International Journal of Psychology* 20:541–67.

———. 1985b. *Body of Power, Spirit of Resistance.* Chicago: University of Chicago Press.

Comaroff, Jean, and John L. Comaroff. 1990. Goodly Beast, Beastly Goods: Cattle and Commodities in a South African Context. *American Ethnologist* 17:195–216.

Comaroff, John L., and Jean Comaroff. 1987. The Madman and the Migrant: Work and Labor in the Historical Consciousness of a South African People. *American Ethnologist* 14:191–209.

Connerton, Paul. 1989. *How Societies Remember.* Cambridge: Cambridge University Press.

Cory, Hans. 1949. *Historia ya Bukoba.* Mwanza, Tanzania: n.p.

Coulson, Andrew. 1982. *Tanzania: A Political Economy.* Oxford: Clarendon Press.

Culwick, A. T. 1939. The Population Problem in Bukoba. Tanzanian National Archives manuscript.

Curtis, Kenneth. 1989. Capitalism Fettered: State, Merchant and Peasant in Northwestern Tanzania, 1917–1960. Ph.D. diss., History Department, University of Wisconsin.

Daniels, E. Valentine. 1984. *Fluid Signs: Being a Person the Tamil Way.* Berkeley: University of California Press.

Dauer, Sheila. 1984. Haya Greetings. Ph.D. diss., Anthropology Department, University of Pennsylvania.

De Boeck, Filip. 1994. Of Trees and Kings: Politics and Metaphor Among the aLuund of Southwestern Zaire. *American Ethnologist* 21(3):451–73.

Devisch, Renaat. 1983. Space-time and Bodiliness: A Semantic Praxiological Approach. In *New Perspectives in Belgian Anthropology, or The Postcolonial Awakening,* ed. R. Pinxten, 13–36. Gottingen: Edition Herodot.

———. 1985. Symbol and Psychosomatic Symptom in Bodily Space-Time. *International Journal of Psychology* 20:589–616.

———. 1993. *Weaving the Threads of Life: The* Khita *Gyn-Eco-Logical Healing Cult Among the Yaka.* Chicago: University of Chicago Press.

Douglas, Mary. 1966. *Purity and Danger: An Analysis of Concepts of Pollution and Taboo.* London: Routledge and Kegan Paul.

Dubisch, Jill. 1993. Reprint. You Are What You Eat: Religious Aspects of the Health Food Movement. In *Applying Cultural Anthropology: An Introductory Reader,* ed. A. Podolefsky and P. Brown, 90–97. Mountain View, Calif.: Mayfield Publishing. Originally published 1981.

Evans-Pritchard, Edward E. 1940. *The Nuer.* Oxford: Clarendon Press.

False Teeth Pulling Affects Gums. 1987. *The New Vision,* 13 November, 4.

Fernandez, James. 1982. *Bwiti: An Ethnography of the Religious Imagination in Africa.* Princeton: Princeton University Press.

Fustel de Coulange, N. D. 1956. *The Ancient City: An Anthropological View of Greece and Rome.* New York: Anchor, Doubleday.

Goody, Jack. 1982. *Class, Culture, and Cuisine.* Cambridge: Cambridge University Press.

Gregory, Christopher. 1980. Gifts to Men and Gifts to Gods: Gift Exchange and Capital Accumulation in Contemporary Papua. *Man* 15:626–52.

Hanks, William F. 1990. *Referential Practice: Language and Lived Space in a Maya Community.* Cambridge: Cambridge University Press.

Hartwig, Gerald. 1976. *The Art of Survival in East Africa: The Kerebe and Long-Distance Trade, 1800–1895.* New York: Africana.

Hugh-Jones, Christine. 1979. *From the Milk River: Spatial and Temporal Processes in Northwest Amazonia.* Cambridge: Cambridge University Press.

Hutchinson, Sharon. 1980. Relations between the Sexes among the Nuer: 1930. *Africa* 50:371–87.

———. 1988. The Nuer in Crisis: Coping with Money, War and the State. Ph.D. diss., Anthropology Department, University of Chicago.

Hyden, Goran. 1969. *Political Development in Rural Tanzania: Tanu Yajenga Nchi.* Nairobi: East African Publishing House.

Inter-territorial Language Committee for the East African Dependencies. 1969. *Swahili-English Dictionary.* New York: Saphograph.

Ishumi, Abel. 1980. *Kiziba: The Cultural Heritage of an Old African Kingdom.* Syracuse: Syracuse University.

Jackson, Michael. 1989. *Paths Toward a Clearing.* Bloomington: Indiana University Press.

Jacobson-Widding, Anita. 1989. Notions of Heat and Fever among the Manyika of Zimbabwe. In *Culture, Experience and Pluralism: Essays on African Ideas of Illness and Healing,* ed. A. Jacobson-Widding and D. Westurlund, 27–44. Stockholm: Almqvist & Wiksell International.

Janzen, John. 1982. *The Quest for Therapy in Lower Zaire.* Berkeley: University of California Press.

Kaijage, Frederick. 1971. Kyamutwara. *Cahiers D'Histoire Mondiale* 13:542–74.

Kajomulo-Tibaijuka, Anna. 1985. Factors Influencing the Cultivation of Firewood Trees on Peasant Farms: A Survey on Smallholder Banana-Coffee Farms, Kagera Region, Tanzania (Rural Development Studies no. 18). Uppsala: Swedish University of Agricultural Sciences.

Katoke, Israel. 1975. *The Karagwe Kingdom: A History of the Abanyambo of Northwest Tanzania.* Nairobi: East African Publishing House.

Kenny, Michael G. 1977. The Powers of Lake Victoria. *Anthropos* 72:715–33.

Laderman, Carol. 1981. Symbolic and Empirical Reality: A New Approach to the Analysis of Food Avoidances. *American Ethnologist* 8:468–82.

Lan, David. 1985. *Guns and Rain: Guerrillas and Spirit Mediums in Zimbabwe.* London: James Currey.

Lass, Andrew. 1988. Romantic Documents and Political Monuments: The Meaning-Fulfillment of History in 19th-Century Czech Nationalism. *American Ethnologist* 15:456–71.

Lefebvre, Henri. 1971. *Everyday Life in the Modern World.* Harmondsworth, England: Penguin.

——. 1991. *The Production of Space.* Trans. D. N. Smith. Cambridge, Mass.: Blackwell.

Lévi-Strauss, Claude, 1966. The Culinary Triangle. *Partisan Review* 33:586–95.

——. 1987. *Introduction to the Work of Marcel Mauss.* Trans. F. Baker. London: Routledge and Kegan Paul.

MacGaffey, Wyatt. 1986. *Religion and Society in Central Africa: The BaKongo of Lower Zaire.* Chicago: University of Chicago Press.

Malinowski, Bronislaw. 1935. *Coral Gardens and Their Magic: A Study of the Methods of Tilling the Soil and of Agricultural Rites in the Trobriand Islands.* New York: American Book.

Maquet, Jaques. 1954. *Le system des relations sociales dans le Ruanda ancien.* Annales du musée royal du Congo Belge. Serie in 8. Sciences de l'Homme. Ethnologie Vol. 1. Tervuren (Belgium).

Marcus, George E. 1986. Contemporary Problems of Ethnography in the Modern

World-System. In *Writing Culture: The Poetics and Politics of Ethnography,* ed. J. Clifford and G. E. Marcus, 165–93. Berkeley: University of California Press.

Marx, Karl. 1906. *Capital, A Critique of Political Economy.* Trans. S. Moore. New York: Charles H. Kerr.

Masquelier, Adeline. 1992. Encounter with a Road Sign: Machines, Bodies and Commodities in the Imagination of a Mawri Healer. *Visual Anthropology Review* 8:56–69.

Mauss, Marcel. 1954. *The Gift: Forms and Functions of Exchange in Archaic Societies,* Trans. I Cunnison. London: Cohen and West.

——. 1979. *Seasonal Variations of the Eskimo.* London: Routledge and Kegan Paul.

Merleau-Ponty, Maurice. 1962. *The Phenomenology of Perception.* London: Routledge and Kegan Paul.

Miller, Daniel. 1987. *Material Culture and Mass Consumption.* Oxford: Basil Blackwell.

Mintz, Sidney. 1985. *Sweetness and Power: The Place of Sugar in the Modern World.* New York: Viking.

Munn, Nancy. 1970. The Transformation of Subjects into Objects in Walbiri and Pitjantjara Myth. In *Australian Aboriginal Anthropology,* ed. E. Berndt, 141–63. Medlands: University of Western Australia Press.

——. 1977. The Spatio-temporal Transformations of Gawa Canoes. *Journal de la Société des Océanistes* 33:39–51.

——. 1983. Gawan Kula: Spatiotemporal Control and the Symbolism of Influence. In *The Kula New Perspectives in Massim Exchange,* ed. J. Leach and E. Leach, 277–308. Cambridge: Cambridge University Press.

——. 1986. *The Fame of Gawa.* London: Cambridge University Press.

Mutahaba, Gelase. 1969. Problems in Effective Social Reform: A Case Study of Land Tenure Reform in Bukoba. M.A. thesis, Department of Political Science, University College, Dar es Salaam.

Newbury, David. 1991. *Kings and Clans: Ijwi island and the Lake Kivu Rift, 1780–1840.* Madison: University of Wisconsin Press.

Oberg, K. 1940. The Kingdom of Ankole in Uganda. In *African Political Systems,* ed M. Fortes and E. E. Evans-Pritchard, 121–62. London: Routledge and Kegan Paul.

Parkin, David. 1969. *Neighbours and Nationals in an African City Ward.* London: Routledge and Kegan Paul.

Pierce, Charles S. 1931–1935. *Collected papers of Charles Sanders Pierce, Vols. 1–6,* ed. C. Hartshorne and P. Weiss. Cambridge: Harvard University Press.

Popenoe, Rebecca. n.d. "Girl's Work is Stomach Work": Female Fatness as a Cultural Ideal Among Sahelian Arabs. Unpublished manuscript, University of Chicago.

Rald, Jorgen, and Karen Rald. 1975. *Rural Organization in Bukoba District, Tanzania.* Uppsala: Scandinavian Institute of African Studies.

Rappaport, Joanne. 1985. History, Myth, and the Dynamics of Territorial Maintenance in Tierradentro, Colombia. *American Ethnologist* 40:27–45.

Reining, Priscilla. 1962. Haya Land Tenure: Land Holding and Tenancy. *Anthropological Quarterly* 35:58–73.

———. 1967. The Haya: The Agrarian System of a Sedentary People. Ph.D. diss., Anthropology Department, University of Chicago.

———. 1972. Haya Kinship Terminology: An Explanation and Some Comparisons. In *Kinship Studies in the Morgan Centennial Year*, ed. P. Reining, 88–112. Washington, D.C.: Anthropological Society of Washington.

———. 1973. The Haya of Northwest Tanzania. In *Cultural Source Materials for Population Planning in East Africa*, ed. A. Molnos, 204–10. Nairobi: East African Publishing House.

Richards, Audrey. 1939. *Land, Labour, and Diet in Northern Rhodesia: An Economic Study of the Bemba Tribe*. London: Oxford University Press.

———. 1959. The Interlacustrine Bantu. In *East African Chiefs*, ed. A. Richards, 27–40. London: Faber and Faber.

Richards, Audrey, and Priscilla Reining. 1954. Report on Fertility Surveys in Buganda and Buhaya. In *Culture and Human Fertility*, ed. F. Lorimer, 344–78. New York: UNESCO.

Roscoe, John. 1911. *The Baganda*. London.

Sahlins, Marshall. 1985. *Islands of History*. Chicago: University of Chicago Press.

Schieffelin, Edward L. 1976. *The Sorrow of the Lonely and the Burning of the Dancers*. New York: St. Martin's Press.

Schivelbusch, Wolfgang. 1986. *The Railway Journey: The Industrialization of Time and Space in the 19th Century*. Berkeley: University of California Press.

Schmidt, Peter. 1978. *Historical Archeology: A Structural Approach in an African Culture*. Westport, Conn.: Greenwood Press.

Seitel, Peter. 1977. "Blocking the Wind": A Haya Folktale and Interpretation. *Western Folklore* 36:189–207.

———. 1980. *See So That We May See*. Bloomington: Indiana University Press.

———. 1986. The Bachwezi in Art and History: Who is Mugasha in Hayaland? Paper presented at the annual meeting of the African Studies Association, Madison, Wisc., October.

Seligman, C. G. 1966. *Races of Africa*. 4th ed. London: Oxford University Press.

Shipton, Parker. 1989. *Bitter Money: Cultural Economy and some African Meanings of Forbidden Commodities*. Washington, D.C.: American Anthropological Association.

Smith, C., and Stevens, P. 1988. Farming and Income-Generation in the Female-headed Smallholder Household: The Case of a Haya Village in Tanzania. *Canadian Journal of African Studies* 22:552–66.

Speke, John. 1863. *Journal of the Discovery of the Source of the Nile*. Edinburgh: Blackwell.

Strathern, Marilyn. 1980. No Nature, No Culture: The Hagen Case. In *Nature, Culture and Gender*, ed. C. MacCormack and M. Strathern, 174–222. Cambridge: Cambridge University Press.

———. 1988. *The Gender of the Gift: Problems with Women and Problems with Society in Melanesia*. Berkeley: University of California Press.

———. 1991. Partners and Consumers: Making Relations Visible. *New Literary History* 22:581–601.

Sundkler, Bengt. 1980. *Bara Bukoba: Church and Community in Tanzania*. London: C. Hurst.

Swantz, Marja-Liisa. 1985. *Women in Development: A Creative Role Denied?* New York: St. Martin's Press.

Taussig, Michael T. 1980. *The Devil and Commodity Fetishism in South America*. Chapel Hill: University of North Carolina Press.

Taylor, Christopher. 1992. *Milk, Honey and Money*. Washington, D.C.: Smithsonian Institution Press.

Thompson, E. P. 1967. Time, Work and Discipline in Industrial Capitalism. *Past and Present* 38:56–97.

Thornton, Robert. 1980. *Space, Time, and Culture among the Iraqw of Tanzania*. New York: Academic Press.

Turner, Victor. 1967. *The Forest of Symbols*. Ithaca: Cornell University Press.

Wallerstein, Immanuel. 1974. *The Modern World System*. New York: Academic Press.

Weiner, Annette B. 1978. The Reproductive Model in Trobriand Society. *Mankind* 11 (Special issue titled "Trade and Exchange in Oceania and Australia," ed. J. Specht and J. P. White):175–86.

———. 1980. Reproduction: A Replacement for Reciprocity. *American Ethnologist* 7:71–85.

Weiner, Annette B., and Jane Schneider. 1989. *Cloth and Human Experience*. Washington, D.C.: Smithsonian Institution Press.

Weiner, James F. 1991. *The Empty Place: Poetry, Space, and Being among the Foi of Papua New Guinea*. Bloomington: Indiana University Press.

Weismantel, Mary. 1988. *Food, Gender, and Poverty in the Ecuadorean Andes*. Philadelphia: University of Pennsylvania Press.

Weiss, Brad. Forthcoming (a). Dressing at Death: Clothing, Time and Memory in Buhaya. In *Surface Signs and Subversions: The Body and Power in Africa*, ed. H. Hendrickson. Durham, N.C.: Duke University Press.

———. Forthcoming (b). The Food That's Never Filling: A Social History of Haya Coffee. *Anthropologie et Société*, special issue on "Culture and Consumption," ed. D. Howes.

White, Luise. 1990a. Bodily Fluids and Usufruct: Controlling Property in Nairobi, 1917–1939. *Canadian Journal of African Studies* 24:418–38.

———. 1990b. *The Comforts of Home: Prostitution in Colonial Nairobi*. Chicago: University of Chicago Press.

———. 1993. Cars Out of Place: Vampires, Technology and Labor in East and Central Africa. *Representations* 43:27–50.

Williams, Raymond. 1973. *The Country and the City*. New York: Oxford University Press.

Willis, Susan. 1991. *A Primer for Daily Life*. London: Routledge.

Young, Allan. 1978. Modes of Production of Medical Knowledge. *Medical Anthropology* 2:97–122.

INDEX

Achebe, C., 183, 185

Agency, 3, 8, 13–14, 59, 126, 220–22

Agricultural practice: and gender, 96, 160, 168; spatial form of, 97–101, 229n.14; temporal form of, 54–55, 112, 160

AIDS, 155, 170–73, 177–78, 179–81, 186, 200, 213–14, 234n.16, 235n.19

Appadurai, A., 12, 13–15, 28

Austen, R., 17

Baganda, 16

Bananas: beer (*embile*), 99, 100, 102; everyday meal (*ebitoke*), 74–78, 84–87, 99, 101–2; plants (*engemu*), 97; roots (*ekisibo*), 54–55, 112; sweet (*obunan*), 72–74, 102. *See also* Agricultural practice; Food

Bastian, M., 210

Battaglia, D., 28, 78, 156, 224

Baudrillard, J., 12

Beattie, J., 16, 47, 56, 86, 122, 158, 159, 200, 213

Beer: distilled banana gin (*enkonyagi*), 61–71, 92, 184, 208; fresh banana (*olubisi*), 61–71, 174; and gender, 87–89; and household space, 37–39, 49; and money, 61–71, 184; preparation, 60–71; and sociality, 88

Binding rites (*okuzinga*) 39–44, 46–50. *See also* Household

Bledsoe, C., 179, 200

Blood (*obwamba*): brotherhood (*okunywana*), 41, 213; and food, 207–8;

as icon of bodily well-being, 207–9, 225–26; menstrual, 96; as power, 212–14; stealing 202–7, 209–19. *See also* Body

Boddy, J., 5, 137, 152

Body: and agnatic relations, 158–65, 168–70, 213; and biomedicine, 215; as cardinal space, 42, 45; and commodities, 158, 204, 207–19; and conception, 90, 139, 169; and drinking, 37; and gender, 160–61, 208; growing fat (*okugomoka*) and wasting away, 142–48, 167; in Merleau-Ponty's phenomenology, 5–7, 163; and pain, 159; and plastic teeth affliction, 155–79; and sexuality, 95, 167–68; and sorcery, 114, 216–19; and teething 158–65

Bourdieu, P., 3, 6, 8, 27–28, 30, 45, 59, 103, 156, 220–26

Bukoba, 22, 184, 187, 203, 205

Carlson, R., 60, 61, 71, 89

Carrier, J., 130

Carsten, J., 66

Casey, E., 156

Certeau, M. de, 3, 12

Cesard, E., 104

Clan (*oluganda*), 16, 18, 20, 21, 22, 234n.10; and blood, 213; and conception, 90; gendered dimensions of, 199, 200–201; and land, 57–58, 176–77, 192–99; and naming, 161–64; and places of origin, 53–55, 56. *See also* Family farms

About the Author

Brad Weiss is Assistant Professor of Anthropology
at the College of William and Mary.

Library of Congress Cataloging-in-Publication Data
Weiss, Brad.
The making and unmaking of the Haya lived world : consumption,
commoditization, and everyday practice / by Brad Weiss.
p.   cm.—(Body, commodity, text : studies of objectifying
practice)
Includes bibliographical references and index.
ISBN 0-8223-1715-7 (cloth : alk paper). —
ISBN 0-8223-1722-2 (paper : alk. paper)
1. Haya (African people)—Economic conditions.   2. Haya (African
people)—Commerce.   3. Haya (African people)—Food.   4. Philosophy,
Haya.   5. Kagera Region (Tanzania)—Economic conditions.   6. Kagera
Region (Tanzania)—Social conditions.   I. Title.   II. Series: Body,
commodity, text.
DT443.3.H39W45   1996
390'.089'967827—dc20   95-37842
                                                              CIP